a seat at the table

OTHER BOOKS BY THE SAME AUTHOR: *Manpower in the Canadian Army: 1939-1945 / Between Arab and Israeli / Megamurder / General Mud*

The struggle for disarmament

a seat at the table

Lt.-Gen. E.L.M. Burns, C.C.,D.S.O.,O.B.E.,M.C.

Clarke, Irwin & Company Limited   TORONTO/VANCOUVER/1972

© 1972 by Clarke, Irwin & Company Limited

ISBN 0-7720-0527-3

Printed in Canada

1 2 3 4 5 JD 76 75 74 73 72

contents

acknowledgements

Work on this historical memoir was begun at Carleton University in 1969, with the support of a research fellowship from the university, and a grant from the Defence Research Board. The main part of the writing and research was done during the year 1970-1, when I was privileged to hold the Skelton-Clark fellowship at Queen's University. My thanks are due to Dr. H. Edward English, Director of the School of International Affairs at Carleton, and to Dr. Hugh Thorburn, head of the Department of Political Studies at Queen's and their colleagues for providing the facilities and the atmosphere of scholarship which greatly helped me in my work.

Mrs. Betty Goetz Lall of Cornell University, one-time secretary of the US Senate Sub-Committee on Disarmament, and later a member of the US Arms Control and Disarmament Agency, very kindly provided me with material and references for the discussion on the treatment of disarmament in the Senate during the 1960's, in Chapter 5.

Mr. Charles Gellner, of the Foreign Affairs Division, Legislative Reference Service, Library of Congress, was most helpful in furnishing records of the hearings of various committees of Congress on appropriations for defence, and related matters.

Mr. George Ignatieff, who succeeded me as leader of the Canadian delegation to the Eighteen-Nation Disarmament Conference, was kind enough to provide information and comment on the negotiation of the draft treaty prohibiting placing of weapons of mass destruction on the sea-bed and ocean floor, and on the draft convention prohibiting the development, stockpiling and production of biological weapons.

Dr. George Lindsey and Messrs. J. H. Trotman and G. D. Kaye of the Defence Research Analysis Establishment read several of the chapters, and I thank them for useful comments and suggestions. They of course bear no responsibility for the opinions expressed throughout the book.

I also wish to thank Mr. Ashok Kapur and Mr. James F. Finan, who assisted me in searching out references at Carleton and Queen's Universities.

Miss Ruth DonCarlos and Mrs. Mary Downey of the Editorial Department of Clarke Irwin were most helpful in preparing the manuscript for the printer, removing errors and pointing out obscurities.

Finally, the patient and efficient labours of Miss Irene McInroy in typing the manuscript are gratefully acknowledged.

chronology

This book is organized by chapters, each dealing with one or more disarmament or armament policy topics. The events are not necessarily referred to in the order in which they occurred. The following outline chronology is intended to help the reader place them in their proper time-sequence.

	1945-8	Communists take over governments in Eastern European states.
SEPTEMBER	1949	USSR explodes an atomic weapon.
JUNE	1950	Korean war breaks out.
APRIL	1950	NATO formed.
	1952	USA explodes thermonuclear device.
	1953	USSR explodes thermonuclear device.
	1953	USA Government takes "New Look" at defence.
JANUARY	1954	J. F. Dulles announces "Massive Retaliation" doctrine.
	1957	J. F. Dulles modifies "Massive Retaliation"; tactical nuclear weapons to be relied upon.
OCTOBER	1957	USSR orbits Sputnik I; after demonstrating ICBM.
DECEMBER	1957	NATO decides forces to be equipped with tactical nuclear weapons.
	1959	U.K., France, USA and USSR agree on Ten-Nation Committee on Disarmament.
		Khrushchev introduces proposal for general and complete disarmament in UN General Assembly.
JANUARY	1960	US Congress informed American ICBM and Polaris programme in progress.
MARCH	1960	Ten-Nation Committee on Disarmament meets.
MAY	1960	American U 2 reconnaissance aircraft brought down over USSR; Paris summit conference fails to meet.
JUNE	1960	TNCD breaks up.
AUGUST	1960	UN Disarmament Commission fails to reactivate disarmament negotiations.
MARCH	1961	USA and USSR agree to negotiate on principles for general and complete disarmament, and to enlarge committee.
SEPTEMBER	1961	President Kennedy introduces USA Programme for General and Complete Disarmament in a Peaceful World at UN General Assembly.
DECEMBER	1961	UN General Assembly approves USA/USSR statement of agreed principles, and Composition of Eighteen-Nation Committee on Disarmament. (ENDC)
MARCH	1962	ENDC meets.

JUNE	1962	Secretary McNamara proposes counterforce strategy, Ann Arbor.
OCTOBER	1962	Cuban missile crisis.
JUNE	1963	USA and USSR agree in ENDC on Washington-Moscow "hot line."
AUGUST	1963	Moscow Treaty banning nuclear tests in atmosphere, under water and in outer space.
SEPTEMBER	1963	USA and USSR declare at UNGA that they will not put weapons of mass destruction in outer space.
JANUARY	1964	President Johnson proposes freeze on strategic armaments.
	1964-8	ENDC mainly occupied in negotiating Non-proliferation treaty.
FEBRUARY	1967	Treaty prohibiting nuclear weapons in Latin America signed.
JUNE	1968	Draft Non-proliferation Treaty agreed to in UNGA.
AUGUST	1968	Warsaw Pact armed forces occupy Czechoslovakia.
NOVEMBER	1969	Strategic Arms Limitation Talks between USA and USSR open at Helsinki.
DECEMBER	1970	Treaty prohibiting weapons of mass destruction on seabed and ocean floor approved by UNGA.
DECEMBER	1971	Draft Convention prohibiting development, production and stockpiling of biological weapons approved by UNGA.

a seat at the table

CHAPTER 1

By way of introduction

It is not surprising that some observers of the international scene have said that the performance of the great powers at the disarmament conferences at Geneva and in the United Nations is nothing but a charade; that they talk disarmament, but what they do is build up armaments. However, it would not be justifiable, on superficial appearances, to condemn the powers as merely dishonest and hypocritical. Nevertheless, during the 1960's the two sides failed to reach any agreement on measures to limit the weapons of mass destruction. Why?

This will perhaps seem a very simple-minded question to many readers. Some might quickly respond that the block is due to the machinations of the American military-industrial complex and its homologue in the Soviet Union. Others might reply briskly that the whole idea is indeed only a dream, and cite the failure of the many past disarmament conferences and breakdown of agreements. They might tell you that you can't change human nature, which is inherently aggressive. They may also ask how one can expect to get an agreement based on mutual trust with those damned communists, who have said that they are going to bury us, whose whole philosophy is that capitalism must disappear, and that it is the duty of all good communists to hasten that disappearance.

There are elements of truth in both these opinions, held by the dovish on one hand and the hawkish on the other. Government policies are decided after weighing advice from several sources. The two most important sources of advice on the question of disarmament are the heads of the military establishment, and the top echelon of officials in departments dealing with foreign affairs – the diplomats. To these should be added, for the United States, certain academic persons who have speculated on how war and diplomacy should be conducted. Some have formed their theories without the discipline of responsibility for the outcome, if they were applied. Others from time to time have occupied positions in government departments which formulate advice.

It would be a mistake to conclude that everyone who works in the Pentagon is a hawk, although naturally the majority of its occupants seem to believe that the surest guarantee of peace and justice is that the armed might of the United States should be incontestably superior to that of any other nation – or perhaps of two or three other nations. Nor should one think that everyone who works in the State Department is a dove. The caution inspired by the persecutions of the McCarthy era is still noticeable, when it is a question of dealing with the Soviet Union.

Now, what do all these observations about the sources from which advice to the US Government on questions of military security and arms control add up to? Simply that the Government, when it has to make a decision on disarmament policy, is subject to conflicting advice, sometimes based on irreconcilable viewpoints. Therefore the policies decided upon inevitably are a compromise. There is nothing essentially wicked or foolish about the attitudes of the advisers at either pole. Nations arm themselves to provide against the danger of coercion or violation of their essential interests by some other nation or nations. But the final goal of arms control and disarmament is also the security of the nation, to improve it by reducing the armaments of other powers. The price for this is a reduction of one's own forces. Therefore, in establishing arms control policies there has to be a dialogue between the proponents of security through armament, and the proponents of security through disarmament. Perhaps polemic would be a more appropriate word than dialogue. It results from this, that the arms control and disarmament policies of any important power at any given time are a compromise between the two lines.

In the United States, where all policies are finally subject to democratic control, and therefore more or less publicly debated, and where the information media are like God in the Episcopalian liturgy, "from whom no secrets are hid," the process of determining military and arms control policy is visible, over a period. It is also possible to identify hawks and doves, through a scrutiny of the proceedings of congressional committees, interviews, articles in periodicals, and so on.

This is not the case, of course, in the Soviet Union, where the final decisions and the processes by which they are reached are shrouded in deep secrecy.[1] A number of American scholars devote themselves to elucidating the policy decisions of the Politburo, and the influences which have determined them, by painstaking study of the Russian press, as well as speeches and writings of the ruling Soviet *élite*. But in spite of these conscientious investigations, we are far from having the same knowledge of the Soviet Union's disarmament positions and policies as we have of those of the United States.

American researchers have produced very good books in which Soviet attitudes towards disarmament are studied in depth.[2] While acknowledging the scholarly detachment with which the authors went about their task, it must be said, nevertheless, that they are Americans, and the main focus of their investigation is on Soviet Union policies and attitudes, and what influences in the Soviet Union bore on their formulation. But to understand why there has been so far no success in limiting and reducing strategic nuclear arms, it is necessary to look at the performance of both of the major participants. The authors of the books mentioned have not omitted to report American disarmament positions as they related to those of the Soviet Union, but they do not say much of the influences within the United States which restricted the scope and negotiability of the measures and programmes of disarmament which the negotiators put forward.

The limitation of strategic armaments proved to be the key issue in disarmament negotiations during the 1960's. Failure to agree on a solution to this problem blocked agreements on other measures of real disarmament, such as the reduction of conventional armaments and conventional armed forces, in which, however, the positions of the superpowers were not too far apart in 1962, if one accepts as sincere the proposals set out in their respective drafts for a treaty on general and complete disarmament.

To understand the reasons behind the proposals for strategic arms

---

[1] In *Adelphi Paper No. 75* (Institute of Strategic Studies) February 1971, Lawrence T. Caldwell sets out views on the influence of "orthodox" and "modernist" factions in the Soviet Union party and military structure. "Orthodox" and "modernist" correspond in their attitudes roughly to American "hawks" and "doves." Although the study is mainly concerned with apparent current attitudes to the Strategic Arms Limitation Talks, the author discusses briefly action and reaction in past phases of the decades-long disarmament-armament dialogue between the superpowers.

[2] Bloomfield, Clemens and Griffiths, *Khrushchev and the Arms Race* (Cambridge Mass.: M.I.T. Press, 1966).

Larson, Thomas B., *Disarmament and Soviet Policy, 1964-68* (New York: Prentice-Hall, 1969).

limitation made during the disarmament conferences of the 1960's, and why none of them led to agreement or visible progress towards agreement, it is necessary to examine the military policies of the two superpowers, including their policies for production of strategic arms, and the doctrines developed for their use in war, or as a deterrent to war.

If the disarmament measures proposed during this period by super-power A are examined from the viewpoint of superpower B, they appear designed to maintain superpower A's military advantages, while eroding those of superpower B. And the reverse is true. In short, the disarmament proposals of the two sides, related to strategic arms, never came near matching, as neither side could offer what looked like a good bargain to the other. Caution, inspired by the warnings of military advisers, limited what was offered by the one side, and what could be accepted by the other side.

An account of the course of all the negotiations on all the measures of disarmament and arms control during the decade would result in a most unwieldy volume. So this book will be focused on proposals for the limitation, reduction and eventual elimination of what are now called strategic arms. The debates on these proposals and counterproposals were carried on in meetings of the Ten-Nation Committee on Disarmament in 1960, and in those of the Eighteen-Nation Disarmament Committee which began in 1962. They were continued through to 1969, when the body was re-named and enlarged, and its meetings became known as the Conference of the Committee on Disarmament.

As adviser to the Government of Canada on disarmament, and leader of the Canadian delegations to those conferences, I took part in all the proceedings from 1960 to the end of 1968. Concerning them I shall be writing from memory, reinforced by the diary I kept throughout. Of course there will be many references to the voluminous records of the conferences – which is about all they have produced, cynics say.

The Ten-Nation Committee on Disarmament was agreed upon by the foreign ministers of the United States, the Soviet Union, Great Britain and France who had been meeting to consider the Berlin problem, in the late summer of 1959. It was composed of five NATO nations and five members of the Warsaw Past: Canada, France, Italy, the United Kingdom, the United States; Bulgaria, Czechoslovakia, Poland, Romania and the USSR. This balanced membership was agreed to in response to the Soviet Union's complaint that in the subcommittee of the UN Disarmament Commission, the organ in which negotiations had previously been carried on, the Soviet Union alone had faced four NATO countries. Canada had been a member of the successive key negotiating bodies ever since 1946, when disarmament had been recognized as of vital importance, because of the menace of nuclear warfare. Thirteen years of negotiation had brought no agreements, but during that period the issues and problems had at least been clarified. All the elements of the disarmament plans and arms control measures, which the TNCD and later the ENDC would negotiate upon, had been discussed at one time or another by the preceding organs. The negotiations were long and complex. For those readers interested in studying them, there are books which competently and concisely tell the story.[3]

On September 18, 1959 Mr. Khrushchev presented the transcendental idea of general and complete disarmament to the United Nations General Assembly. After it had been discussed in the First Committee, the Assembly passed a resolution setting as the principal task for the Ten-Nation Committee on Disarmament, "to work out in detail and agree upon measures leading towards the goal of general and complete disarmament under effective international control."

This set the stage for disarmament negotiations at the beginning of the 1960's. At the end of the decade, in November 1969, the United States and the Soviet Union, the superpowers which possess at least ninety per cent. of the strategic armament in the world, began bilateral negotiations for its limitation. These two events may be called epochal in the chronicle of disarmament negotiations, and so define the limits of the period covered by this book.

Both superpowers had voted in favour of Resolution 1378 of November 20, 1959, which stated in its preamble that, "the question of general and complete disarmament is the most important one facing the world today." In its operative section it called upon ". . . Governments to make every effort to achieve a constructive solution to this problem." But as already mentioned, during the following decade, far from disarming, they actually multiplied their arsenals of nuclear weapons many times. France went ahead with a programme to make herself a nuclear power. China in 1964 exploded a nuclear device, and thus achieved nuclear power status. The Chinese are gradually developing bombs and vehicles for them which will eventually give them real deterrence capacity. Great Britain, the third country to explode a thermonuclear bomb, has not greatly increased her nuclear deterrent force during the period of the 1960's, and it remains minimal in comparison with those of the superpowers.

---

[3]Noel-Baker, Philip, *The Arms Race* (London: Atlantic Books, 1958).
Nutting, Anthony, *Disarmament, an Outline of the Negotiations* (London: R.I.I.A.—Oxford, 1959).

So the reflective reader may ask: Why do the nations continue these negotiations which in twenty-five years have produced only a few relatively fragile arms control measures, while the race in building the most destructive armaments goes on and on, and no agreement to stop it seems to be in sight? The answer is that the world, especially the part of it represented in the United Nations, fears the immeasurable death and destruction which would ensue if the terrific arsenal of nuclear weaponry were ever employed in war.

What comes through very clearly, in the annual debates in the United Nations General Assembly and in the innumerable conferences and demonstrations held throughout the world, is that the nations which don't possess nuclear weapons want the nuclear powers to abolish them. And it is fair to say that the overwhelming majority of citizens in the nuclear power nations would be happy if this could be done. The governments of the nuclear powers must take account of this mass of opinion, both domestic and external, and, whatever their private doubts and confusions on whether to rely on nuclear armament or on disarmament for their security, in the face of world opinion they must stand in favour of disarmament – with the unspoken reservation, of course, that it will be on their own terms. And so the negotiations must go on.

From the beginning of these negotiations, in 1946, the Soviet Union, by its continuous advocacy of the prohibition of all use of nuclear weapons, and their total abolition, has presented itself in a favourable light to the non-possessing nations, especially in the Third World. The United States, in contrast, has often been made to look as if its policy was really "Love that Bomb." But the Soviet Union's continued build-up of its nuclear armoury has somewhat eroded, as of recent years, the noble image that its "Ban the Bomb" propaganda may have created.

Results in the decade of disarmament negotiations have been meagre. Nevertheless, several agreements, more or less successful in reducing the threat of nuclear war, have been concluded. They are measures of arms control; not of disarmament. Some of them will be discussed in their bearing on the prime question of limitation of strategic arms. Potentially the most important of these is the Non-proliferation Treaty, opened for signature on July 1, 1968. Whether it will be effective in preventing the increase of the number of nuclear powers will depend on whether those now existing (the United States, the Soviet Union, Great Britain, France and China) limit and eventually reduce their armaments, especially long-range nuclear weapon vehicles.

The policies of the superpowers for waging nuclear war, and also for avoiding it are of the highest import to Canada. When, during the 1950's, a potential enemy became able to deliver nuclear weapons of immeasurable destructive power to the North American continent, it took away the security from overseas attack which Canada had enjoyed for more than a century.

As Canada has neither the desire nor the resources to become a first-class nuclear power, and has renounced the intention to produce nuclear weapons, it would clearly be an immediate gain to our national security if the strategic armament of the superpowers (and lesser nuclear powers) could be abolished. Canada has supported disarmament and arms control proposals, including general and complete disarmament, which are intended to lead to this result.

But we have not promulgated, at any time, a disarmament policy of our own. This does not mean that we did not have one. In a later chapter, the policy guidelines approved by the Cabinet in January 1961 will be set out. However, prior to that, and afterwards, in the negotiations we followed the lines of policy developed by our powerful allies. It was not that we had nothing to say. I will try to point out, in the pages which follow, how on certain issues we worked to move our allies, in particular the United States, in directions which our government thought would be more productive of results.

The problem of disarmament, as it appeared through this decade, was to get agreement between the superpowers. We tried to forward this through persuasion and argument; private persuasion with our American partners, and public argument with the Soviet Union.

On some issues, we felt more in agreement with the attitudes of non-aligned members of the negotiating bodies than with those of our allies. Lafontaine has a fable about two bulls fighting. A frog who was watching them groaned, and on being asked why, replied that, as a result of the combat, one of the bulls would be driven into the frogs' marsh and would trample many of them to death. Not only the non-aligned but also allies who do not possess nuclear arms sometimes feel rather like those frogs, and wish there were more signs of the superpowers considering what might happen to the frog-nations in their potential nuclear tramplings in the earth-marsh.

In today's world, it is part of our foreign policy to join in an alliance for our security. That being so, we have had to respect the interests of our more powerful allies, especially the United States, which spreads its nuclear umbrella over the North American continent and Western Europe.

It will not be debated here whether or not Canada would be safer, or make a better figure in the world, if we were neutral. But in the disarmament negotiations in which I have participated, it has never seemed to me that, had we been neutral, our influence would have been greater than it was as a member of the NATO alliance. How can influence be weighed anyway? Has not somebody said that influence is what you think you have, so long as you do not try to use it?

CHAPTER 2

Cold war and hot weapons, 1945-1960

In the last chapter it was said that in order to understand the terms of disarmament proposals advanced during the sixties, and why they were not accepted, one had to examine the military policies of the superpowers, which among other effects have produced the strategic arms race. But to understand the military policies, one must go back to the political circumstances and the attitudes of the superpowers which lay behind them. If there had been no fear, envy and rivalry, the superpowers would not have been moved to spend vast amounts of money and energy in arming.

Most readers will have a general idea of how the American-Russian alliance in World War II was transformed into the antagonism of the cold war. It is a story which has been told in innumerable articles and books. Still, it may be useful to recapitulate the facts in somewhat elementary terms, for those who have not concerned themselves with the subject recently.

Even during the period of alliance, trust had been minimal. The Russians didn't frankly disclose their war aims and strategy to the western allies, nor did the western allies have full confidence in the Russians. This was understandable, in view of the Soviet-Nazi agreement of 1939, which left Hitler free to set off World War II. The uneasy relations of the Soviet Union with the West since 1917 prevented any full and free understanding and cooperation.

After Japan surrendered in August 1945, the Russians, looking at the United States, saw a military giant with a weapon of incalculable power – the atomic bomb. The Third Reich was completely defeated. The Soviet Union did not acknowledge that the West had much to do with the victory, and it had a plan for protecting itself in future from the overland invasions under which it had suffered in both world wars. But the United States, with the power practically to destroy an enemy society without invasion, or prior defeat of its land army, posed a new kind of threat. This threat had to be met, and the USSR adopted two means of meeting it. First, Russian scientists and engineers were set to master the secret of making the atomic bomb, and this they did sooner than the West had calculated. Second, besides building a zone of buffer states between the historic invaders and its own territory, the USSR kept large conventional forces mobilized, which the West European nations saw as capable of invading them with little or no warning, and sweeping across Germany and France to the North Sea and the Channel.

The succession of takeovers of governments of East European states by communist parties, in the benevolent presence of the Soviet army, culminated in the seizure of power in Czechoslovakia. This event, together with Soviet pressure on Berlin, and the ever-present threat of the massive Soviet forces, inspired the creation of the North Atlantic Alliance in 1949, and the balance-of-power policies which ensued. The threat of invasion by the Soviet armies was countered by the threat of the use of the nuclear armament of the United States.

But to Russian strategists, the converse was also true. The United States was inhibited from the use of nuclear weapons by the Russian ability to invade the territory of its European allies. Later, when the USSR had acquired nuclear weapons and the medium-range bombers and rockets to deliver them to all parts of Western Europe, the European NATO partners, unable to defend themselves from a completely devastating nuclear assault, remained hostages to guarantee that the United States would not initiate a preventive war.

These, then, were the elements of the political situation which were compounded into attitudes of fear and hostility, generating the arms race and the confrontation in Europe, which was the most dangerous sector. There, opposing armed forces were closest together, and there the vital interests of both sides were more directly threatened. But the polarization was global, and erupted into war in Korea in 1950.

During the Eisenhower administration, Secretary of State John Foster Dulles developed the policy of containing the expansion of communist influence and control. To Americans, this seemed purely defensive policy,

COLD WAR AND HOT WEAPONS, 1945-1960

preventing the spread of the communist infection by a sort of *cordon sanitaire*. To the Russians it seemed encirclement, an attempt to confirm and eventually to strangle the socialist states. We may think this fear unreasonable, in view of the extent of USSR territory, but "encirclement" did form one of the main themes of USSR propaganda against "imperialism" in the cold war.

In the pages which follow it will not often be necessary to refer to political events which affected the atmosphere in which disarmament negotiations were taking place. But the political conflict was ever present, like a thick fog obscuring the vision of disarmament goals and ways to reach them. The miasma impeded the efforts of the policy-makers and negotiators on each side to agree on measures which would be significant in lessening the threat of nuclear war.

To state thus plainly the obstacle to achieving effective measures of disarmament, or limiting the nuclear armaments of the superpowers, is not to imply that we must despair of reaching the goal. The obstacle can conceivably be overcome if leaders (and those led) on each side in time perceive that their fears of what the adversary may do or intend to do are not really justified. The world is large enough to accommodate the true interests of both the United States and the Soviet Union. It is not inevitable that they should clash everywhere, or clash anywhere to the point of armed conflict.

Attemps to limit and control armaments need not and cannot wait on the conciliation of American and Russian interests and policies everywhere in the world. Agreements, such as the Moscow Test Ban and the Non-proliferation Treaty, go to prove that the superpowers have common interests and can cooperate. This erodes the concept that their interests are unchangeably antagonistic. Conversely, every announced build-up of armaments reinforces the impression of implacable hostility, the implied intention to destroy, and thus degrades the conditions of trust and good faith necessary for success in any negotiation leading to a durable agreement.

The year 1960 fell in a period when there was much uncertainty among American strategic thinkers as to how nuclear weapons should be employed, and indeed what should be the roles of all the United States armed forces.

When the American monopoly of nuclear weapons had been broken by the Soviet Union's first nuclear explosion in September 1949, United States strategists then had to assume that the USSR would build up its stock of nuclear weapons and the aircraft to deliver them at a rate of increase not much inferior to the growth of the American strategic forces.

In 1949, also, the communists under the leadership of Mao Tse-tung achieved control over mainland China. These untoward events caused President Truman to have the National Security Council review foreign policy, the military forces required to support it, and the strategies for the use of those forces. The two prime factors in the situation, existing and foreseen, were the following.

First, the USA and its allies, particularly in Europe, were critically weak in conventional forces compared to the Soviet Union and its allies. Second, it was estimated that by 1954 the Soviet Union would be able to launch a very destructive nuclear attack on the United States.

The report of the National Security Council, NSC 68, was very important in the development of United States military policies, as it was the first comprehensive examination since the end of World War II of the problems facing the nation and its allies, and the possible solutions. In the face of the multiple threats presented by the imbalance of conventional forces and the depreciation of the deterrent effect of the existing American superiority in nuclear weapons, NSC 68 recommended "an immediate and large-scale build-up in our military and general strength and that of our allies with the intention of righting the power balance and in the hope that through means other than all-out war we could induce a change in the nature of the Soviet system."[1]

In 1950, the invasion of South Korea by the Republic of North Korea appeared as additional evidence that the Soviet Union was determined to extend the area under communist rule; in this case by proxy. This resolved most of the doubts which for a while had caused the administration to hesitate to implement the recommendations of NSC 68. These doubts were due mainly to the political consideration that a great increase in the defence budget, with the consequent raising of taxes, would be resented by the taxpayers, to the disadvantage of the Democratic party. Then the war in Korea called for a great increase in spending on the conventional forces, which had dropped to low levels following the rapid US demobilization after the end of World War II. The competition between the services for the available funds created confusion or difficulty in determining global military policies.

There was a long controversy as to whether the build-up of military strength should be for the purpose of establishing a strong "mobilization base" for fighting a war which would essentially resemble World War II, or whether it should be mainly concentrated on increasing the potential

---

[1]Quoted in *The Common Defense*, Samuel P. Huntingdon (Columbia University Press, 1961), page 51.

of the strategic arms – nuclear weapons and their vehicles. Those who favoured the second course argued that the advent of the nuclear weapon and the extraordinary development of the means for its delivery would mean that the future wars between great powers, if they should occur, would be decided in the course of the first exchanges. That was to say that another World War would be settled in a matter of days; not of years. Therefore, to prepare for a long World War II type of conflict would be senseless, diverting money and effort from building up the weapons systems, which would be decisive.

The question of which policy should be followed was not resolved until some years later, when the issues gradually clarified. Deterrence emerged as the ruling policy. This required the maintenance of a degree of strength in the American nuclear delivery forces, which would inhibit the USSR from initiating any military action which carried a risk of developing into a major war. But as both sides built their nuclear arsenals to fantastic heights, measured in the capacity to destroy, American strategic thinkers realized that it was not just Soviet Union aggression that must be prevented, but the outbreak of nuclear war. This necessitated a re-thinking of the American policy of relying on nuclear weapons as the main source of military power, to be used in every serious armed conflict. When this was comprehended, the conclusion followed that the United States armed forces must have the resources and organization to enable them to fight limited wars, without recourse to nuclear weapons.

These developments in policy will be referred to again as necessary in later chapters. For the present, the discussion here will be limited to the decisions taken in regard to the "strategic armaments" (nuclear weapons and the means for their delivery) in the years 1950-1. So long as the USA had a monopoly of the atomic weapon, the US Air Force could remain relatively small. Its striking power could not be seriously reduced by a surprise attack by Soviet aircraft carrying only high explosive bombs. But now that the potential enemy could deliver atomic weapons, the situation had changed. The American force now had to be large enough so that it could not be eliminated in a surprise nuclear attack, and had to be in a state of readiness to strike back immediately at the enemy's strategic air force. The measures taken by the United States between 1950 and 1953 to meet the perceived threat included developing the thermonuclear weapon, increasing its nuclear stockpile, and greatly increasing the numbers of vehicles capable of delivering the nuclear weapons against targets in Soviet Union territory.[2]

President Truman was faced with taking the very important decision

[2]Huntingdon, *op. cit.*, pages 61-2.

as to whether the United States should make a thermonuclear (or fusion) bomb in the face of very divided opinions among his advisers. His main reason for deciding that the weapon should be developed was that it seemed likely that the Soviet Union would eventually build one, and was perhaps actually engaged in the effort to do so.

This estimate, as is well known, proved correct, for the Soviet Union exploded its thermonuclear device only a year after the United States had proved its own. The development of this new weapon, with a thousand-fold more explosive power than the atomic (or fission) bomb, very obviously added to the dangers of a war in which strategic nuclear armaments would be used, and accelerated the trend towards a strategy of deterrence.

In 1951 and 1952 new and extensive studies on air defence and tactical nuclear weapons were initiated by the US Air Force. Both of these aspects of military action grew more important, resulting in changes and shifts of emphasis in American strategic policy in the ensuing years.

During the Korean war, the Air Force expanded. In 1949 began the "rejuvenation" of the Strategic Air Command, which had been in existence since 1946. But its capacity to deliver the atomic weapon was limited, and depended on the controversial B 36 bomber, and on other aircraft which were of World War II vintage. However, in the middle 1950's, the B 47 intermediate-range bombers began to come into service, and the B 52 intercontinental bomber was under active development.

The next cycle in American military policy began in 1953, with what was called the "New Look." The inspiration to have a new look at defence policies arose from the easing of tensions when the Korean war ended, and a superficial softening of Soviet Union attitudes when Stalin died. Then there was the perennial motive for a government's examination of its military policies – to reduce the military expenditure if possible, and either cut taxes, or spend the money saved on some object more beneficial to society or to the prospects of the political party in power.

It was possible for the Eisenhower administration to take this New Look because of the build-up of American military strength under the previous administration, which had generally followed the recommendations of NSC 68. By 1954, the SAC had a large fleet of B 47 medium-range bombers operating from overseas bases, and adequate supplies of improved atomic bombs. It could have virtually destroyed the Soviet Union as a modern industrial state, together with a great part of its population, with little chance of the Soviet Union retaliating in an effective way against the territory of the United States. But – even as in 1970 – the effect of continued high rates of spending on the armed services was feared as being likely to have adverse effects on the economy and well-being of the nation. This gave impetus to the search for a cheaper way to preserve the security of the United States and its allies. The Eisenhower administration took a less pessimistic view of the balance of forces as between the USA and the USSR in the years after 1954 than did their Democratic predecessors. It seems President Eisenhower and his advisers underestimated the ability of the Soviet Union to develop and produce strategic armaments at a rate which would threaten the comfortable American superiority which existed in 1953.

A new study by the National Security Council was carried out, and after considerable debate on its contents, the following main features emerged as its recommendations for American strategy and military policy. It warned that Soviet military power would continue to grow, and recommended extensions of the continental defence against airborne nuclear attacks. The policy of containment of communist expansion should be maintained, and more than ever, nuclear airpower should be relied on for implementing that policy. Later the study argued that it could no longer be assumed that large-scale war could be waged without recourse to nuclear weapons. The President approved the recommendations of the paper, including authorization for the military to plan on using nuclear weapons in any future conflicts if militarily desirable. The importance of the roles of strategic air power as a deterrent to aggression and of the lately-developed tactical nuclear weapons were emphasized. The theory was that American possession of both strategic airpower and tactical nuclear weapons would reduce the needs for high levels of manpower in the three services overall, while enabling the policy of containment to be pursued. It was also hoped that a reorganization on the lines proposed would eliminate the need for large American forces to be stationed overseas, and that some of those existing at the time could be withdrawn. There was also increased stress laid on the need for improving and increasing the power of the continental defence against air attack.

Much public attention, and much criticism, was aroused by one interpretation of the military policy which the United States might follow as a result of the New Look. This was in Mr. John Foster Dulles' speech before the Council of Foreign Relations in New York on January 12, 1954. He said he was announcing a distinctively new policy, based on decisions made by the National Security Council. The essential of this policy was:

. . . to depend primarily upon a great capacity to retaliate, instantly, by means and at places of our own choosing. Now the Department of Defense and the Joint Chiefs of Staff can shape our military establishment to fit what is our policy, instead of having to be ready to meet the enemy's many choices. . . . As a result, it is now possible to get, and share, more basic security at less cost.

This became known as the doctrine of massive retaliation. It certainly did have a massive simplicity, but it was not long before that simplicity was lost. A barrage of criticisms elicited clarifications and explanations over the next few months amounting virtually to a retraction. Nevertheless the defence programming and military policy pursued by the United States over the next few years were in the main oriented towards massive retaliation, and remained so until at least 1959.[3]

One line taken to counter the criticisms of the massive retaliation policy was to point out that the United States had acquired a system of tactical nuclear weapons which would enable it to exercise military force, without depending on large conventionally armed forces. This would limit the situations where massive retaliation would need to be used to meet threats to the security of the United States or of its allies.

Mr. Dulles stated that tactical nuclear weapons:

Can utterly destroy military targets without endangering unrelated civilian centers. . . . If the United States became engaged in a major military activity anywhere in the world . . . those weapons would come into use, because, as I say, they are becoming more and more conventional and replacing what used to be called conventional weapons.[4]

The North Atlantic Council decided in 1954 to integrate tactical nuclear weapons into the NATO forces, as a substitute for the increase of conventional forces which had been agreed to at the Lisbon Conference, but which had never been attained.

Some years later, in October 1957 (the month of Sputnik I) Mr. Dulles published an article which showed how the doctrine of massive retaliation had been softened during the three and a half years since he had announced it.

The United States has not been content to rely on a peace which would be preserved only by a capacity to destroy vast segments of the human race. . . . The resourcefulness of those who serve our nation in the field of science and weapon engineering now shows that it is

[3]Bernard Brodie, *Strategy in the Missile Age* (Princeton University Press, 1959).
[4]Quoted in Huntingdon, *op. cit.*, page 80, from a report in *The New York Times*, March 17, 1955.

possible to alter the character of nuclear weapons. It seems now that their use need not involve vast destruction and widespread harm to humanity.[5]

By the mid-1950's, the "balance of terror" had come into being. The change was due to two main factors: first, the increasing power of the Soviet Union to deliver nuclear weapons to targets on United States territory, and second, the growing stockpiles of thermonuclear weapons. The assumptions on which the New Look strategy had been based in 1953-4 were rudely shaken. By 1955, the Soviet Union had shown that it had made considerable progress in the production of long-range bombers, and that in aircraft design and development it was near to equalling American achievements. Then evidence was picked up by radar that the Soviet Union was testing ballistic missiles of 800 miles range in large numbers. The Killiam committee appointed by the US administration to inquire into the matter of missile development gave warning that unless the USA speeded up its programme, the Soviet Union would achieve a decisive lead in this branch of weaponry by 1960. And then in 1957 came the Soviet announcement of successful testing of a ballistic missile of inter-continental range, followed by the proof furnished to the world by the flight of the first Sputnik.

As we shall see in the next chapter, the first reaction of the American authorities was to order acceleration of their own missile development programme. The Strategic Air Command element in the Air Force increased in importance, and absorbed a greater proportion of the total US military budget. Then a debate developed on what should be the limits of increase of the strategic armaments. Should the USA do whatever was necessary to maintain superiority over the USSR nuclear strategic forces, or would a stage be reached in the increase of bombers, missiles and nuclear weapons when further increase would be irrelevant – when the capability popularly known as the possession of "overkill" would be reached? The debate on whether to adopt one or other of the two policies now identified as "Superiority" and "Sufficiency" continued. More and different delivery systems were added to the armoury, until the late sixties. It is apparently still not settled, in spite of President Nixon's report to Congress on February 18, 1970.[6] This continued ambivalence must create great difficulty in determining American positions for the Strategic Arms Limitation Talks.

---

[5]*Foreign Affairs.*

[6]*U.S. Foreign policy for the 1970's* (Washington, D.C.: US: Government printing office, 1970).

CHAPTER 3

American defence policies, 1959

What fuels the arms race is reciprocal fear. In the last chapter, we noted Soviet fears of the United States air power and atomic weapons, and then the fears generated in the United States when the Soviet Union had built nuclear weapons and aircraft which could deliver them on North American territory. In 1957, the Soviet Union tested a ballistic missile of intercontinental range, following this with the spectacular earth-orbiting of Sputnik I. This demonstration that the Soviet Union could hit the continental United States with a nuclear weapon, delivered by means against which no defence existed, reinforced American fears of the Russian conventional armed might which threatened Western Europe. The uneasiness with which American legislators saw the situation, and the advice given by American military men for the preservation of the security of the United States (and of her allies) come out plainly in the congressional hearings on the Department of Defense estimates for the financial year 1960, which took place beginning in January 1959.

General Nathan Twining, then Chairman of the US Chiefs of Staff, had said in his statement to the committee that the Soviet Union was implacably hostile to the United States, that its eventual goal was a Moscow-dominated, communist-controlled world, and that its leaders aimed to achieve clear military superiority over the United States. But for the next five years (1959-64) Russians would not be confident that they had gained such an advantage as would make it practicable for them to initiate a general war – according to United States intelligence estimates. The reasoning was that if the United States deterrent power continued to be built up, the Soviet Union would not hazard the attack.[1] However, the Soviet Union believed that its great conventional strength and its growing nuclear capabilities forced caution on the United States.

The estimates of the Soviet Union's ability to inflict damage on the United States which were presented to the committee were not published in the record. However, some ICBM's could hit the continental USA, and damage could also be inflicted by the submarine-launched air-breathing missiles which the USSR possessed. For the year 1959, the greatest threat would be from nuclear weapons delivered by aircraft. Of course, the United States had a great superiority in intercontinental long-range bomber aircraft. General Twining also testified that the United States was even ahead in the competition to deliver nuclear warheads on the adversary's territory by missile. The Thor missiles installed on bases in England could deliver more megatonnage to the Soviet Union than the USSR's ICBM's could deliver to the United States. General Twining remarked: "We have a terrific advantage over the Soviet because we are around his periphery. . . . He is trying to get us out of there, out of Europe, out of these bases."[2]

In further discussion, it was pointed out that the USSR was reported to have a considerable number of IRBM's, and that these had the ability to take out the US Thor missiles in England, which were not hardened. General Twining admitted that this could happen, but the result would be that such an action would give an unmistakable warning to the United States. "The first shot he fires, SAC goes and we have him over the barrel." Then the several alternative means of delivery of nuclear weapons to Soviet territory were referred to: Titans would be in hardened emplacements; some of Atlas would be. These ICBM's were in production or shortly would be. The Regulus (an air-breathing missile) would be deployed on USN ships around the world (it was phased out when Polaris became operational). And above all, Polaris would be deployed around the world also, and be very difficult for the USSR to find and counter.[3]

There followed some discussion of the readiness to fire and accuracy of the Soviet ICBM's (data not public) and this, of course, was important in relation to the Soviet's ability to launch a preemptive strike. After Mr.

---

[1]House of Representatives Hearings on Department of Defense Appropriations for Financial Year 1960, page 20.

[2]*Ibid.*, page 40.

[3]*Ibid.*, page 45.

Mahon, the chairman of the committee, had remarked that he would feel much safer in 1959 than in 1960, presumably because it was forecast that USSR ICBM's would become operational in 1960, Mr. McElroy, the then Secretary of Defense, said:

> If you mean they can do us a lot of damage, there isn't the slightest question about that, because we have no way at this time to stop the ICBM's from coming in. Their [USSR's] only protection, however, is to use their missiles with surprise, to inflict upon us such a complete destruction of our retaliatory power that we cannot give them the same treatment in return. That is the point at which General Twining's discussion of the accuracy in hitting targets comes into play. If only 25 or 30 of those hit the target to which they are directed, you know perfectly well that there are going to be available major retaliatory forces in addition to those that we get off with the warning that we get from our ballistic early warning system. These forces will be able to inflict destruction right back on the Soviets.

Mr. Laird, who became Secretary of Defense in 1969, in 1959 and 1960 was a member of the committee. He observed:

> Is not the whole question here . . . one of balance? The main thing we should be concerned with is that we have the proper balance. . . . Certainly the chart shows that we do have balance as far as deterrent balance is concerned.[4]

We see from these extracts from the proceedings of the committee that in January 1959 the problems of nuclear war were being discussed in categories which have persisted until the present: the enemy's capacity to deliver a disarming strike, the retaliatory capacity which would remain after such a strike, and the balance between opposing forces required to provide effective deterrence.

There was some more discussion of the accuracy of Soviet missiles during the testimony of Secretary of the Air Force Douglas. Mr. Flood suggested that the Air Force had estimated the probable accuracy of the Soviet ICBM at a range of 5,000 miles as ten miles. Secretary Douglas corrected him, and stated an estimated Circular Error Probability (CEP) of a number of miles (not printed in the record). From the context it presumably must have been less than ten miles. The Air Force estimated that

---

4*Ibid.*, page 41.

the accuracy would improve in 1962 but that the American missiles would be more accurate.[5]

Thus, at this early stage in the study of the problems of long-range nuclear war, the congressmen, or some of them, appreciated the importance of the accuracy of the ballistic missile, in calculations of the possibility of a preemptive strike. As an examination of the controversies over the ABM and the MIRV in 1968-9 will show, it is possible by using different values of CEP to vary drastically the calculated probability of delivering an effective preemptive strike (or take-out of the opposing missile force). The data on which the CEP of a missile is based is mainly observation of the impact of the warheads in the tests carried out of both USA and USSR missiles. In order to get adequate range, and not endanger people, the target areas are in the Atlantic or Pacific oceans. Both the USA and the USSR have made a practice of observing the results of the other's tests. However, the data obtained, and the calculations which obtain a CEP from this data are kept highly secret, and have never been disclosed to the public. Consequently, the independent researcher, or would-be critic of the claims of the military to extraordinary degrees of accuracy, and hence capacity for disarming strikes by ICBM's, is unable to disprove such claims, or, on the other hand, to be convinced of their soundness.

Secretary McElroy was asked whether he thought the possibility of war was any greater than it was during the previous year. The Secretary of Defense replied that the demonstration of resolution shown by the USA during the last year in Lebanon, in the Taiwan Straits, and in Berlin had shown the USSR that the USA was not unwilling to commit its forces to the defence of the free world against armed aggression. And he believed that every time one of such situations was resolved "by a further demonstration of our resoluteness as a people," the danger of future war would be reduced.

The Secretary of Defense reviewed the state of development and production of the United States' ballistic missiles. The first units of the IRBM, Thor, had already been deployed in the United Kingdom, and additional units of both Thor and Jupiter (another IRBM) would be deployed in the course of the next eighteen months. The production programme for Thor and Jupiter would be completed during the fiscal year 1960 (July 1, 1959 to June 30, 1960). Eight squadrons in all were to be produced. The Atlas ICBM had successfully completed a full-range test and was well along in production. By the end of June 1959 the first few operational Atlases

---

[5]*Ibid.*, page 895.

would be in position. The Titan, another ICBM, was being developed with high priority. Testing began, and it should have been operational before the end of June 1959, considerably earlier than had been anticipated. Development of the Minuteman was progressing rapidly, "on the expanded scale proposed by this committee last summer." The Hound Dog air-to-ground missile designed to be fired from the B 52 intercontinental jet bomber was approaching production. Construction of the first five submarines equipped to fire the Polaris missile was well along, and the first lot of these were expected to join the fleet during 1960.[6]

Later it was discussed whether both Atlas and Titan should be produced. The Titan programme had been undertaken as an insurance against Atlas not being satisfactory. But although Atlas had been developing well, it was considered desirable to keep the Titan programme going. The evaluation of neither missile had progressed to the point that it would be desirable to increase production plans. Mr. Mahon suggested that the development production and deployment of Minuteman should be pursued on a crash basis. The Secretary said that while this had been considered, his technical advisers did not recommend it, but rather that the development of the missile should continue with "all practicable speed."[7]

Funds were to be provided for the development of the B 70, a very high performance intercontinental jet bomber (the development of which is still going on) and for a new air-to-ground ballistic missile which would be a follow-on to Hound Dog. (This was the Skybolt system, cancelled by Mr. McNamara in 1961, to the embarrassment of the British Government, which had relied on it to maintain the effectiveness of the V-bomber delivery system for its nuclear deterrent.)

As for Polaris-launching submarines, six had been started, three more would be started in 1960, and three more in 1961, "without prejudging the number of additional submarines needed thereafter."

Some of the committee members expressed surprise that the estimate of Russia's ability to strike the United States was much lower than in previous years. It was even said that sometimes it seemed that the intelligence estimates were "tailored" to fit the budget demands. This, of course, was firmly denied. No doubt some of the committee men had in mind the "bomber gap" (that is, that USSR intercontinental bombers, at projected rates of production, would outnumber the USA's equivalent aircraft) that had been threatened in the early fifties, and was found to be non-existent later. It now had apparently been replaced by a "missile gap." General

---

[6]*Ibid.*, page 5.
[7]*Ibid.*, pages 92, 93.

Twining remarked at the meeting that he thought the intelligence was now probably accurate as regards the planes. The Russians had not built the aircraft which US intelligence estimated they were able to do.

Secretary McElroy gave a brief exposition of the working of the "worst case hypothesis" in planning. He observed that the figures as to the number of missiles the Russians might have were "not anything like a firm statement as to what they will do. This simply says what they may do."[8] Then, as the date for which the forecast was made came nearer, a closer estimate as to what the USSR actually had would become possible. But the Department of Defense had to take account of the outside estimate in its planning.

Mr. Laird remarked that two years ago the projection of USSR bomber production was more than twice as high as the figures which had just been given. He assumed that while two years ago the US intelligence was projecting capabilities, the current figures were firm, solid intelligence. Since the Chiefs of Staff had the responsibility of protecting the country, they had a tendency to be liberal in their estimates when they did not have sound intelligence. General Twining and Secretary McElroy agreed that this was so.[9]

General Twining acknowledged that he had reported to the committee in former years that the Air Force predicted that by 1959 the USSR would have 600 or 700 of the intercontinental bomber types. However, it did not build them, presumably because of difficulties in production and operations. And he thought that perhaps it would build relatively few, and concentrate on the ballistic missile field.[10] (Statements of Mr. Khrushchev a year later confirmed this hypothesis. He went so far as to say that the missile had made the bombing airplane obsolete.)

The SAC dispersal and alert programme had been accelerated in the past year. This programme was undertaken in order to lessen the possibility of a considerable number of the intercontinental bombers being destroyed at their bases by missiles. Studies in preceding years had shown that they could be very vulnerable, as at the time the USA had no adequate ballistic missile warning system.

The Secretary of Defense had decided in January 1958 that the Army should go ahead with the research and development of the Nike-Zeus anti-missile missile. The Army had been working on Nike-Zeus for the previous eighteen months (that is, since June 1956). It was a development of the previous Nike series of anti-aircraft ballistic missiles. There

8*Ibid.*, page 44.
9*Ibid.*, page 185.
10*Ibid.*, page 18.

had been some confusion of responsibilities, as the Air Force had been working on an anti-missile system called Wizard. We see that the anti-ballistic-missile (ABM) programme, which was to develop into such a controversy in 1968-9, had a long period of gestation.[11]

Later in the hearings, General White, Chief of Staff of the Air Force, was asked to what extent targets in the USSR were identified and located. General White replied:

> We believe we know the major, significant military and industrial targets today. Some may be under construction that we do not know about yet, but in the normal course of events, based on history, we will have knowledge of them before too long.[12]

Probably General White's confidence that all important targets would be located was due to the U 2 flights over the Soviet Union, a secret intelligence-gathering programme which only came to light dramatically in May 1960 when Gary Powers' U 2 plane was brought down by a missile in Soviet territory – an event which caused the breakdown of the intended Summit Conference in Paris.

---

[11]*Ibid.*, page 373.
[12]*Ibid.*, page 887.

CHAPTER 4

Khrushchev's general and complete disarmament

As already remarked, a new phase in disarmament negotiations began when Mr. Khrushchev made his proposals for general and complete disarmament in the United Nations General Assembly on September 19, 1959.[1] On that occasion he said:

> Everything indicates that the time has come to usher in a period of international negotiations, conferences and meeting of statesmen in order that, one after another, the pressing international problems should find their solution.[2]

He went on:

> In order that the principles of peaceful coexistence should become completely established in relations between the States, it is necessary, in our opinion, to put an end to the cold war.

Taken at its face value, the famous principle of coexistence is acceptable to almost everyone, except the most extreme hawks. But there are

[1]Official Records of the General Assembly Fourteenth Session, 799th plenary meeting.

[2]The statement found a belated echo in a sentence in President Nixon's 1969 inaugural address: "After a period of confrontation we are entering an era of negotiation."

wide divergences between national viewpoints as to the elements from which a state of peaceful coexistence is to be created. And as for the cold war, although the international climate has improved greatly since the Stalin era, the atmosphere in 1959 and even in 1970 was chilly rather than temperate, let alone warm. This brings to mind the often-asked question: Must disarmament wait on improved international relations, or is disarmament necessary before international relations can really improve?[3] It is the relations between the NATO countries and the Warsaw Pact bloc which now are in question. Perhaps the relations between China and the rest of the world will be of equal importance in the long run.

Mr. Khrushchev began his exposition of the need for general and complete disarmament by rehearsing the facts that one hydrogen bomb released a greater amount of energy than all the explosions set off by all countries in all wars known in the entire history of mankind. There was no spot on the earth today that could not be hit by nuclear-headed rockets. Such tremendous potential for destruction could not be ignored.

If a nuclear war were allowed to start, there would be tens and even hundreds of millions of human victims. There would be no difference between front and rear, between soldiers, women and children. Many large cities and industrial centres would be reduced to ruins. Radioactive contamination would long continue to maim and kill people in future generations.[4]

The military expenditure of all states in 1959 totalled approximately $100 billion annually. It was time to call a halt to this senseless waste of resources and energy, preparing for war and destruction. (In the decade since 1959, the anual expenditure on armed forces and armaments was estimated to have grown to $180 billion.)

---

[3]See Selwyn Lloyd's statement to the UN General Assembly, September 17, 1959 (UNGA official records, 798th plenary meeting): "The second great problem is disarmament. There are some who say that you can have no disarmament without political settlements, but others who say that you will not get political settlements while the present race in armaments continues. The truth is that if we can get political settlement it will make agreement on disarmament easier; if we can get an agreement on disarmament, it will make political settlements easier. Progress in either field will cause a correspondingly favourable reaction in the other field."

The obvious conclusion from the above argument is that the nations should press ahead with negotiations in *both fields*.

[4]For recent authoritative information, see the 1968 Report of the Secretary General of the United Nations, transmitting the study of his consultative group on the "Effects of the Possible Use of Nuclear Weapons and the Security and Economic Implications for States of the Acquisition and Further Development of these Weapons."

Mr. Khrushchev observed that the question of control (verification) had been one of the main difficulties in arriving at agreements in disarmament negotiations. The Soviet Union was for strict international control over the implementation of a disarmament agreement. But it was, and always had been, against a control organization which could collect military intelligence before there was actual disarmament. The USSR was in favour of genuine disarmament under control, but against control without disarmament.

Here we have a statement of the Soviet Union dogma on control (verification). "Control over disarmament, but no control over armaments." This clashes with the conviction of the NATO countries that control of any agreed reduction of nuclear weapon vehicles had to provide not only that destruction of those vehicles should be witnessed, but also that there should be procedures to ensure that those vehicles which remained did not exceed the agreed limits – which would require some kind of a controlled stocktaking before the disarmament process began. We shall be returning to this problem as we consider the proposals for reduction of nuclear weapon vehicles in 1960 and successively later.

Many states, Mr. Khrushchev said, feared that disarmament measures would particularly affect those armaments in which they were superior to other nations, or which they believed were especially necessary to themselves. This being so, in the atmosphere of the cold war and of mutual suspicion, no state – and he said he was speaking seriously and not making propaganda – could reveal its military secrets, the organization of its defences and war production without impairing its national security.

(This was the Soviet Union's justification for refusing to accept "control over armaments.")

Why did disarmament have to be "general and complete"? Mr. Khrushchev said that so long as disarmament was conceived of as only partial, and it was assumed that some armaments would remain after the implementation of a disarmament agreement, nations would be apprehensive that an attack on them could still be launched. Therefore the very possibility of wars being unleashed must be ruled out. So long as large armies, air forces and navies with nuclear weapons and their vehicles existed, so long as general staffs worked out plans for war and young men were taught to wage it, there would be no guarantee of peace.

The Soviet Government had come to the firm conviction that the way out of the deadlock lay through general and complete disarmament. The essence of its proposal was that over a period of four years all states should effect complete disarmament and should no longer have the means to wage war. Land armies, navies and air forces should cease to exist;

general staffs and war ministries should be abolished; military educational establishments should be closed. Tens of millions of soldiers, sailors and airmen should return to peaceful, creative labour. Military bases in foreign countries should be dismantled. Nuclear weapons should all be destroyed, and their production should cease. Nuclear energy should be used exclusively for peaceful purposes. All military ballistic missiles should be eliminated, and rockets in the future should be used only for space exploration and other scientific purposes. States should retain only strictly limited and agreed numbers of police (militia) who should be equipped with small arms only. Their function would be solely to maintain order and protect the personal security of the citizens.

Many writers have dismissed general and complete disarmament as a mere utopian dream. However, if one tries to formulate a programme of disarmament, the main object of which would be to preserve the world from nuclear war or the threat of it, it becomes difficult to find a point at which the process can stop short of the degree of disarmament projected for the final stage in the Soviet Union draft treaty on General and Complete Disarmament[5] and in the United States Basic Principles for General and Complete Disarmament in a Peaceful World.[6] If the process did not go so far as the abolition of all specialized means of delivering the nuclear weapon – rockets, bomber aircraft, missile-launching submarines – and the dismantling of all nuclear weapons, the possibility of a war in which nuclear weapons would be used would still remain. And even if nuclear disarmament were accomplished it would not be enough, if the great powers still retained large conventional armaments and armed forces enabling them to fight each other in World War II style. Should this happen, there would be a race to rebuild the nuclear weapons and the means of their delivery. As many observers have pointed out, the knowledge of how to build a nuclear weapon cannot be wiped out, even if the existing weapons could be. Therefore, it would be necessary for the nations to reduce conventional as well as nuclear armaments to a point where war between the major powers would be almost an impossibility, because of lack of means to carry it on.

This argument in favour of the idea of general and complete disarmament would perhaps be convincing if international politics were regulated by rationality. Policies which the best of reason can formulate are distorted by fear, suspicion, distrust, envy and malice. It is not easy to predict when these failings will be overcome sufficiently to ensure the control and elimination of international violence.

---

[5]ENDC/2.
[6]ENDC/30.

Yet in spite of all the justifiable doubts as to the feasibility of general and complete disarmament, and of the good faith of the Soviet Union in proposing it, and in spite of the scornful criticism heaped on it by "realists," its attraction for the majority of nations was expressed by the unanimous vote (including, of course, the votes of the NATO powers) for Resolution 1378, on November 20, 1959, calling for governments to seek a constructive solution to the problem of general and complete disarmament.

Later, Mr. Khrushchev said that if the Western powers were not ready to embark on general and complete disarmament, "the Soviet Government is ready to come to agreement with other States on the appropriate partial steps of disarmament and the strengthening of security."

That is to say, the Soviet Union was prepared to discuss a number of measures that have come to be classified as arms control. Among those which Mr. Khrushchev mentioned were reduction of foreign troops on the territories of Western Europe, within a zone of control and inspection; a nuclear-free zone in Central Europe, conclusion of a non-aggression pact between the NATO States and the Warsaw Treaty States, and the prevention of surprise attack. While the terms in which these measures were presented were clearly biased in favour of the Soviet Union and its allies, and so were never discussed in any depth in the TNCD or the ENDC, it is to be noted that in 1969 the NATO members began seriously studying what is now called Mutual Balanced Forces Reduction – that is, the first of Mr. Khrushchev's proposals to which the others are more or less related.

Some American scholars believe that the Soviet Union's advocacy of general and complete disarmament was a propaganda play, rather than a serious proposal to reduce armaments and the resultant tensions. It could create a peace-loving image of the Soviet Union in the Third World and the more credulous elements of the public in Western countries. It may have reflected a Russian "ideological propensity for total solutions," and a tradition going back to the Litvinoff proposals in the 1920's, and the nineteenth century. It may even have been produced to give Mr. Khrushchev a momentous theme to expound at his appearance in the 1959 United Nations General Assembly.[7]

The same authors note that Mr. Khrushchev took great interest in propagating the Soviet Union disarmament policies, the main lines of which probably accorded with his personal views.[8]

---

[7]See *Khrushchev and the Arms Race*, Bloomfield, Griffiths and Clemens, page 143.

[8]*Ibid.*, page 179.

Only the day before Mr. Khrushchev made the speech of which extracts have just been given, the Rt. Hon. Mr. Selwyn Lloyd, then Foreign Secretary of the United Kingdom, had spoken to the General Assembly, and had set out the British ideas for a programme of disarmament. Some of the things he said are important because they illustrate the gradual approach to disarmament which the West favoured, as opposed to the radical or transcendental quality of Khrushchev's propositions. The proposals first put forward by the NATO group at the Ten-Nation Disarmament Committee Conference were in general based on the line given in Mr. Selwyn Lloyd's speech and this line derived from proposals put forward by France and Britain in the 1957 meetings of the previous (five-nation) disarmament committee.

Mr. Lloyd said that the British aim was to move forward towards the abolition of all nuclear and other weapons of mass destruction, and towards the reduction of other weapons and armed forces to levels which would rule out the possibility of aggressive war. Obviously, this would have to be done in stages.

In the first stage, it was hoped to confirm the prohibition of testing of nuclear weapons, on which the United States, the Soviet Union and the United Kingdom were then negotiating. This would be an important step towards dealing with the difficult question of halting the spread of nuclear weapons. There should also be a conference on halting the production of fissile material for the purpose of making nuclear weapons – the so-called "cut-off." The other measures proposed for the first stage of disarmament did not relate closely to the limitation of nuclear weapons or their vehicles.

For the second stage, the "cut-off" should be implemented. Military stocks of fissile material should be transferred, under international supervision, to non-weapons uses.

In the third stage, the ultimate objective, there should be a prohibition on the manufacture of nuclear, chemical, biological and other weapons of mass destruction, and of their use. The possibility of controlling the remaining stocks of weapons of mass destruction, and then eliminating them should be reexamined. As progress was made in dealing with the remaining stocks of weapons, conventional armaments and military manpower would be reduced to the levels required for international security only.[9]

It will be seen that there were certain ideas on disarmament common to the British proposals and those of the Soviet Union, as presented by

[9]See official record of the 798th meeting of the UN General Assembly, September 17, 1959.

Mr. Khrushchev. The main issue in the negotiations on the control of the weapons of mass destruction was not the final goal, but the programme or procedures which should be adopted for reaching it. Or perhaps it would be more exact to say that this was ostensibly the main issue.

M. Jules Moch, who had represented France at numerous previous disarmament conferences, again stressed a point that he had been making for some years. Through the inability of the great powers to agree in 1946 on a compromise solution to the problem of stopping the production of fissile material for weapons use (the Baruch plan of 1946, rejected by the USSR), the building up of stocks of nuclear weapons and the fissile material for them had "passed the point of no return." That is, they had proliferated to the extent that no feasible system of verifying that all weapons and material had been eliminated could be devised, even if agreement could be reached that such drastic nuclear disarmament should be carried out.

Was the same mistake to be made in regard to missiles, long-range bombers, the "vehicles" for conveying the nuclear weapons to their targets? ICBM's and intercontinental bombers were very large objects, and as yet there was not an overwhelming number of them. If it were agreed to limit and eventually reduce their number, it should be possible to verify that parties to the agreement were fulfilling their obligations.

In the French view, it was necessary to give high priority in any disarmament programme to measures prohibiting the development and production of all such vehicles – satellites, rockets, supersonic and long-range bombers, ocean-going submarines, aircraft-carriers. If this priority were accepted by the other parties to the negotiations, a programme could be developed. As a first stage, existing weapons and construction programmes could be declared to an international disarmament organ, testing should be publicly notified and controlled, and the third stage would see the prohibition and destruction of existing stocks of the vehicles.[10]

Some further elucidation of M. Moch's argument may be useful. By the late 1950's a very great number of nuclear weapons had been manufactured, and technology was progressively reducing them in size, while increasing or maintaining the explosive power. Suppose it had been agreed between the nuclear powers that no more nuclear weapons should be produced, and that, pending their eventual total elimination, each of the nuclear powers should retain only 100 of them. If any of the contracting powers should act in bad faith, and retain a larger number of nuclear bombs and warheads than the stipulated 100, it would be an impossible

---

[10]See UN Document A/A1/821.

task to detect their presence in a country the size of the Soviet Union or the United States – or even Great Britain. Both sides professed that disarmament should be under "strict international control." But could there be "strict international control" to ensure that there were no clandestinely-retained nuclear weapons? Remembering that most of the nuclear weapons at this time were not larger than a big barrel or a hogshead, and that the scientists assured us that the uranium in them could not be detected by searching with Geiger counters or any other radiation-measuring device, one can see that a really effective degree of verification had become impossible.

But on the other hand, ICBM's and aircraft of intercontinental range are very large objects, and would be most difficult to conceal from international disarmament inspectors. So the Moch argument came to be accepted, that is, it was conceded that the most easily verifiable way to check the arms race would be to apply restrictions to the nuclear weapon vehicles, neither so numerous nor so easily concealed as the nuclear weapons. The restrictions to be applied to the nuclear weapons themselves would be, in a sense, secondary, and could come later. Mr. Khrushchev, at a later date, employing one of his agricultural metaphors, observed that nuclear weapons without their means of delivery would be as harmless as so many "cucumbers lying in a barn." While not exactly true, it puts the idea across.

The excerpts from statements by Messrs. Khrushchev, Selwyn Lloyd and Moch in the 14th UN General Assembly set forth, in a general way, the thinking of the principal members of the Ten-Nation Committee on Disarmament. This conference was to begin the following March (1960), at Geneva. The important principle in regard to strategic arms limitation (as the process would now be called) enunciated by M. Jules Moch should be particularly noted.

The representatives of the United States, the United Kingdom, Italy, France and Canada arranged to meet together at Washington between the end of the 1959 UN General Assembly and the opening of the Ten-Nation Disarmament Conference. Their purpose was to put together a negotiating position, using the proposals which had been advanced by the Western countries at the UNGA. The United States had not proposed any specific measures or programme relating to disarmament. However, it was known that a "task force" under the direction of Mr. Charles A. Coolidge, a Boston lawyer, was preparing a report for the US Government, on disarmament and related topics. It was expected that the report would be used to determine the United States contribution to the eventual Western position. But the Coolidge report, although completed and presented to the US Administration, never was made public, nor were its recommendations communicated to the allied participants in the TNCD. We assumed that the recommendations, for one reason or another, had been found unacceptable by President Eisenhower and his advisers, and that the report had been pigeon-holed. This was perhaps due to the attitudes of the military authorities and the politicians who believed in security through armament.

Before describing the efforts of the five NATO representatives to construct a position for the TNCD, it will be appropriate to review the proceedings of the House of Representatives hearings on Department of Defense appropriations for the fiscal year 1961, and also to examine US military policies and strategy, especially in relation to Khrushchev's general and complete disarmament proposal. One effect of the Coolidge report fiasco was that when the Western representatives met on January 25, 1960, the United States representatives had no firm instructions as to the measures they were to advocate for inclusion in the Western proposals.

CHAPTER 5

American and Soviet defence policies

The hearings on Department of Defense appropriations for the financial year 1961 began in January 1960. This was less than two months after the United Nations General Assembly had adopted Resolution 1378 on general and complete disarmament. The United States had voted for it, thereby ostensibly accepting the ideas which it set forth, of which the most important were that the Assembly,

> Considering that the question of general and complete disarmament is the most important one facing the world today,

> Calls upon Governments to make every effort to achieve a constructive solution to this problem. . . .

> Expresses the hope that measures leading towards the goal of general and complete disarmament under effective international control will be worked out in detail and agreed upon in the shortest possible time.

Mr. Gates, who had succeeded Mr. McElroy as Secretary of Defense, observed at the beginning of his testimony in the 1960 hearings:

> We cannot assume at this time that negotiations with the Soviets will result in agreements that will ease our defense problems. There is

nothing to justify a belief that the Soviets will make substantive concessions which will reduce our security requirements, in fact, the Soviet Union is increasing its military capabilities, especially its missile delivery systems.[1]

What the committee chiefly wanted to hear about, it seems, was how the United States projected programme of building ICBM's compared with the programme of the USSR. Mr. Gates admitted that if the estimated Soviet production of ICBM's and missiles launched from submarines (air-breathing, at the time) was compared with the plans for the deployment of American ICBM's and Polaris missile submarines, the Soviet Union might "enjoy at times a moderate numerical superiority during the next three years" (that is, 1960, 1961, 1962). But after mid-1962 the USA would begin to catch up. Even if the Russians produced somewhat more of the vehicles than they were expected to do, this would not give them ". . . a strategic posture which might tempt them to initiate a surprise attack." The overall United States quantum of armament, offensive and defensive, in a conflict in which nuclear weapons would be used would be too powerful a deterrent. Mr. Gates said:

> Our retaliatory forces are capable of carrying out their assigned missions. Manned bombers are still, for both ourselves and the USSR, the primary means of delivering heavy nuclear weapons. . . . In this category the United States far exceeds the USSR.[2]

Secretary Gates stressed that although the Soviet Union was expected to have large numbers of ICBM's, according to US intelligence estimates, they would not have the accuracy required to destroy the American ICBM's in the hardened silos in which it was intended to place them.[3]

Funds were being provided for additional Atlas and Titan ICBM's, to a total of twenty-seven squadrons, and to prepare for the production of Minuteman. Both Atlas and Titan were being continued in production because, while more Atlas missiles could be made operational at an early date, the Titan had greater "growth potential." The Thor-Jupiter programme would be completed soon. Four Thor squadrons and three Jupiter squadrons were being provided through the military assistance programme to England, Italy and Turkey.[4]

---

[1]House of Representatives hearings on Department of Defense Appropriations for Financial Year 1961, page 2.
[2]*Ibid.*, page 3.
[3]*Ibid.*, page 4.
[4]*Ibid.*, pages 8, 149, 159.

The production of Polaris submarines was going ahead at a faster rate than had been anticipated in the previous year's hearings. Nine were already in commission, and twenty-three were under construction or conversion. The first Polaris missile systems would be operational towards the end of 1960.

Secretary Gates and General Twining made the point that theretofore the Department of Defense had been quoting figures on future numbers of Soviet Union missiles based on what, theoretically, it could produce. The figures this year, however, were based on an intelligence estimate of what the Soviet Union probably *would* do, rather than on what it *could* do. It had been stated formerly that the Soviet Union could have three times more ICBM's than the United States in the period 1960-3. Current intelligence estimates were that the Soviet Union superiority in ICBM's would not be nearly so great.[5]

Reading the questions by congressmen, and the replies by officers and officials, it can be seen that the issue of the "missile gap" was looming large in the presidential election year of 1960. The Democrats would attempt to show that the Republican administration of President Eisenhower had allowed the Soviet Union to get a dangerous lead over the United States in the missile race. The Republicans, of course, would lay stress on the overall strong deterrent position of the United States military forces, as had been brought out in the testimony referred to.

Mr. Laird asked:

Mr. Secretary, do you think that in view of some of the statements that have been made publicly by certain individuals, a few Members of Congress, that we might mislead the Soviet Union into a position where they might miscalculate our deterrent possibilities?

Secretary Gates replied:

I think it is unfortunate that these statements are made that give the impression that we are . . . open . . . to a surprise attack. . . . I have a good deal of respect for the Soviet Union's intelligence. . . . I do not think they are going to be misled by these statements. . . . But I do think it is harmful to us in international negotiations, to our foreign policy discussions, to our position in the eyes of the world, to allow . . . false impressions to be circulated.[6]

Mr. Laird observed that after having listened to the testimony presented, he wondered whether in fact the USA might have planned for pro-

---

[5]*Ibid.*, pages 23, 25.
[6]*Ibid.*, page 126.

ducing more missiles than would be necessary, to provide a deterrent against a possible USSR attack in 1966. "How much retaliatory force do you need to deter a big war?" After further discussion off the record, Secretary Gates said that it was not yet decided how many Minuteman and Polaris would be built. If the department were quite sure of the technical reliability of these armaments, the programme might be speeded up. The requirements for effective deterrence would have to be reviewed annually, in the light of what the Russians would do.

There you have the classic rationale for an arms race. Nation A bases its policy for acquiring armaments on either catching up to, or keeping ahead of Nation B; while Nation B is acting reciprocally.

Dr. York, the scientific adviser to the Department, explained what was meant by the term "deterrent gap," which he was said to have originated. He said:

> The question is not whether we have more missiles than they have, but whether our strategic deterrent can or cannot survive the first attack. If it can, then there is no deterrent gap. . . . The conclusion here . . . is that there is no deterrent gap. Whether there is or is not a missile gap, there is not a deterrent gap.[7]

The whole strategic situation and the military policy relating to the means of delivering the nuclear weapons was exhaustively discussed. What has been given above is a very condensed précis of the questions and answers to questions relating to that part of the hearings. It is obvious that the principal anxiety of the congressmen was that the Soviet Union seemed to have got ahead in production of intercontinental ballistic missiles, which greatly increased the vulnerability of the continental United States to nuclear attack. They wanted to be reassured that the administration was exerting every effort to close the so-called missile gap. The political overtones of the inquiry, as I have said, were very easily perceived.

A good deal of interest, mingled with incredulity, was aroused by the report of Khrushchev's speech to the Supreme Soviet on January 14, 1960. The United Press International had him saying that Russia had built up the greatest nuclear rocket striking force in the world. The Soviet Army wielded such means of warfare and such firepower as no other army had ever had. The USSR had outstripped the West and was "several years" ahead in the designing and production of intercontinental ballistic missiles. Nuclear weapons would continue to be produced until the Western powers agreed to a ban. In the meantime the rocket-striking

---

[7]*Ibid.*, page 136.

force was taking the place of the Air Force, and the production of some bombers had been discontinued. Mr. Khrushchev also said that the strength of the Soviet armed forces, which then stood at 3,623,000 men, would be reduced by 1,200,000, because the new types of armament now at the disposal of the USSR were so powerful.

The agenda of the meeting of the Supreme Soviet was labelled "Disarmament – A Way to Strengthen Peace and Ensure Friendship Between Nations," but the UPI report did not say much about disarmament. Mr. Gates, however, was apparently familiar with the general and complete disarmament proposals, for when he was asked whether the defence programme contemplated in the 1961 budget might be changed if the United States were given assurances that the USSR would really do what Mr. Khrushchev had said it would, he ended his brief reply with the following words:

> I do not think people are going to take very seriously the idea that the Russians are going to throw away all their arms and have a foreign policy based on no military strength. We are not taking it very seriously in the Department of Defense. . . . In the disarmament proposal he made to the United Nations it was a pretty blanket elimination of every bit of military power. I think this is only a tactic and that the long-range objective remains unchanged.[8]

We have seen that in 1959 and 1960 members of the House Committee were most zealous in seeking assurances that the armaments of the United States should not be outmatched by those of the Soviet Union. Security against nuclear attack was to be gained by being incontestably the stronger. When we come to look at the proceedings of the Congress in regard to the alternative means of seeking security against the enormous threat of nuclear war – that is, through disarmament or arms control – it is hard to find any considerable or continuing interest in the matter. It was not until the Kennedy administration established the Arms Control and Disarmament Agency in 1961, and began effective moves towards agreement on a treaty prohibiting the testing of nuclear weapons, that hearings began to be held. Over a score of years prior to this, senators made hardly more than a dozen speeches advocating a programme of disarmament to be negotiated with the Russians. And there were far fewer speeches in the House of Representatives.

There were several reasons for this. First, perhaps, is the general proposition that politicians interest themselves only in those causes in

[8]*Ibid.*, pages 54, 55.

which the voters are perceived to be interested, or could be interested. And for the United States electorate, disarmament was not one of those causes. Furthermore, this was the period of the cold war, and distrust of the intentions of the Soviet Government was deep-seated. Soviet rejection in 1946 of the Baruch plan seemed to many Americans a rejection of the idea of collaboration in the control of the nuclear danger, and instead a challenge to a contest in building armed strength, perhaps with world domination as a goal. This generated scepticism as to the possibility of negotiating effective agreements with the Russians, although there was a vague sentiment that disarmament – if it could be accomplished – would be a Good Thing.

Nevertheless, some of the speeches by senators showed real vision. In 1950, Senator Millard Tydings said:

. . . We must lay aside the futile attempts to outlaw these new weapons by dealing with them alone. . . . I am not advocating that this nation shall disarm while every other nation shall remain armed. I am advocating that all nations enter into an agreement to disarm gradually over a period of years, on a schedule agreed to, under the eyes of each other, with constant worldwide inspection to see that disarmament is progressively carried out. That is the only way we can ever disarm, the only way which we can successfully outlaw the hydrogen and atomic bombs . . . if civilization and humanity are to find security on this earth, they cannot find it by partial disarmament, they must find it by complete disarmament, plus inspection before, during and after disarmament.[9]

In 1951 Senator Flanders proposed in a speech in the Senate:

. . . disarm completely in every weapon and to any degree above the few small arms required for maintenance of civil order. The essential, of course, is that the carrying out of this disarmament must be progressive and must be done under the direction and under the inspection of the United Nations itself.[10]

The Senator addressed a letter to the President, which carried the signatures of thirteen members of the Senate and nine members of the House, suggesting that the United States put forward a proposal along these lines in the United Nations. He also suggested, as part of his plan, a United Nations police force, "in accordance with the original intention of the

---

[9]Congressional Record, Volume 96, February 6, 1950, page 1478.
[10]Ibid., Volume 97, February 12, 1951, page 1199.

Charter which shall be superior in size and armament to any forces available to the member nations."

These ideas had no impact at the time, but they are essentially similar to the basic ideas which Mr. Khrushchev put forward in his advocacy of general and complete disarmament, and were included in the United States "Outline of Basic Provisions for a Treaty of General and Complete Disarmament in a Peaceful World," laid before the Eighteen-Nation Committee on Disarmament in 1962.

In 1953 the Senate passed a resolution, No. 150, which set out five principles, essentially similar to those Senators Tydings and Flanders had suggested. This resolution was supported by a number of senators and passed in an atmosphere of general agreement. It had been inspired, in part, by an address of President Eisenhower, on April 16, 1953, and was intended as "advice" of the Senate to the Executive on this element of foreign policy. However, this was the only resolution in this period by either House or Congress which dealt with the substantive conditions of disarmament.[11]

In a speech on July 13, 1956, Senator Flanders proposed that the United States and the Soviet Union should agree together to ban ICBM tests, and further testing of the thermonuclear bomb.[12] A year later Senator Hubert Humphrey, Chairman of the Subcommittee on Disarmament, of the Senate Committee on Foreign Affairs, proposed in a speech on June 17, 1957 that the United States should try to reach agreement with the Soviet Union to control (and presumably limit) the construction of intercontinental and intermediate-range ballistic missiles.[13] He foresaw that unrestricted competition in building these armaments would impose a great burden on both nations. But it was not until 1969, twelve years, several thousands of missiles and billions of dollars later that this idea was accepted, and the superpowers commenced the Strategic Arms Limitation Talks. Senator Humphrey's suggestion was made before the Soviet Union had launched Sputnik I, and demonstrated an ICBM. That no attention was paid to his suggestion and those of his colleagues, at the time, has been explained by the attitude of the military and the executive as revealed in the appropriation hearings.

In a speech on February 3, 1958, the then Senator Lyndon Johnson proposed an agreement under United Nations auspices, to prevent the

---

[11]Disarmament and Security: A Collection of Documents 1919-55; US Senate, Subcommittee on Disarmament, 84th Congress, 2nd Session 1956, page 788.
[12]Congressional Record, July 13, 1956, page 12614.
[13]Ibid., June 17, 1957, page 9332.

extension of the arms race into outer space. This idea found a place in both the United States and the Soviet Union programmes for general and complete disarmament, and eventually was dealt with as a separate, partial measure, first by declaration by the two powers in the United Nations General Assembly, and later in the Outer Space Treaty.[14]

Senator Humphrey made an important speech on February 4, 1958, advocating regional disarmament agreements, the banning of nuclear weapon tests, and the reduction of fissile materials for weapons purposes.[15] The speech received a large measure of public support, as evidenced by the exceptional amount of favourable mail the Senator received. On December 6, 1959, he made a speech advocating a reduction of intercontinental ballistic missiles, a ban on their testing, and a world-wide system of protection against surprise attack. In June 1960, when the TNCD was meeting in Geneva, he presented his ideas on a first-stage disarmament agreement. This would include a prohibition of the production of long-range bombers.[16]

As this narrative of disarmament develops, it will be seen that many of the Senator's suggestions listed above were incorporated in United States disarmament proposals at the Geneva conferences. Whether the ideas were original to those who made the speeches, or whether they were suggested to them by officials or persons outside government who were working on disarmament, is not material. What should be considered briefly, however, is how much the Executive consulted the Senate on the positions to be taken by the United States delegations to the disarmament conferences, and in the United Nations. One would think that this would have been done systematically, since the Senate would have to consent to any treaty which might result from the negotiations to which the proposals related.

A general observation regarding the reluctance of the Executive to consult with the Legislative Branch, under the American system of government is that, especially when the two branches are under control of different parties, the Executive Branch sometimes is suspicious that Congress wants to obtain information to use for partisan political ends. The Legislative Branch tends to think that the Executive deliberately withholds information in order to increase its position of power. The Executive dislikes interference by the Congress in policy-making, in the foreign field, and sometimes seems to fear that if confidential information

---

[14]*Ibid.*, Volume 104, February 3, 1958, page 1484.
[15]*Ibid.*, February 4, 1958, pages 1607-31 and January 27, 1960, page 1420.
[16]*Ibid.*, June 24, 1960, page 14189.

is given to senators or representatives, they may leak it to the media, which could interfere with successful negotiation.

The conflicting interests which operate in the formulation of arms control policy in the Executive have been briefly touched on. The agency or administrative unit charged with the responsibility for drawing up disarmament positions had to contend with opposition, suspicion and foot-dragging in varying degrees from the departments of the Government which might view the proposals as likely to threaten the security of the United States, or at least their own prerogatives, influence and share of the public funds. First of the reluctant dragons was, of course, the Department of Defense, for obvious reasons. Second was the intelligence community, particularly in relation to revealing its capacity for collecting information about enemy forces, armaments and military installations. The Atomic Energy Agency, with its important programme for the development and testing of nuclear weapons and their components sometimes proved reluctant. And lastly, opposition came from certain elements in the State Department, which sometimes viewed certain disarmament proposals (such as non-proliferation) as likely to upset relations with allies, or clients for military assistance programmes.

In 1960, the Secretary of State, the Hon. Christian Herter, created a Disarmament Administration by executive order. This was the precursor of the Arms Control and Disarmament Agency set up by the Kennedy administration in 1961. The creation of this agency required hearings in the Senate and the House, and, from this period on, Congress paid more attention to disarmament and arms control measures, especially to the prohibition of the testing of nuclear weapons, and the non-proliferation treaty. But these arms control measures will not be discussed at length, being peripheral to the main subject of this book, which is the negotiations and proposals for the limitation of arms of mass destruction (strategic arms), and the forces which inhibited progress in this vital area. However, as the narrative develops, there will be references to the views expressed in the Congress on various measures.

Following Stalin's death, Malenkov, who succeeded him as Prime Minister, allowed the people of the Soviet Union to be informed of the terrific damage which nuclear weapons could cause – information which had been withheld under the Stalin régime. Malenkov and other authorities went so far as to say that nuclear wars could destroy communist as well as capitalist society. When Khrushchev in turn became Prime Minister, at first he opposed this conclusion, but later came around to accept it in essence. In 1956 he revised the Leninist tenet that war with the "imperialists" was inevitable, and the other dictum (adapted from Clausewitz), that war was an instrument of politics.[17]

Khrushchev's conclusion that nuclear war could not be a means of advancing the socialist revolution is illustrated by the remarks that it would not be possible to build communism on the radioactive rubble left by a nuclear war,[18] and that "the atomic bomb does not adhere to the class principle."[19]

The Chinese, early in the course of their long polemic with the Soviet Union, challenged the ideas that war was not inevitable, and that nuclear war was a supreme danger, to be avoided at almost any cost. They asserted that the USSR was too concerned by the nuclear menace, and that because of this, Soviet Union military policy failed to serve the needs of world revolutionary movements.[20]

As we have seen, the US Strategic Air Command had been expanded greatly because of the anxieties created by the Korean war. This was about the time when Khrushchev reached the pinnacle of power. The Soviet military were greatly concerned by the possibility of a US surprise nuclear strike on their country. But Khrushchev had begun to believe that the USA had no intention of initiating a nuclear attack, and that nuclear war was improbable. The question he had to decide was whether or not to opt for a deterrent posture, with some inferiority to the USA in armament, or whether to attempt to achieve Soviet Union superiority in that armament, the capability to "win" a war in case deterrence failed. Should the build-up of the armed forces, including intercontinental missiles and bombers, have first call on the resources of the Soviet economy, when the need to improve the condition of agriculture and general standards of living was acute? Apparently Khrushchev decided for deterrence, and not to attempt to reach superiority. Nevertheless, in frequent public statements he exaggerated the power conferred on the USSR by its nuclear armament and delivery systems.[21] Whether this was deliberate bluffing, to induce the rest of the world to agree to his programme for general and complete

---

[17]Garthoff, *Soviet Strategy in the Nuclear Age* (New York: Praeger, 1964), pages 6, 7.

[18]*Pravda*, December 13, 1962.

[19]*Pravda*, July 14, 1963, "Open letter to the Central Committee of the Soviet Union."

[20]Wolfe, Thomas W., *Soviet Power and Europe, 1945-1970* (Baltimore: Johns Hopkins, 1970), page 131.

[21]In 1960, Mr. Khrushchev asserted to the General Assembly: "Recently I was in a factory, and I saw rockets coming out like sausages from a sausage machine." UN Doc. A/PV. 900 para. 189.

disarmament, or merely to enhance Soviet prestige, we shall probably never know.

Most Soviet military leaders would have preferred a policy aimed at attaining superiority, and were not very happy with Khrushchev's decision. His emphasis on the deterrent effect of missiles seemed to them to be likely to lead to a lack of proper balance in USSR forces. When funds were being allocated for defence, missile development got the biggest share, which left little for strengthening the other military elements. The marshals thought that the nuclear deterrent would be credible only if the Soviet Union could fight any kind of war – all-out nuclear, limited nuclear, or with conventional armaments alone.

Although the terms were different, this controversy paralleled that in the United States between the military who wanted to have the *matériel* to "win" a nuclear war, and those (mainly civilian officials or academic exponents of strategy) who maintained that the proper purpose of nuclear armament was deterrence, and that there could be no victory in a nuclear war.

In his speech to the 1960 Conference of Communist World Parties[22] Khrushchev indicated that there would be a more active Soviet Union policy in the underdeveloped countries. That is to say, that the USSR would be prepared to support revolutionary wars and insurgencies. But as it turned out, the Soviet Union did little to put this proposed policy into effect. As the 1960's went on, the Russian leaders realized that if the USSR and the USA should confront one another in a war originating in the Third World, it could build up to a global nuclear war, which was to be avoided at all costs.

As we have seen, NATO decided in 1957 to arm itself with tactical nuclear weapons, and to rely on them to meet any serious aggression by Soviet Union conventional forces. The USSR was very apprehensive of the danger which would arise if the Federal Republic of Germany had a part in the use of nuclear armament. At this time Soviet Union technology had not progressed very far in developing tactical nuclear weapons. Khrushchev and his advisers had to determine the priorities between building up strategic nuclear armament, to reduce the American preponderance, and extensive development of tactical nuclear arms. Hence it took some years before the Soviet forces in Europe caught up with the NATO forces in this respect.

I have referred to Khrushchev's speech to the Supreme Soviet on

---

[22]Khrushchev, "For New Victories of the World Communist Movement," *Kommunist,* January 1961.

January 14, 1960. In it he observed that any future war would be of short duration, and that it was probable that the issue would be determined in the initial phase. However, the enormous territorial expanse of the Soviet Union would enable it to survive and retaliate, if it took care to disperse and hide its own strategic forces.

In proposing to rely on their new long-range weapons of mass destruction instead of ponderous conventional armies, the USSR, it could be said, was more or less following the same lines as had the United States in its New Look policy. However, a difference came later. When the United States modified its New Look-cum-Massive Retaliation strategic ideas, it proposed to rely, in the European confrontation, on the tactical nuclear weapons which it had developed, while the Soviet Union relied on the threat to European NATO countries of its MRBM's, IRBM's and medium-range bombers.

Even after the Soviet Union had begun to deploy tactical nuclear weapons, these could not be used, they considered, without the hostilities developing into a "strategic" nuclear exchange (that is, intercontinental, and counter-city in Europe). Khrushchev held steadfastly to the view that any warfare in Europe would be likely to escalate to the limit.[23] He held this view even after it had been rendered somewhat dubious by the dissensions within NATO arising from US pressures to build up conventional forces, so as to provide for the strategy of "flexible response" conceived during the Kennedy administration. (The theory of "flexible response" – of which more will be said later – was that an aggression by Warsaw Pact forces should be met by employing conventional or nuclear armed forces as appropriate to the dimension of the enemy offensive, but in a carefully controlled manner, in the hope of avoiding escalation into a full-scale nuclear war.)

Khrushchev's changes in the military policy and the manpower reductions did not greatly alter the strength of the forces deployed in the Western theatre, that is, in the territory of the Warsaw Pact allies, and the western part of the Soviet Union. In 1961 Marshal Malinovsky[24] gave a speech in which he laid stress on the nuclear armament of these forces, and the increase in their battlefield mobility and firepower conferred by new equipment. Tactical nuclear weapons and nuclear-armed tactical aircraft would be relied on in future to prepare an attack, more than the traditional Russian use of massed artillery. This announced policy appeared to respond to the arguments of the Soviet military who continued

---

[23]Khrushchev, Reports of speeches, *Pravda*, November 29, 1957 and January 15, 1960.
[24]Malinovsky, R.Ia., Report to 22nd Party Congress, *Pravda*, October 25, 1961.

to urge that the Soviet Union must be able to continue to fight a war even after an all-out nuclear exchange.

Their view was that after the initial nuclear blasting at all ranges and at all targets, large conventional forces would be needed to occupy Europe and consolidate victory,[25] and, as already remarked, maintaining large conventional forces in the European theatre could be justified as another element of deterrence.

The Soviet Union politico-military problem in Europe was complex. To continue to hold the European countries as hostages against United States attack, by the threat of their intermediate- and medium-range nuclear missiles and preponderant conventional forces, would operate against the political strategy which sought to detach the European NATO allies from the United States.

In the Khrushchev period, the Soviet Union military theorists categorized wars as (a) general world war, (b) imperialist wars, and (c) wars of national liberation.[26] It had become a firm element in Soviet military theory that any world war would be fought using nuclear weapons for unlimited ends, and between rival socialist and imperialist coalitions.[27] There was a sporadic tendency to argue that the West was bent on attacking the Soviet Union and its allies if a favourable occasion should arise. Soviet theorists were beginning to pay more attention to the possibility of surprise nuclear attack, and frequently charged that the USA was planning to stage such a surprise attack in a preventive war against the Soviet Union.[28] This kind of argument continued into the early 1960's. However, during the conference of experts on the prevention of surprise attack, which was held in Geneva in November and December of 1958, the Soviet delegates seemed not much interested in the technical possibilities of lessening the danger of an intercontinental surprise attack with nuclear weapons, and pushed their own proposals for inspection and observations systems in Europe as a part of a disarmament plan for the region.[29]

Soviet strategists usually pictured general war arising out of a crisis in Europe. If hostilities began there, they were highly likely to escalate into

[25]Wolfe, T. W., *Soviet Strategy at the Crossroads*, pages 110-15, 139-46, 172-6.
[26]Marshal Sokolovsky et al., *Soviet Military Strategy* (Prentice-Hall, 1963), pages 282, 283.
[27]Wolfe, *op. cit.*, pages 111-15.
[28]Khrushchev, *For Victory in Peaceful Competition with Capitalism* (New York: Dutton, 1960), pages 33, 491.
[29]*The United Nations and Disarmament, 1945-1970*, page 75. For a more detailed account of this conference see *Why ABM*, J. J. Holst (Elmsford, N.Y.: Hudson Institute Press, 1969), Chapter 12.

a general nuclear war. But towards the end of the 1950's there was less insistence on the inevitability of war, in Soviet military writing, and more confidence in the possibility of nuclear deterrence. This could have been due, in part, to Khrushchev's growing conviction that there were "soberminded" elements as well as hawks within the United States leadership.

As noted above, when Khrushchev came into power he had to decide on what should be done about building a bomber force. He decided to depend primarily on missiles to provide a deterrent to United States attack, and he settled for a modest intercontinental bomber force, accompanied by a numerically larger medium-range bomber force, which could threaten the European NATO countries, and the American overseas bases. Russian military leaders did not agree with Khrushchev's view that the bomber was becoming obsolete, and they advanced the same arguments in favour of retaining a large bomber force that were heard from American Air Force generals.

While Mr. Khrushchev was in power, the USSR devoted much effort to building up a strong defence against bombing attack. It included fighter aircraft directed by ground control centres, anti-aircraft artillery and surface-to-air missiles, of which there was a large deployment around Moscow.[30]

Soviet Union research on ABM's is supposed to have commenced at the same time as they began to produce long-range offensive missiles. In October 1961, Marshal Malinovsky reported that the problem of destroying a missile in flight had been successfully solved.[31] Khrushchev stated in July 1962 that the Soviet Union had developed an anti-missile missile which could hit a fly in outer space.[32] In 1963 there was a discussion in the US Senate on the possibility that the USSR had already begun siting ABM defences around Leningrad.[33] But apparently Khrushchev had taken no decision on deploying an ABM system, although no doubt he had sanctioned preparatory work.

In this and preceding chapters we have reviewed the superpowers' military policies in regard to long-range nuclear-weapon vehicles as they were in the year 1960, during and after the Conference of the Ten-Nation Committee on Disarmament. In the next chapter we shall examine, in the light of these policies, the proposals put forward by the two sides in the TNCD.

[30]Sokolovsky, *op. cit.*, page 307.
[31]*Pravda*, October 25, 1961.
[32]*The New York Times*, Statement by Khrushchev, July 17, 1962.
[33]Thomas, John R., *Role of Missile Defense in Soviet Strategy and Foreign Policy* (McLean, Va.: Research Analysis Corporation, 1965), page 1.

CHAPTER 6

Western proposals, 1960

When the representatives of the five NATO members of the Ten-Nation Disarmament Committee met in Washington on January 25, 1960, they were faced with the task of drawing up proposals for a programme of "measures leading towards the goal of general and complete disarmament under effective international control," to quote from the concluding operative paragraph of General Assembly Resolution 1378/XIV. We expected that the Soviet Union would present a draft treaty based on the "Declaration of the Soviet Government on General and Complete Disarmament."[1]

In the outline programme contained in the Soviet Union Government's declaration, there was no measure for limiting or reducing the numbers of nuclear weapons or their vehicles in the programme until the third stage, in which it was proposed that all these armaments and also "air force equipment" should be destroyed. In the first two stages conventional arms and forces and overseas bases would be eliminated.

This was almost the reverse of the priority suggested by M. Jules Moch. Leaving the elimination of nuclear vehicles to the last stage gave the western delegates the impression that the Soviet Union believed itself to be well ahead of the United States in the development of long-range

[1] UN Document A/4219; September 19, 1959.

ballistic missiles, and wished to preserve this advantage as long as possible during the process of disarmament.

We have noted the claims of Mr. Khrushchev about the power of the Soviet Union's intercontinental rockets, and their superiority in this new and alarming type of armament. But the Russian military no doubt had access to the information that had been laid before the House Committee on Defense Appropriations (and possibly information on certain points not published in the record). They may have perceived that the so-called "missile gap" would soon be closed by the United States, and that the Soviet Union might indeed soon find itself outproduced in ICBM's and other highly developed means of delivering the nuclear weapon.

Although at the time little attention was paid to it, a hint had been received that the USSR might be willing to change its priorities. Mr. Timerbaev, a member of the USSR Permanent Mission to the United Nations in New York, had a conversation about mid-February with Mr. P. C. Dobell, who was then a member of the Canadian Mission. Mr. Timerbaev, who had been a member of a previous Soviet Union delegation to a disarmament conference (and who has subsequently been concerned with disarmament questions), said that the USSR was disturbed by reports that the USA would place principal importance, in its proposals for disarmament, on the reduction of conventional forces in the first stage. He hoped that, if the USA position was not yet firm, they would propose real measures of disarmament in the field of nuclear weapons and missiles in the early stages. Mr. Dobell pointed out that this suggestion did not conform with Mr. Khrushchev's September 19 proposals, which stressed reduction of manpower and conventional forces in the first stage, and left elimination of nuclear weapons and missiles until the third stage. Mr. Timerbaev said that this aspect of the Khrushchev proposals was an attempt to conform to the pattern of the Western approach in the past. However, these proposals were not intended to be detailed or inflexible. He was sure that, if the West should desire to advance the timing of disarmament in fields other than conventional, the USSR would be glad to negotiate on that basis.

Now, although Soviet Union diplomats who have taken part in disarmament negotiations on occasion are willing to talk in a relaxed way about possible variations of positions their government has taken up publicly, they do not go so far as to suggest anything which they know has not been under consideration in the organs where official advice is formulated. Certainly it is difficult to conceive of even the most accessible Russian diplomat suggesting anything which he knows would be unacceptable to the authorities on the levels above his. So we had a hint of the possibility of the Soviet Union changing the priority between measures of dealing with conventional arms and forces, and those dealing with nuclear armaments. But it was several months before this change was brought to the negotiating table as a firm Soviet Union proposal.

From the inception of, and indeed from the beginning of preparations for the Ten-Nation Conference, the Canadian representatives devoted particular attention to the possibility of checking development of the new class of nuclear weapon vehicles, the intercontinental and other long-range nuclear-headed rockets. As already mentioned, it would be to Canada's advantage if there could be a limit to the means of delivering the devastating thermonuclear weapons across the Atlantic. If there were a nuclear war between the two superpowers, Canada, situated between them, could hardly expect to be immune from the effects – radioactive fallout, and warheads falling short of their intended targets. The argument advanced by M. Moch for according priority to the elimination of the nuclear weapon vehicles in the disarmament process had impressed the Canadian authorities as logical and sound.

A special committee had been set up in the Department of National Defence to examine the probable development of new means of waging war, including missiles. General Charles Foulkes, then Chairman of the Chiefs of Staff Committee, arranged for this special committee to collaborate with officials of the Department of External Affairs who were dealing with disarmament matters. Studies of the problem of control (verification), and of measures for the halt in production and subsequent reduction of missiles were undertaken. Unfortunately there were no immediate dividends from these studies, for reasons which will be explained as the history of the negotiations is developed. The fact is mentioned here, however, as showing that the Canadian authorities recognized at an early period the vital character of the control of the long-range nuclear weapon vehicles (or "strategic arms") in any plan for disarmament.

Shortly before the meeting of the Western Five, I had a conversation with Dr. George Kistiakowsky, then special scientific adviser to President Eisenhower. The subject of how to control any measure for limitation or reduction of long-range ballistic missiles was discussed in a general way. Dr. Kistiakowsky believed that the Soviet Union would not abandon its traditional policy of secrecy, and would continue to refuse to allow inspections on its territory. This would render it very difficult to devise any scheme for effective verification. However, he predicted that it would be possible for satellites to scan Russian territory and discover missile sites.

He also agreed with the idea that there could be a stalemate in the race to produce bigger and better and more ballistic missiles, and that, when that occurred, prospects for control of this arms race would be brighter. One must be impressed by Dr. Kistiakowsky's ability to foresee developments, and also by the fact that it took until 1969 for the idea of stalemate and the advisability of negotiations for limitation of the race in strategic weapons to be accepted.

The meeting of the Western Five began as scheduled, with Mr. Frederick Eaton, the representative of the USA, acting as Chairman. It was noticeable that the US apparatus for dealing with the negotiation and disarmament generally was on a very modest scale. For example, Mr. Eaton and his assistants were housed in several rooms in an old house not far from the old State Department offices. The house, which had been acquired by the Government with other land as a building site, was somewhat dilapidated inside, and the officials were more than somewhat crowded. One could not help contrasting the accommodation and numbers of the United States staff responsible for disarmament with the size of the Pentagon and its establishment of 30,000 or more. One hoped that this disproportion did not exactly represent the value placed by the US Administration on peace and disarmament on the one hand, and warlike preparations on the other.

Even at this early stage we began to think how the concerns and activities of the Ten-Nation Committee on Disarmament could be harmonized with those of the North Atlantic Council (the NATO political body). Mr. Jules Leger, then Canadian Representative on the Council, had drawn the attention of our authorities to this problem. The question of coordination did not become acute until the negotiations on a nonproliferation treaty began to show signs of approaching agreement in 1966. The delays which then occurred, through the necessity of gaining the concurrence of the NATO partners, are another story, and not related closely to the problems of control of strategic arms. However, there was always a divergence between the interests of the representatives of the NATO countries in the ENDC and those in the North Atlantic Council. One group was concerned mainly with strengthening military means of gaining security; the other with reducing those military means by agreement with the potential adversary for balanced mutual scaling down of armaments and forces. During the 1960 negotiations, the NATO members of the TNCD sent regular written reports to the North Atlantic Council. When the ENDC began to meet in 1962, the method of coordination was for representatives of the NATO countries in the TNCD and ENDC to attend meetings of the North Atlantic Council every two weeks or so, report what had been going on in the disarmament conference, and answer questions. Excepting the representatives of one or two countries, the Council seemed to take little interest in these sessions, and one got the impression that they shared the view of so many militarily-oriented persons, that disarmament was all moonshine, and that nothing to upset the quiet routine of the NAC was likely to emerge from Geneva.

When the Western Five assembled on January 25, the Americans produced a critique of the Khrushchev GCD proposals, which the British, French and Canadian delegates felt to be too negative and too permeated by suspicion of Soviet Union motives. I suggested to my colleagues that the West should go to Geneva determined to test whether the Soviet Union's professed desire for disarmament was sincere. For this purpose we should not simply reject their proposals, but should criticize them in a constructive way, with a view to reaching a programme acceptable to the West. For this we should have a position offering practical means of arriving by degrees at a safer world – peaceful and disarmed.

Mr. Eaton's first commentary on the British and French proposals was not at all encouraging. He said the United States could not discuss reductions in conventional forces, the missile control item, nor the conference on nuclear cut-off. However, he said this was a preliminary reaction, as definite instructions had not yet been received from the administration. The delay in formulating instructions may have been due to the current political uproar over the alleged missile gap, and other deficiencies in defence arrangements, in a presidential election year. This delay continued until the 15th of February.

In a discussion on February 12 of the tactics which the Soviet Union delegation might adopt at the TNCD, I pointed out that all nations had endorsed the idea of GCD in the UNGA Resolution 1378/XIV, and therefore we could not avoid accepting it as a *goal* in the TNCD negotiations. Otherwise the Soviet Union representatives could accuse the West of rejecting in the TNCD what they had accepted in the United Nations. We should endeavour to have a plan which would define more specifically and realistically what GCD should be, and indicate a method of reaching the goal by degrees, consistent with the actuality of international relations. This was generally agreed to. The British and French delegates, Sir David Ormsby-Gore[2] and M. Jules Moch, said that if there were no concerted Western plan to put on the negotiating table when the TNCD opened on March 15, they would be obliged to present the U.K. and French plans, as proposed

---

[2]Now Lord Harlech.

at the UNGA, and this would be unfortunate as showing disagreement on disarmament policy among the NATO countries.

It was naturally worrying not to know what the USA would be prepared to agree to when the negotiations opened at Geneva. To judge from the tone of the American press, disarmament was far from the thoughts of the general public. The great concern was to catch up with the Russians in space rocketry, and close the "missile gap."

About this time I had an unofficial conversation with the late Mr. Allen Dulles, then head of the Central Intelligence Agency. Some of the things he told me suggested the information which the House Appropriations Committee must have been getting, but which was not reproduced in the record. He said that the Americans could detect firing of all Russian ICBM's and of some IRBM's. He doubted that the Soviet Union then had ICBM's in operational sites. Nor did they have solid-fuel rockets.

The United States would like to carry out tests in the atmosphere on new warheads for Polaris and Minuteman. (Presumably these tests were carried out after the Soviet Union abrogated the moratorium on nuclear weapons testing in January 1961.)

Finally on February 15 the US view on what the West should propose at the opening of the TNCD was disclosed. It was not stimulating, being made up of bits and pieces from previous disarmament proposals. On the whole it looked more like a plan for avoiding disarmament than for effectively controlling armaments. However, by February 19, as a result of criticisms and suggestions by other delegations, a fairly presentable Western position paper had been put together. It covered three stages of disarmament. The French delegation, however, was dissatisfied by the lack of provisions for real control of nuclear weapon vehicles in the early stages, and later, after the proposals had been referred to the French Government, raised quite strong objections. The Canadian criticism of the plan was that it should have earlier and more effective provisions for the control of missiles.

The US authorities, and presumably mainly the military authorities, were not at all pleased by Canada's supporting a measure for the early curbing of the race in long-range missiles. On one occasion Mr. Eaton, in a jocular way, remarked to the Canadian delegate that Canada could give away her missiles if she liked – the USA was not going to give away theirs. Canada, of course, had no missiles at that time.[3]

---

[3]It was only later that we acquired "Honest Johns" (range about twenty miles) and Bomarcs (anti-aircraft defence missiles) from the USA. The warheads for these were always kept under firm United States control.

The real difference between the French and the Americans was over whether nuclear weapon vehicles, including the so-called "nuclear-capable" weapons (that is, those which could deliver either conventional or nuclear explosive warheads), should be limited in the first and second stages of the disarmament programme. The British position was about midway between those of the Americans and French. The Americans and the British possessed the nuclear weapons and means for their delivery, which provided the deterrent on which the defence of Europe against possible Soviet Union aggression was thought to depend. Hence they were unwilling to barter away these armaments at the beginning of negotiations, and in the existing political situation.

On March 6 there was a conference in Ottawa between the Chairman of the Chiefs of Staff Committee and the top External Affairs officials concerned in disarmament, to decide what position Canada should take at the conference in regard to the control of long-range nuclear weapon vehicles. They discussed whether the disclosure of the existing strength of the USA in intercontinental bombers and missiles would affect the deterrent. The Chairman of the Chiefs of Staff thought that it would. No conclusion was reached, but the Canadian delegation was to receive instructions in time for the meeting of the Western Five, which took place in Paris on the 8th of March.

At the Paris meeting, M. Moch explained the position of the French Government. Although he thought certain amendments desirable, eventually he said that he would put the proposals to his government. On March 9 they were finally agreed to, although no one was very happy about them. Nevertheless, it was decided they would be released to the press on the day before the TNCD opened. They were presented to the North Atlantic Council on the 10th of March. There was not much comment from representatives of those states not participating in the TNCD. There was another meeting of the Council on the 12th of March. Mr. Eaton had gone to Geneva to discuss procedural arrangements with the Russians, so I appeared for the Five to explain points about the proposals, and answer questions. There was no serious criticism of the plan. Some delegations reserved the right to comment at a later date. All wanted to be kept abreast of and be consulted on any further steps. That ended the preliminary negotiations among the Western Five, and the TNCD Conference opened on March 15, 1960.

The "Plan for General and Comprehensive Disarmament in a Free and Peaceful World,"[4] submitted by the five Western powers to the TNCD

4Document TNCD/3.

on March 16, 1960, contained the following paragraphs in the preamble:

> The ultimate goal is a secure, free and peaceful world in which there shall be general disarmament under effective international control and agreed procedures for the settlement of disputes in accordance with the principles of the United Nations Charter.

> The task of the Ten-Nation Disarmament Conference should be to work out measures leading toward general disarmament, which can only be attained by balanced, phased and safeguarded agreements.

Although the first stage provided for reductions of manpower and conventional armaments, the only positive measure relating to missiles was the following:

> Prior notification to the International Disarmament Organization of proposed launchings of space vehicles and the establishment of co-operative arrangements for communication to the International Disarmament Organization data obtained from available tracking facilities.

This provision for notification of rocket launchings was left out of later Western disarmament proposals, as the United States became confident that it could detect them by electronic and other distant operational systems under its own control.

It was also proposed that joint studies should be undertaken in this stage on the feasibility of the following measures which were to be included in the second stage, and the means which could be taken to verify compliance with them.

> The prohibition against placing into orbit or stationing in outer space vehicles capable of mass destruction, to be effective immediately after the installation and effective operation of an agreed control system to verify this measure.[5]

> Prior notification to the International Disarmament Organization of proposed launchings of missiles according to predetermined and mutually agreed criteria, and declarations of locations of launching sites, and places of manufacture of such missiles, with agreed verification including the on-site inspection of launching sites of such missiles.

---

[5]This was eventually adopted as a separate arms control measure, first by declaration of the USA and the USSR at the 1963 UNGA, and later as Article IV of the Treaty on Principles Governing the Activities of States in the Exploration and Use of Outer Space 1966.

The proposal extended the "notification" measure of the first stage. Its provision for declaration of launching sites and manufacturing facilities foreshadowed the sort of control for eventual limiting or eliminating of long-range missiles for purposes of war, which the Western delegations thought necessary in the early sixties.

> The cessation of production of fissionable materials for weapons purposes immediately after the installation and effective operation of an agreed control system to verify this measure, conditional on satisfactory progress in the field of conventional disarmament.

> Agreed quantities of fissionable material from past production to be transferred under international supervision and control to non-weapons uses, including stockpiling, immediately upon the installation and effective operation of an agreed control system to verify the cessation of production of fissionable material for weapons purposes.

This became one of the "package" of arms control measures advocated by the USA, and supported by its allies in the ENDC and the UNGA, which could be put into effect before agreement on a general disarmament treaty. Its relationship to the general problem of control of strategic armaments will be discussed later.

> A disarmament conference with other states having significant military capabilities, called to consider their accession to the disarmament agreement, including their acceptance of appropriate reductions of limitations of their respective force levels and armaments.

It was obvious that if there were eventually to be general and complete disarmament, as the Soviet Union had defined it, or even to the extent that the United States Government might contemplate at that period, all other nations with "significant military capabilities" would have to disarm as well. The participants in the TNCD had the People's Republic of China particularly in mind.

In the third stage of the Western disarmament plan, the following measures "regarded as necessary for achieving the ultimate goal" were to come into effect.

> Reduction of national armed forces and armaments by progressive safeguarded steps . . . to levels required by international security and fulfilment of obligations under the United Nations Charter to the end that no single nation or group of nations can effectively oppose enforcement of international law. . . .

Prohibition of production of nuclear, chemical, biological and other weapons of mass destruction, further transfer to fissionable materials to peaceful use, and further steps, in the light of the latest scientific knowledge, to achieve the final elimination of these weapons.

Measures to ensure the use of outer space for peaceful purposes only.

Control of the production of agreed categories of military missiles and existing national stocks and their final elimination.

The above extract from the Western powers' "Plan for General and Comprehensive Disarmament" includes only those articles which bear on control or limitation of long-range nuclear weapon vehicles (strategic arms). It is not too easy to disentangle the points which relate to this most important class of armaments from the plan as a whole. It dealt also with conventional armaments and armed forces, and with measures for ensuring a peaceful world when it became disarmed (such matters as peace-keeping forces and means of resolving disputes under the principles of international law, in accordance with the ideals of the United Nations).

It is to be noted that the measures which the Western Five laid on the table at Geneva on March 16 did not entail any immediate and effective action to lessen the menace of nuclear weapon vehicles of intercontinental range.

CHAPTER 7

Ten-Nation Committee, first session

When the TNCD opened on March 15, 1960, each delegation made a short statement. In mine the following passage was included:

> The present and terribly dangerous form of the armaments race is the competition in building ballistic missiles and other means of delivery of nuclear explosives. The Canadian Government holds the view that it is of the greatest urgency to take early measures to stop this race in nuclear armaments. There are just two alternatives: a continuation of the race, whose only end can be nuclear war, with unimaginable death and destruction; or its cessation, a resolve to control and then abolish this kind of weapon and move towards a peaceful world.

> Every nation, every alliance, claims that its armaments are for defensive purposes only. Yet fear of aggression, fear of being attacked by surprise, persists. What is the main element of this fear? It is fear of the unknown, fear of what the adversary may be doing, and this results from the secrecy surrounding armaments and other preparations for war.

> So long as there is great secrecy about these matters there will be fear of the unknown, of surprise, of aggression. This fear causes nations and alliances to strive to outstrip in armaments any possible adversary. The only way to remove the fear is mutual disclosure of actual

positions, exchange of information, and, by this means, the establishment of a degree of mutual confidence in order that effective measures of disarmament may be undertaken and that the pervading fear may eventually disappear.

It is easier to point out what we know ought to be done than find the means of doing it. To find the means to dissolve this complex of secrecy, suspense and fear; that is the first task of this Ten-Nation Committee as the Canadian delegation sees it.[1]

There was nothing original about the views expressed in the passage quoted. They were held by the majority of states which did not possess nuclear weapons. However, emphasis was placed on the halting of the race in missiles and other means of delivery of the nuclear weapon – a point not stressed by other delegations, except the French. The passage about the importance of breaking down the barrier of secrecy was intended to support the first stage proposals of the Western plan, which called for declaration of stocks of long-range nuclear weapon vehicles and related information.

Mr. Zorin, the representative of the Soviet Union, first extolled the merits of the USSR plan for General and Complete Disarmament, and its leading exponent, Mr. Khrushchev. He then went on to say that there were still forces in the world which resisted general disarmament. He meant to imply, of course, that these forces existed only in the capitalist world – not at all in Holy Russia. Towards the end of his speech he commented on the Western proposals, which, as mentioned above, had been published, although they had not yet been placed on the table at the conference. He said they did not "contain the realistic provisions for carrying out general and complete disarmament." Previously, although without referring specifically to the Western published proposals, he had suggested they only called for "lengthy study of various technical problems and forms of control over armaments, as well as measures for allegedly ensuring the security of states." It must be admitted that Mr. Zorin's criticism had a good deal of justification.[2]

Sir David Ormsby-Gore, the British representative, referred to the lack of trust and the political differences which divided the countries meeting in the conference, and said that for proposals to be acceptable, they must give equal security to all. Comprehensive disarmament, which was the goal of the West, had to be carried out by successive stages, in which

[1]*Verbatim Record; Ten-Power Disarmament Committee* (London, HMSO, 1960), Comd. 1152, page 7.
[2]*Ibid.*, page 18.

forces and armaments should be steadily decreased, but throughout a satisfactory military balance had to be maintained between the two groups (that is, NATO and the Warsaw Pact).[3]

M. Jules Moch, representing France, said that what the world expected of the conference and hoped for above all, was nuclear disarmament. Conventional weapons and the strength of armed forces were secondary considerations. Once again he stressed that the control of the long-range nuclear weapon vehicles had become the crucial problem in the disarmament complex.[4] The negotiations which followed in the TNCD and in the early sessions of the ENDC were to find the West and the East at odds over many aspects of disarmament and arms control, but it began to be realized, by 1963, that the control of an increase in "strategic arms" (long-range nuclear weapon vehicles) constituted the key problem to be solved if there were to be any real progress towards disarmament.

In his statement the United States representative, Mr. Eaton, emphasized the American view that general disarmament could only take place in a world of sufficiently stable international institutions and relations to allow the settlement of international disputes by resort to legal and political means, instead of by force of arms, exercised or threatened. This viewpoint, which seems very logical, was not immediately helpful in arriving at effective arms control agreements. In one passage Mr. Eaton said:

> We must patiently address ourselves to the task of designing a workable plan of general disarmament, in a world in which man can live at peace with himself, where freedoms will flourish, secure from the fear of invasion by forces of oppression. A world at peace under law, this is the goal – disarmament, a means of achieving it.[5]

The references to "freedoms secure from the fear of invasion by forces of oppression" were hardly calculated to put the Soviet Union representatives in a conciliatory state of mind.

Mr. Eaton went on to elaborate the concept of gradual, step-by-step progress which was held by all Western participants. But this ran counter to the Soviet Union's overt approach, which called for the negotiation as soon as possible of a treaty on general and complete disarmament, to be completed in four years, or not much longer. And the negotiations in the TNCD during the following months can be described as mainly wrangling

---

[3]*Ibid.*, page 22.
[4]*Ibid.*, page 11.
[5]*Ibid.*, page 26.

and jockeying for propaganda positions over which of the two approaches to disarmament was the proper one to undertake.

On March 17, Mr. Nosek, the Czechoslovakian representative, asked several questions about the Western plan, of which the following related to nuclear disarmament.

> The proposal of the Western delegations contains no explicit provision concerning the banning of the use of nuclear weapons. We should like to know if there is any intention to make a declaration concerning these significant measures and, if so, at which stages.

> The proposal of the Western delegations does not provide for destruction of nuclear weapon stockpiles. . . . In the view of the authors of the Western proposal . . . when will the complete liquidation of deposited weapons take place?[6]

The first of these questions related to the Soviet Union's propaganda proposals to "Ban the Bomb" which it had been pushing in various milieux and with various approaches since 1946. It may be admitted that it is not unreasonable to propose that if the powers really did begin to eliminate all nuclear weapons in a programme of general and complete disarmament, at some stage they should establish a convention with effect in international law to the effect that the use of nuclear weapons would be prohibited. Hence Mr. Nosek's question had point. But it raises the general question of whether such a declaration would be credible and reassuring to the world at large if considerable stocks of nuclear weapons were still being retained.

The West had a special reason not to undertake to abstain from the use of the nuclear weapon – or even from first use of it, which was a variant of the "Ban" also proposed. This reason was, as mentioned above, that the security of Western Europe in the face of the great superiority of the Warsaw Pact powers' conventional forces and armaments, depended on the deterrent provided by the United States nuclear war capability. It was thought that if the Western nuclear powers bound themselves not to use the nuclear weapon, the credibility of the deterrent might be compromised, and a temptation might be offered to the Eastern bloc to use their military superiority to execute a territorial coup – for example to eliminate or further compromise the Berlin enclave.

The second question of the Czechoslovak delegate indicated the

---

[6]*Ibid.*, page 53.

somewhat equivocal character of the Western provisions for the eventual elimination of nuclear weapons. This and similar questioning by the other Eastern delegations caused the West to strengthen the provisions in this respect in the revised plan which was produced later in the conference.

On March 21, Sir David Ormsby-Gore criticized the Soviet Union proposals which had not been developed in more detail than as presented in the UNGA by Mr. Khrushchev. He said that the Soviet Union proposals so far presented were quite imprecise, and hardly merited the name of a plan. More clarification than had been furnished up to then would be needed before they could receive the necessary detailed consideration.[7]

Mr. Zorin replied to the points made by the British representative, and in particular to his criticism that the Soviet Union plan had no measures for dealing with nuclear armaments until the last stage of the disarmament process. He reminded the conference that the Soviet Union had always, in its previous proposals for disarmament, stressed the importance of dealing with the threat of nuclear war at an early stage. But in view of the insistence of the Western powers that "they cannot give up nuclear weapons on the ground that the Soviet Union possesses superior armed forces and conventional armaments," the Soviet Union, in the GCD proposals, had left the reduction of these armaments to the end. Mr. Zorin then went on to argue that if conventional armaments and armed forces were reduced as provided for in their GCD proposals, it would be impossible for any nation to carry out an aggressive war, because there would be no armies to occupy the territory of the defeated enemy – consequently no logical purpose in initiating a war. This argument reflected the strategic views of the Soviet Union military at that time, that without large armed forces it would be impossible to conduct an offensive war, because territory could not be occupied. If nuclear weapons only were used, the only consequence would be the extermination of the peaceful population and the destruction of the material and cultural assets on the enemy territory.

At the end of his speech Mr. Zorin said that, however, if the Western powers were ready to accept a complete ban on atomic and hydrogen weapons, to eliminate them from national arsenals and destroy all stocks of them, right at the beginning of the disarmament programme, the Soviet Union would agree. It had always determinedly advocated the total prohibition of nuclear weapons, at any stage of the disarmament programme.[8]

---

[7]*Ibid.*, page 93.
[8]*Ibid.*, pages 95-8.

Mr. Zorin's statement substantiated the hint that we had received un-officially that the Russians would be ready to change the order of priorities in their GCD proposal. This is what they did, in the revised programme, submitted to the TNCD on June 7, 1960 which we shall be examining in the next chapter.

On March 22, Sir David Ormsby-Gore harked back to the question of the "Ban," and the timing of the elimination of nuclear weapons in the USSR proposals. He said that the *final* elimination of nuclear weapons would have to be left until the last stage, but that the U.K. position was that disarmament should proceed by balanced stages and that provision for nuclear disarmament should be made at all stages *pari passu* with provisions for conventional disarmament. He went on to say that there was some confusion as to whether the Eastern countries were proposing that the prohibition of nuclear weapons should come in the last stage, or in one of the earlier stages.[9]

On March 25 I made a statement on behalf of the Canadian delega-tion, supporting the peacekeeping proposals in the Western plan, and arguing that such provisions would be necessary in any plan for GCD.

Later, in the statement, answering Mr. Zorin's argument that it would be impossible for a nation to commit an aggression if it had only nuclear armaments, and no large conventional forces, I said:

I think a moment's consideration will show that a great Power posses-sing missiles could use them to threaten a smaller State if it did not fall in with the desires of the great Power and act according to its interests. It would not be necessary to threaten the destruction of large cities and their population; a threat of exploding nuclear weapons in some part of the smaller state, perhaps in an area important to its economy, after due warning so that the population could be evacu-ated, might be sufficient to break the will of the smaller nation. I hope that no great nation possessing these engines of destruction would ever actually make such threats, but how could the small nations which do not possess nuclear weapons and rockets regard the world and themselves as secure while even after conventional weapons had largely disarmed there were great Powers possessing nuclear weapons, ballistic missiles and their means of delivery? It is a fact that weapons of this kind create far more fear in the world today than any others, as many speakers in this Conference have said.[10]

---

[9]*Ibid.*, page 105.
[10]*Ibid.*, page 161.

The conference went on wrangling, mainly about its purpose and procedure, until April 26, when the Western Five presented a "proposal concerning principles and conditions for general and complete disarmament under effective international control."[11] This document was intended to clarify the basic positions of the Western powers, and to bolster their programme submitted at the beginning of the conference[12] which, as we have seen, had been criticized effectively by the Eastern delegations. None of the Western delegations was entirely satisfied with our programme, which, as recorded above, had been put together rather hastily. In it divergent views held by the members of the Five on some important points, particularly on the timing of measures for the limitation and reduction of long-range weapon vehicles, were imperfectly reconciled.

The most important passages from the "Principles and Conditions" document are the following:

a / Disarmament must be carried out by stages, each stage to be completed as rapidly as possible although no fixed timetable can be laid down in advance for the process as a whole;

b / Nuclear and conventional measures must be balanced so that no country or group of countries will obtain, at any stage, a significant military advantage and so that equal security for all will be maintained and thus international confidence progressively increased;

c / Disarmament measures must be effectively controlled throughout by an International Disarmament Organization within the frame-work of the United Nations, to ensure that compliance with these measures is verified from their entry into force and that there is no evasion throughout the disarmament process and thereafter;

d / Disarmament measures must be negotiated progressively according to the possibility of their early implementation and effective control.

The final goal of a programme of general and complete disarmament under effective international control must be to achieve the reduction and limitation of all types of forces and weapons to the levels required by each State for its own internal security and fulfilment of its obligations under the United Nations Charter and the elimination of all weapons surplus to those required for those purposes. The programme must also provide for the use of outer space for peaceful purposes only and for the final elimination of weapons of mass destruction and their means of delivery.

---

[11]TNCD/5.
[12]TNCD/3.

Principles (a) and (d) state the Western position calling for gradual progress towards more stringent disarmament measures as international confidence increased. Principles (b) and (c) are important in their relation to the problem of limiting and then reducing strategic arms (weapons of mass destruction). The document has some importance as a forerunner of the principles agreed in 1961 between the USA and the USSR for the guidance of the Eighteen-Nation Committee on Disarmament, which will be discussed in due course. But its introduction did not improve the tone or substance of discussions in the TNCD, which adjourned on April 29, in view of the summit conference to be held in Paris in May, between President Eisenhower, Chairman Khrushchev, Prime Minister Macmillan and President de Gaulle.

Why the proposed 1960 "Summit" did not meet is a well-known story. An American U 2 reconnaissance and photographic aircraft was shot down in the Soviet Union, just before the conference date. This gave the Russians proof that the United States had been conducting photographic surveillance of their territory for a considerable period, enabling much strategically important information to be obtained. A great outburst of indignation and recrimination by Mr. Khrushchev followed, echoed by all the USSR media, employing their usual propaganda techniques. President Eisenhower took the responsibility publicly for the programme of what the Soviet Union called espionage, and Mr. Khrushchev asked for an apology and a promise not to repeat this type of offence, as a condition for attending the conference. President Eisenhower could not accept this condition, and the conference was off.

The TNCD communiqué, issued at the meeting on April 29, had set June 7 for resumption of the negotiations. Western delegations, after the summit debacle, were in considerable doubt as to whether the conference would indeed resume. However it did, and the Soviet Union delegation presented a new programme for GCD, which showed certain important changes from that put forward at the 1959 UNGA.

CHAPTER 8

Ten-Nation Committee, second session

The "Basic Provisions of a Treaty on General and Complete Disarmament," submitted by the Soviet Government to the TNCD on June 7, 1960[1], changed its position in regard to the elimination of nuclear weapon vehicles. The timing was advanced, as Mr. Zorin had hinted that it might be.

The introductory part of the document mentioned that some powers, notably France, had expressed the view that disarmament should begin with the prohibition and destruction of nuclear weapon vehicles. It went on to say that the Government of the USSR still considered the order of priority of disarmament measures provided in its proposal of September 18, 1959 was well suited for bringing about general and complete disarmament. Nevertheless it was ready to agree on a different order if this would be more acceptable to the Western powers. The Soviet Government therefore proposed that it should be agreed that the process of general and complete disarmament should begin during the first stage, with the prohibition and destruction under international control of all means of delivering nuclear weapons to their targets, and with the simultaneous liquidation of military bases in foreign territories.

It was then stated magnanimously that the Soviet Union was prepared

---

[1]TNCD/6 Rev. 1.

to take this step, ". . . despite the fact that it had a generally recognized superiority in the most modern and effective means of this kind, namely, intercontinental rockets."

Passing to the detail of the measures which the Soviet Union now proposed for the three stages of disarmament, we find the following:

First Stage.

1 / All means of delivering nuclear weapons will be eliminated from the armed forces of States; their manufacture will be discontinued and they will be destroyed. Such means include:

- strategic and tactical rockets, pilotless aircraft of all types, and all military aircraft capable of delivering nuclear weapons;
- surface warships that can be used as vehicles for nuclear weapons;
- submarines of all types;
- all artillery systems, as well as other means, that can be used as vehicles for atomic and hydrogen weapons.

Paragraph 2 provided for the withdrawal of troops from foreign territories to their own country, and the closing down of foreign military bases.

Paragraphs 3 and 4 proposed to prohibit placing "any special devices" in orbit; warships from leaving territorial waters and military aircraft capable of carrying nuclear weapons from flying beyond national boundaries. Launching of rockets would be only for peaceful purposes, under agreed arrangements, including inspection of their launching sites.

Article 5 called for non-proliferation of nuclear weapons (eventually to be embodied in the Non-proliferation Treaty of 1968, after four years of negotiation in the ENDC).

Article 7 outlined the control measures proposed, including those related to control of strategic arms which follow:

On-site international control will be established *over the destruction*[2] of rocket weapons, military aircraft, surface warships, submarines and other means which can be used as vehicles for atomic and hydrogen weapons.

. . . control will also be established at airfields and ports, to ensure that they are not used for military purposes. At the same time, rocket launching sites, with the exception of those maintained for peaceful purposes, will be destroyed. . . .

---

[2]Italics added.

The control organization will have the right to inspect without hindrance all enterprises, plants, factories and shipyards previously engaged wholly or in part in the production of rockets, aircraft, surface warships, submarines and any other means of delivering nuclear weapons, in order to prevent the organization of clandestine production of armaments which can be used as vehicles for atomic and hydrogen weapons. By agreement, permanent control teams may be established at some plants and installations.

International inspection teams dispatched by the control organization will have the right to carry out a thorough examination of rocket devices to be launched for peaceful purposes, and to be present at their launching.

At first sight, these provisions seem quite comprehensive. What prevented their acceptance by the West was that they provided for control *over disarmament only,* over the *destruction* of what each side might declare as its holding of the various vehicles. There was no provision for verifying the numbers of such vehicles before the disarmament process began. Hence, the West argued, there was no certainty that some might not be retained clandestinely. After the destruction of all others had been accomplished, even a few vehicles could provide a means of "nuclear blackmail."

But the Russians refused to entertain provisions for control measures which would require a count of the vehicles before disarmament measures began. They pointed out that such measures would disclose the deployment of the Soviet Union missiles which constituted the main element of their deterrent. The deterrent would then be exposd to a preemptive strike, which in view of the balance of long-range nuclear weapon vehicles at that time was certainly more of a possibility than it has been since the mid-sixties. In justification of this fear, and of the measure for withdrawal from and closing down of all foreign bases, the representative of Romania quoted a statement made by Admiral Arleigh A. Burke, the United States Chief of Naval Operations, in April 1959 (just a year before) as follows:

The United States has the ability right now, in being, to destroy the Soviet Union. We can do it in several ways, and several times over, with our powerful Strategic Air Command of the United States Air Force, with carrier striking forces of the United States Navy, with tactical air forces and with intermediate range ballistic missiles, which are now being installed on certain European sites.[3]

---

[3]TNCD/PV 16.

In the second stage of the proposed programme, chemical, biological and other weapons of mass destruction would be prohibited, their manufacture would be stopped and stockpiles would be destroyed, under international control.

It is especially to be noted that only in the second stage would there be reductions in armed forces and conventional armaments, measures which in the original 1959 USSR proposals for GCD took place in the first stage. If the measures proposed by the Soviet Union were implemented in the order suggested, the effect would be that the superiority in conventional armaments and armed forces of the Warsaw Pact in Europe would be left intact, while the nuclear armaments on which the West relied to deter the East from aggressive use of that military superiority would be abolished. Naturally, this made the new USSR proposals unacceptable, and during the three weeks until the conference ended the West devoted much of its effort to criticizing them, and exposing their imbalance. At the same time, the Western delegates had to admit to themselves that their own March 16 disarmament plan looked very feeble. The Soviet proposal to do away with all means of delivering the nuclear weapon in the first stage of disarmament, even if really a piece of gamesmanship, would doubtless be acclaimed by those nations which were neutral or had no nuclear arms. From June 7 on, there were discussions among the Western Five on the necessity for producing a more attractive disarmament plan.

At the United Kingdom reception in honour of the Queen's birthday (June 9), I had a conversation with Sir David Ormsby-Gore and Mr. Zorin. The latter wanted to know when the West would begin to discuss the new Soviet Union plan seriously. Ormsby-Gore said he was awaiting instructions, and observed that the plan needed to be more balanced as between nuclear and conventional disarmament. He also asked how it could be verified that all vehicles would be brought to the place where they would be destroyed, and that there were none kept and concealed elsewhere. Zorin said that the United States claimed to know all about the deployment of USSR weapons, and as the West's bases and missile sites were known, there should be no room for deception.

At the TNCD meeting that day I had made a statement in regard to the new USSR proposals, saying:

> . . . the Canadian delegation does appreciate the adoption of certain of the ideas that were put forward in the Western proposals. These are. . . . the prohibition of the launching into orbit or the placing in outer space of devices carrying weapons of mass destruction . . . and the control over the launching of rockets for peaceful purposes . . .

another important modification to the original Soviet plan appears in paragraph 9 of the third stage, that measures to maintain peace and security in accordance with the Charter of the United Nations shall be carried out, and that States shall undertake to place at the disposal of the Security Council as required, contingents of police (or militia) from those retained by the said States.[4]

Although these changes did not affect the central disarmament problem, it seemed desirable to welcome Soviet agreement to some of the Western proposals, to help in keeping the atmosphere favourable to compromise on more important questions.

In introducing the new Soviet Union proposals, Mr. Zorin had said that M. Jules Moch had repeatedly stressed the need to prohibit and destroy the means of delivering nuclear weapons to their targets. He went on to suggest that the new proposals had met the French position.[5] On June 13, M. Moch replied to this, saying that certain French ideas appeared to have been adopted, but that the presentation, the methods of application, and the general philosophy were not in conformity. Although some of the proposals called for attention by the French delegation, there were others which they could not accept because, if adopted too soon, they would jeopardize Western security before adequate disarmament measures had been applied and effectively controlled.[6]

Ever since the conference had opened the Western delegates had been obliged to adopt what amounted to stalling tactics. It was difficult simply to criticize the Soviet Union plan, with nothing better than our March 16, 1960 programme to offer in its place. I recall a meeting with Sir David Ormsby-Gore at which we discussed how our plan could be improved. This was part of a series of discussions on the subject, and on June 17 Mr. Eaton flew back to Washington to get approval for a new set of proposals which would have more disarmament content in the early stages. They were designed to give the West a better negotiating position, or at least to improve its appearance in the eyes of the world.

There were several TNCD meetings between June 17 and 25, at which the atmosphere deteriorated, with accusations by the Soviet Union and other Eastern representatives that the USA and the West did not really want disarmament, and were not negotiating seriously. They made these accusations public in a press release on June 22, in which it was said:

---

[4]*Verbatim Records; Ten-Power Disarmament Committee* (London, HMSO), Comd. 1152, page 672.
[5]TNCD/PV 33.
[6]TNCD/PV 37.

There is a growing impression that the United States of America and its allies do not wish to make progress in the negotiations on disarmament, but to make them mark time indefinitely, or, in general, to bring about their failure.

This allegation was, of course, repudiated by Western representatives, who pointed out that since the presentation of the new Soviet Union plan they had been seeking explanations of some of its features, which they found unclear or impracticable. It was also pointed out that Mr. Eaton had returned to Washington in order to get new instructions from his government, necessary for progress in the new situation.

Mr. Eaton returned on June 25 with the new programme, which had been approved by President Eisenhower. The Western delegates spent part of the next day discussing it with the USA delegation, and were seeking approval of their governments to support it. But at the meeting on the 27th, a Monday, Mr. Zorin led off with a statement announcing that the Soviet Union would no longer participate in the proceedings of the TNCD. He said, in part:

It has become quite obvious that the Western Powers are trying to avoid discussing the new Soviet proposals, and that once again they have no intention of conducting serious and fruitful negotiations on disarmament. . . .

Under such circumstances the participation of the Soviet Union in endless discussions in the Ten Nation Committee would, objectively speaking, merely confuse world opinion. . . . The Soviet Union naturally cannot be an accomplice in deceiving the peoples of the world. In view of this, the Soviet Government is breaking off its participation in the Ten Nation Committee. . . .[7]

Mr. Zorin said, however, that his government was willing to take part in disarmament negotiations in the future, and that it would pursue the matter at the next session of the UN General Assembly.

The representatives of the four other Warsaw Pact states following in turn, made statements practically identical in sense. The Polish representative, Mr. Naszkowski, who was in the chair, refused to recognize any Western representatives asking to speak, and at the conclusion of their five addresses, the Warsaw Pact delegates picked up their papers, and, as *The Economist* reported it, they shuffled out of the hall like waiters avoiding the eye of an impatient diner.

---

[7]*Verbatim Records T.P.D.C.* (HMSO), pages 881-2.

The five Western delegations determined to continue the meeting by themselves. They called in the press to hear what they had to say, and each representative spoke, voicing indignation at the proceedings of the Warsaw Pact delegations. Mr. Eaton, with the concurrence of the other Western delegations, tabled the revised programme in the name of the United States. The following is a resumé of the modifications to the March 16, 1960 plan.

The programme's introduction redefined the requirements of "General and complete disarmament in a secure, free and peaceful world," to include:

> The cessation of production of all kinds of armaments, including all means for delivering weapons of mass destruction, and their complete elimination from national arsenals, through progressive stages, except for those armaments agreed upon for use by an international peace force and agreed remaining national contingents.[8]

It will be noted that this statement did not exclude the possibility that the international peace force might be armed with nuclear weapons and the means for their delivery. The second article in stage three also allowed for this. The reason for this opening being left was the argument advanced in some quarters, especially in the United States, that if the nations of the world really disarmed themselves, and depended on an international force for their protection against aggression, that force should have at its disposal the ultimate weapon. Otherwise, some villainous dictator might clandestinely provide himself with nuclear armaments, and blackmail the rest of the world. I argued against leaving nuclear armaments in the hands of the eventual international peace force. My main reason was that it was inconceivable that the United Nations would authorize nuclear arms being used by a force that was intended to maintain peace and security in a disarmed world, or indeed support a general and complete disarmament treaty which provided for the contemplated peace force to have nuclear armament.

The whole issue was highly theoretical, but the Eastern delegation, in the course of the negotiations, noted the exception to the proposed destruction of all nuclear weapons and their vehicles. They attacked it, as indicating that the West did not really want to destroy all nuclear arms, but to keep some, over which it might exercise control through a subservient United Nations majority.

Measures in stage one of the new programme included measures

---

[8]TNCD/7, June 27, US plan.

which had been moved up from stage two of the March 16 plan, viz., the prohibition of orbiting or stationing in space of weapons of mass destruction, measures of inspection and observation to limit the possibility of surprise attack, and reduction of armed forces (of the USA and USSR to 2.5 million; later to 2.1 million), with concurrent sequestration of a related proportion of conventional armaments.

In stage two, the forces of the superpowers were to be reduced to 1.7 million. Armaments, "including nuclear, chemical, biological and other weapons of destruction in existence and all means for their delivery shall be reduced to agreed levels, and the resulting excesses shall be destroyed or converted to peaceful uses."

In stage three, it was provided that:

Forces and military establishments of all States shall be finally reduced to those levels required for the purpose of maintaining internal order and ensuring the personal security of citizens and of providing agreed contingents of forces to the internal peace force.

The international peace force and remaining agreed contingents of national armed forces shall be armed only with agreed types and quantities of armaments. All other remaining armaments, including weapons of mass destruction and vehicles for their delivery and conventional armaments shall be destroyed or converted to peaceful uses.

The new programme of the United States was never discussed in formal negotiations, and indeed is not of great importance in regard to the question with which this study is concerned. It did represent a more positive approach to the central problem of disarmament, that is, the checking of the race in strategic arms. When negotiations were again resumed, by the Eighteen-Nation Committee on Disarmament, the United States produced a more generous programme, which we shall be examining in later chapters.

Even as the Warsaw Pact delegations walked out of the conference, Mr. Khrushchev declared that the Soviet Union was ready to resume disarmament negotiations after an interval. He had written to the heads of governments of the Western states participating in the Ten-Nation Committee on Disarmament, and his letter to Mr. Macmillan contained the following observations:

. . . The Soviet Government . . . has come to the conclusion that the Western Powers, to judge by the position adopted by their representatives in Geneva, do not wish to conduct serious talks on disarmament.

. . . This is shown by the continuing arms race which is being conducted by the Powers referred to and also by the fact that, in the course of the discussions of questions of disarmament in the Committee, they are trying to create only the appearance of negotiation and in so doing to deceive people sincerely striving for a solution of the disarmament problem.

Taking all this into account, the Government of the USSR has come to the conclusion that it must break off its participation in the fruitless discussion in the Committee of Ten in order to set before the next regular session of the General Assembly of the United Nations Organization the question of disarmament and of the position which has arisen over the carrying out of the resolution of the General Assembly of November 20, 1959, on this question.[9]

Mr. Khrushchev's self-righteousness was tiresome, of course, but it is true that the United States, in particular, was driving ahead with the production of several nuclear weapon delivery systems, with much publicity being given to the need to eliminate the missile gap. But there was no indication that the Soviet Union was not also producing more ICBM's, and the MRBM's and IRBM's already deployed were a monstrous threat to the European NATO countries.

While the negotiations had certainly not been gratifying to the Eastern participants, they had not been so sterile as to justify their abrupt breaking-off. Progress had been made towards bringing the positions of the two sides together in some of the measures discussed. The real reason for the walk-out may have lain in Khrushchev's anger at President Eisenhower's refusal to apologize for the U 2 reconnaissance programme, and a consequent feeling that he had been led up the garden path during his recent visits to the United States. What some of his colleagues may have regarded as his credulity, and his too enthusiastic commitment to GCD may have created political difficulties for him. And we can be sure that the Russian military authorities threw their weight on the side of those who probably said, "You can't ever trust the Americans, this proves it again." (As we know, many Americans and individuals in allied countries are fond of saying, "You can't ever trust the communists.")

However, in his speech in East Berlin after leaving Paris, Khrushchev was willing to state: "If we can't get a working agreement on the settlement of disputed international issues with the present leaders of the USA

---

[9]*Verbatim Records T.P.D.C.* (HMSO), Annex 12 page 938.

or with the president who takes over from Eisenhower, we'll wait until the president after that."[10]

Surveying the negotiations on general and complete disarmament which covered a period of about nine months, from enunciation by Khrushchev in September 1959 to miscarriage at the end of June 1960, what conclusions or lessons can we draw?

The first impression is apt to be of the lack of realism of the exercise – a debate among ten of the most heavily armed nations in the world (incidentally, those most threatened by the effects of nuclear war, if it should break out) on how they and the rest of the world would get rid of their armaments and prepare to live peaceably, all within a period measured in years; not decades. Twelve years after the TNCD conference, the nations are more heavily armed than ever and the armouries of nuclear weapons have grown enormously. Nevertheless the United Nations continued to pass resolutions calling for the successive disarmament committees (ENDC, CCD) to busy themselves with negotiations calculated to achieve GCD. But it is now tacitly admitted that while GCD should be the eventual goal, it can only be reached by a process of adding to the arms control measures already achieved, and so building up international confidence. The way to general disarmament will only be open when the world is able to believe that force of arms will no longer be employed by the most powerful nations in settling disputes with their neighbours. Meanwhile it is universally recognized that for real progress some agreement must be reached on the limitation of strategic arms (long-range nuclear weapons vehicles). Preliminary talks on this matter were held between the USA and the USSR at Helsinki during November and December 1969. Further meetings have been held in Vienna and Helsinki alternately.

Can we assess the true purposes of each side in the TNCD conference in Geneva from March 15 to June 27, 1960? How ready were the governments of the states represented to put into effect the measures included in the plans and programmes then put forward? A first answer would be that it is much easier to determine what each side was *unwilling* to accept, than what they were willing to agree to. They were most reluctant to accept any proposed measure which they believed might degrade the security which they hoped would be ensured by their armaments and armed forces.

When we analyse the proposals of the two sides, we see that they were

---

[10]Current digest of the Soviet Press, No. 20 (1960) page 5. Quoted in *Khrushchev and the Arms Race.*

calculated to retain their own real or supposed strategic advantages – or, at least, not to give anything away. General and complete disarmament, by doing away with the means of waging long-range nuclear warfare, would abolish the most dangerous threat to the security of the Soviet Union; and, of course, also the threat of direct and immediate attack on the North American continent. The reduction and eventual disappearance of conventional armaments and forces, as contained in the proposals for general disarmament of both sides, would remove the threat to Western Europe of the Soviet superiority in these elements of armed force.

But the United States, looking at the complex situation, seemed to give greater weight to maintaining the armaments estimated to be required for national security, and as a deterrent against the Soviet threat to Europe, than to the problematical long-term security which might be achieved by a disarmament agreement. In particular, the United States was making strenuous efforts to overcome the supposed advantage of the Soviet Union in intercontinental missiles, and was unwilling to negotiate about early reduction of these vehicles, or long-range bombers.

The Soviet Union reversed priorities in its programme for general and complete disarmament, by switching the abolition of nuclear weapon vehicles from the last stage to the first stage. This change could well have been inspired by a calculation that it was not to its advantage to let the race with the USA in this type of armaments continue. The USSR effort might be surpassed in spite of very great expenditure of economic resources, for which it had other urgent requirements.

The principal overt points of difference between the approach of the Soviet Union and its allies, on the one side, and the United States and its allies on the other, were the following.

The West believed that the approach to disarmament had to be gradual, building up confidence by agreements on the less difficult problems, while the Soviet Union strenuously urged crash or revolutionary action, as set out in its plan for general and complete disarmament in four years.

The Soviet Union maintained that control (verification) should be applied only to the actual destruction of nuclear weapon vehicles and other important armaments, while the West insisted that the *total stock* of these categories should be verified before destruction commenced, to insure that none were retained secretly.

These differences were doubtless due in part to the desire of each side to seem to be "negotiating from strength," and the intentions of both superpowers to continue building long-range nuclear weapon vehicles, and other mass destruction armaments.

As we shall see, in discussing the later negotiations in the Eighteen-Nation Disarmament Conference, these differences persisted, through relatively minor changes of position by the two sides, and no doubt constitute the basic problems with which the negotiators in the Strategic Arms Limitation Talks have to grapple.

After the walk-out of the Warsaw Pact representatives from the TNCD at the end of June 1960, there was a pause in negotiations relating to strategic armaments. Talks resumed only after agreement had been reached in 1961 on the terms on which the further parleys should be conducted.

CHAPTER 9

UN Disarmament Commission meeting, 1960

After the lamentable breakup of the Ten-Nation Committee, there was no body in which to carry on negotiations on general and complete disarmament, or arms control measures. However, the Canadian disarmament negotiating apparatus was kept busy. The Hon. Howard Green, Secretary of State for External Affairs, had adopted disarmament as his number one object of policy, and sought every occasion and means to get substantive negotiations going again in 1960 and 1961. But he had little success. A brief account of the activities during this period may illustrate the limits of Canadian influence in international affairs.

The superpowers, for divers reasons, were not anxious to resume formal talks. Mr. Khrushchev, although he professed to be ready to recommence negotiations at any time, probably realized that not much could be accomplished during the political turmoil of a United States presidential election year, even if both sides were basically serious about disarmament. Eisenhower would not be in the presidential race, and Khrushchev may have felt that with a new man in the White House, there could be a new and more favourable disarmament deal.

Also, the Chinese had been attacking his disarmament policies in international communist meetings, and this had important repercussions in the power struggle going on at the time in the obscure recesses of the

Kremlin.[1] In 1959 the Soviet Union had withdrawn the aid it had previously furnished to China in developing nuclear technology, and this rankled with the Chinese, who concluded that the USSR and the USA were conspiring to prevent them from achieving the status of a nuclear power, and that disarmament agreements were part of the plot. But it was not until a year or so later that the Chinese made world-wide propaganda on this, no longer confining it to meetings of the communist camp. During the UNGA, towards the end of October 1960, Mr. Winiewicz, Deputy Foreign Minister of Poland, told Canadian representatives privately that the USSR did not want to proceed with disarmament negotiations at that time, owing to its ideological dispute with China.

As for the American officials concerned with disarmament, they saw no advantage in going ahead with negotiations, as a new administration might change the disarmament policies developed up to that point. In the middle of an election campaign it would be almost impossible to obtain government permission to modify positions and to operate with the flexibility which would be essential if real negotiations were to take place. So both superpowers were willing to take a lengthy recess from the negotiating table, and therefore were unresponsive to arguments from Mr. Green and others that disarmament could not wait.

After the walk-out, while the Canadian delegation to the TNCD was waiting for orders, we did studies on arms control measures. One was the non-dissemination of nuclear weapons, which had been brought to the fore by Mr. Frank Aiken, Foreign Minister of Ireland, at the UNGA in 1958 and 1959.[2] He proposed prohibiting the acquisition of nuclear weapons by countries not possessing them. This idea appealed to the Canadian Government, especially as we had declared we should not produce nuclear weapons ourselves, in spite of having all the necessary resources to do so. So non-dissemination became Canadian policy, and was advocated by the Minister and Canadian representatives on all relevant occasions. Finally, after long drawn-out negotiations, the Non-proliferation Treaty was agreed upon in June 1968.

The semantics in the change of name of this important arms control

---

[1]See *Soviet Policy-Making*, Ed. Juviler and Morton (New York: Praeger, 1967), pages 204, 205.

[2]In 1959 a resolution (1380 XIV) put forward by the Irish delegation was adopted. It called on the TNCD to consider the feasibility of an agreement under which the powers producing nuclear weapons would refrain from handing over the control of such weapons to any nation not possessing them, and the powers not possessing such weapons would refrain from manufacturing them.

measure are of some interest. When the Irish first introduced the subject, the word was non-dissemination – non-spreading – and its meaning was taken to be stopping the acquisition of nuclear weapons by those nations which did not have them. Then some purist in the US State Department must have concluded that while dissemination could denote a nuclear power giving nuclear weapons or information on how to make them to a non-possessor, it did not cover the case of a nation creating nuclear weapons without outside aid. But both (undesirable) cases of increase in the number of nations possessing nuclear weapons and the sovereign right to fire them off could be called *proliferation*. So the Americans began to use the term non-proliferation, and other nations followed. (The Russians did not use separate words for dissemination and proliferation; both were *rasprostranyennie*.)

But then representatives of some states began to point out, to the embarrassment of the nuclear powers, that *they* were proliferating by adding to their own stockpiles of nuclear weapons. Mr. Vishnu Trivedi, leader of the Indian delegation during the period when the ENDC was negotiating the NPT, invented the terms "vertical proliferation" to describe the addition to stockpiles by nuclear powers, and "horizontal proliferation" to mean the spreading of nuclear weapons capability to additional nations. This terminology became popular among non-possessing nations.

The other arms control measure which the delegation studied was the prohibition of the use of chemical and biological agents in war. The Geneva Protocol of 1925 purported to do this, but some important nations, including the United States, had not ratified or adhered to it. It was also thought that its terms were not sufficiently comprehensive, in view of the "progress" which had been achieved since 1925 in thinking up more powerful agents, and new techniques for their employment. This was due to the chemical warfare establishments maintained by the great powers, nominally only for research on how to defend both military and civilians against gas and living pathogens.

Chemical and biological weapons, in disarmament contexts, were generally included in the class of "weapons of mass destruction," although during most of the decade of the sixties they received very much less attention than the nuclear weapon. Occasionally proponents of a "Ban the Bomb" resolution would point out that the great powers had not resorted to chemical warfare during World War II, in spite of the invention of nerve gases, potentially much more lethal than any previously-known agent. It was argued that this restraint was owing to their having signed the Geneva Convention. Therefore, the Ban-the-Bombers contended, if a convention could be agreed upon which would in similar fashion prohibit the use of nuclear weapons, it would also be likely to be observed. The flaw in this argument is that the effects of using nuclear weapons could be so enormously greater than those of using chemical weapons that they were not to be equated. While a first strike with nuclear weapons might decide World War III, experience had shown in World War I that, even when used by surprise, gas did not produce decisive victory, and, after the first occasion of its use on a large scale, not even important tactical success. Its use merely added to the general unpleasantness of war for each side. Hence military men in World War II, while apprehensive that the enemy might use gas, and insisting on a great deal of training in defence against it, never advocated departing from the engagements of the Geneva Convention as a means of winning battles, or the war. It should be remembered that most great powers, in ratifying the protocol, reserved the right to retaliate if an enemy used chemical weapons against them. And it followed that if they were to be able to retaliate they must have stocks of chemical weapons with which to do so – and a scientific establishment busily studying both defensive and offensive possibilities of chemical warfare.

It seemed to me in 1960 that Canada might promote a renovation of the Geneva Protocol in the disarmament milieu. There was still a remnant of feeling in the country against gas in war owing to our soldiers having been victims of it in the Second Battle of Ypres, in April 1915. Later, I discussed with Norman Robertson, then Under-Secretary of State for External Affairs, whether Canada should make strengthening the Geneva Protocol a special concern of ours and he agreed that it would probably be a good move. However, the issue was not of great importance compared to other arms control questions. Also, the involvement of our defence research establishment in the defensive aspects of chemical and biological warfare, cooperating with the U.K., the USA and Australia, made it awkward for our Government to start an agitation against what our scientists were studying. It was not until 1968 that the prohibition of chemical and biological warfare became a big issue in the ENDC and the UNGA, and this followed mainly as a result of propaganda against American use of "riot-control" gas and chemical defoliants in Vietnam.

About the third week in July 1960 it was decided to disband the Canadian Delegation to the TNCD. I returned to Canada and became involved in arrangements for a meeting of the United Nations Disarmament Commission. This organ was first established in January 1952 to carry forward the tasks originally assigned to the Atomic Energy Commission and the Commission for Conventional Armaments. The membership of both these bodies had been that of the Security Council, plus Canada, when we were not a Security Council member ourselves. The membership of the newly constituted Disarmament Commission was to be the same. As several years passed with no disarmament agreement reached in the Commission or its subcommittee (of which Canada was also a member) other nations began to press for membership. But it proved impossible to get a consensus on what states should be included in a limited expansion, and the final (Russian) solution was to include all the hundred-odd members of the United Nations, which made it far too cumbrous for a negotiating body. However, in theory this unwieldy committee retained the responsibility for disarmament matters in the United Nations. So it had been agreed, among the Western Five, that we should call for it to meet, in order to decide what might be done to continue the discussions on general and complete disarmament, which the General Assembly had demanded so urgently during the previous session. It could also afford an opportunity to make propaganda that the walk-out of the USSR and its allies from the TNCD demonstrated their insincerity, their unwillingness to negotiate in substantive terms. Mr. Green was particularly active in pressing for a meeting of the UNDC. At this time he had thoughts of developing a home-grown Canadian disarmament plan, featuring provisions for an international peacekeeping force, and non-dissemination of nuclear weapons.

For some time he had been wanting a more independent Canadian disarmament policy. During the NATO ministers' conference in Istanbul in May of 1960, to which he had brought me along with his usual panel of advisers, he had told us that Canada must not be afraid to disagree publicly with the United States in disarmament negotiations; that we should not be dragged along at the tail of the United States war chariot. If the disarmament negotiations failed, he felt Canadian opinion would not tolerate it, unless we had made our disagreement with the American position clear. Norman Robertson and I gently argued against such a proceeding. We suggested that public disagreement should only be a last step, after private attempts to get our allies to accept our viewpoint had failed, and when the question on which we were at odds was of the highest importance. A few days later I had a discussion on this subject with the Hon. George Drew, then High Commissioner for Canada in London. While he favoured the government line on disarmament, he thought that in pressing our views we must "consider the facts of life" and our position in NATO and NORAD.

These discussions illustrate one of the problems of Canadian representatives in trying to exercise influence in international affairs, if it happens that our opinions and interests do not fit in with those of the

United States. If private argument and persuasion fail to win American acceptance of our position, should we publicly disagree? We might get a glow of moral satisfaction from, so to speak, nailing our theses to the cathedral door, but would we be more likely to achieve our object? Of course, one can imagine issues on which we should maintain our position if we felt sure it was right, and that of the United States was wrong, but the question would have to be a very important one to make it worthwhile to risk the deterioration of relations with the great ally whose power guarantees our security in the nuclear age, and with whose economy ours is so linked that disruption could have the severest effects. If we had no influence *with* the United States, what influence should we have *against* them? These are generalities, and one can only make judgements of right and wrong in specific cases. During the disarmament negotiations of the 1960's, while our delegation sometimes expressed viewpoints which were not precisely those of the United States, on the whole we maintained the line which had been worked out in the conferences between the representatives of the NATO powers which were held almost daily. During the ENDC sessions, sometimes one of the eight non-aligned nations' representatives would say that Canada was the ninth non-aligned member of the Committee. But this was only a joke – or intended as flattery.

We have already looked at what the United States and the Soviet Union were doing to equip themselves with nuclear weapon vehicles. We can now devote a few paragraphs to Canada's modest efforts to follow the nuclear fashions, and provide our forces in Europe and Canada with tactical nuclear weapons. The government seems to have agreed with our allies to acquire the vehicles, without full understanding or consideration of the consequence that when the vehicles became operational, they would have to be provided with nuclear bombs or warheads. In the early sixties, whether or when to get these nuclear munitions became a burning political question which divided Mr. Diefenbaker's Cabinet, and helped to bring about its fall from power.[3]

When it was decided that the NATO forces should be equipped with tactical nuclear weapons in January 1957, Mr. Diefenbaker signed the protocol on behalf of Canada. During 1958, following suspension of the production of the Avro Arrow (Canadian-developed) aircraft, the Department of Defence apparently decided that the obsolete F 86 fighter

---

[3]For a detailed account of these developments, see *A Renegade in Power*, P. C. Newman, Chapter 23; also *Canada's Changing Defence Policy, 1957-1963*, Jon B. McLin (Baltimore: Johns Hopkins Press, 1967), Chapters IV, V and VI.

aircraft, with which the RCAF division in NATO was equipped, should be replaced by an advanced aircraft designed for the strike-reconnaissance role. After certain negotiations this turned out to be the Lockheed F 104. The Army was not to be left out of the atomic parade. It was to get a battery (four) of Honest John rockets, which were nominally dual purpose. That is, they could carry either a high-explosive warhead, or a nuclear one. But the intention of the military throughout was that it should be a nuclear weapon vehicle. To use it to throw H.E. didn't make sense, from a cost-effectiveness viewpoint.

In May 1959, General Lauris Norstad, USAF, the Supreme Allied Commander, Europe, visited Ottawa, and briefed the Cabinet on what the strike part of the strike-reconnaissance role meant – delivering tactical nuclear weapons.[4] (These "tactical" weapons ranged in explosive power from the twenty kilotons of the Hiroshima bomb upwards.) The available literature does not disclose what members of the Cabinet were present at this briefing. From subsequent developments it does seem that perhaps the Cabinet as a whole – certainly some members of it – did not understand the implications of the decision to equip the RCAF with the F 104.

In June 1959 General Pearkes, the Minister of National Defence, announced that 200 of this type of aircraft would be built by Canadair in Montreal, and that eight squadrons of them would be operational by May 1963. The version produced in the Montreal plant would differ from the prototype F 104 (Starfighter) and would bear the identification number CF 104. It is alleged that the RCAF specified modifications to the structure which would prevent it being used to deliver high-explosive bombs. It was designed only for nuclear weapon delivery; originally it had been dual-purpose. It was also adapted for reconnaissance, seen chiefly as searching for suitable mass targets for nuclear attack.[5]

When Mr. Diefenbaker announced the suspension of production of the Avro Arrow on September 23, 1958, he also said that negotiations were under way to get Bomarc anti-aircraft missiles from the United States. These could have either high-explosive or nuclear warheads. What was apparently not realized at the time was that no high-explosive warhead had been designed for the version of the missile which we were to get. This does not seem to have been understood even after Mr. Diefenbaker's later statement, on February 20, 1959, that Bomarcs were being acquired for two positions, to extend the anti-aircraft missile network being constructed by the United States – and this, although negotiations for obtain-

---

[4]McLin, *op. cit.*, page 116.
[5]Newman, *op. cit.*, page 346.

ing the complementary nuclear warheads apparently had been begun at this time.[6]

The Cabinet split started when Mr. Green realized that the acquisition of this aggregation of nuclear-weapon vehicles meant that Canada would be becoming a nuclear weapon user, though not an owner. (The nuclear warheads for the vehicles would be kept under strict United States control, in accordance with the MacMahon act.) A political author wrote that Mr. Green was ". . . profoundly convinced that Canada's adoption of nuclear warheads would nullify the nation's influence in the vital business of helping along disarmament negotiations between the major powers."[7] Whether his conviction on this point was "profound" or not, he certainly disliked the idea of having nuclear weapons in the hands of Canadian forces. Being a man of great tenacity of purpose, he, with others of his Cabinet colleagues who disliked the idea of nuclear armament, managed to prevent a Cabinet decision to acquire nuclear warheads, through 1961 and 1962, and until the Conservative government went out of office following the 1963 election.

Despite fears that Canada's influence in the disarmament negotiations would be diminished if we entered arrangements which would allow our forces to deliver American-owned nuclear weapons if war should erupt in Europe, or if North America were attacked, it does not seem to me that there was any difference in the way our colleagues at the disarmament table looked at us, before and after we had lost our "nuclear virginity," as some scoffing journalists put it. By that time we had established the Canadian position as strongly in favour of reduction of the long-range (strategic) nuclear weapon vehicles. From time to time we emphasized that we could long ago have made ourselves a nuclear bomb, but had determined not to, that we were against the proliferation of nuclear weapons, and strongly for a complete ban on testing nuclear weapons. The Big Nukers, with their vast array of population-destroying apparatus, could hardly reproach us, and the anti-nuclear non-aligned did not want to alienate us, as they saw us as the nation in NATO whose views were nearest to their own.

In December, I submitted a memorandum to Mr. Green arguing against the acquisition of the F 104's and Honest Johns – on military, as well as disarmament grounds.[8] Briefly, the arguments were that the use of tactical nuclear weapons would escalate into all-out nuclear war. As

[6]*Ibid.*, page 348.

[7]*Ibid.*, page 341.

[8]The arguments are reproduced in part in Appendix I. The creation of a joint NATO nuclear force was also opposed.

the United States would control these weapons, they were likely to hesitate to authorize their employment if it seemed to them that this would probably result in a nuclear holocaust in their homeland. Also, the USSR would probably soon equip its forces and those of its allies with tactical nuclear weapons, which would neutralize the hoped-for advantage to the West. A preferable solution would be to strengthen the conventional forces of the NATO alliance to attain a better balance with the conventional forces of the Warsaw Pact.

By a parallel process of thought, many American strategic analysts came to adopt the same ideas a few years later. Mr. McNamara's strategy of flexible response was based on somewhat the same considerations.

The UN Disarmament Commission finally met on August 16, in New York. The non-aligned nations had prepared a resolution calling for the resumption of disarmament negotiations, but it was clear that they did not think that the TNCD would be the best kind of body for the purpose, and that they wanted representation on whatever committee should replace it. This was reasonable, and had been proposed by the Soviet Union. But it was also clear that there would be the same difficulty as had been met with in constituting the Disarmament Commission. It would be a problem to decide what nations should be added to the five NATO and five Warsaw Pact countries, in order that the group would be restricted enough in number to be suitable for negotiations, yet generally representative of the United Nations membership. It took another year of intermittent negotiation before the USA and the USSR produced a proposal which was accepted by the General Assembly, not without some grumblings and mutterings from the countries left out.

After three days of discussion the UNDC passed a resolution based on the non-aligned proposal. The principal operative paragraph was that the Commission:

> *Considers it necessary and recommends* that in view of the urgency of the problem continued efforts be made for the earliest possible continuation of international negotiations to achieve a constructive solution of the question of general and complete disarmament under effective international control.

The Commission also recommended that the fifteenth (1960) session of the General Assembly, which was to begin in just a month, should give "earnest consideration to the question of disarmament."[9]

---

[9]Doc. DC/182/Corr. 1, August 18, 1960. Reprinted in *Documents on Disarmament, 1960,* page 224.

In the early days of this session, on September 20, 1960, President Eisenhower addressed the General Assembly. In speaking of disarmament (or arms control) he made two proposals, which related to the control of strategic armaments. He observed that recently the Antarctic had been declared "off limits" to military preparations, and that this gave hope that the principles which had been enshrined in the Antarctic Treaty could be extended to an even more important sphere – outer space. As we have seen, proposals to this end had been included in the Western March 16, 1960 Plan for GCD and in the USSR June 7, 1960 revised outline treaty.

President Eisenhower's second proposal was ". . . terminating, under verification procedures, all production of fissionable material for weapons purposes." Each nuclear power would turn over a quantity of the material to the International Atomic Energy Agency for the benefit of countries developing nuclear power for peaceful purposes. Since 1958 this had been one of the United States package of arms control measures, and it still remains one. During the ENDC negotiations, it was periodically brought forward, with some elaborations, by the USA delegation. But the Soviet Union representatives generally dismissed it rather peremptorily, alleging that it was not an effective measure of disarmament, and would do little to remove the danger of the outbreak of nuclear war. Western delegations felt that the real reason for the Soviet Union's objection was that the United States had far larger stocks of weapons-grade fissionable material than it did, and proposed to make this advantage permanent. The Soviet Union probably needed all the U 235[10] they had for the nuclear weapons they were planning to build.

To complete the "cut-off" story, in his letter to the ENDC when it resumed sessions in January 1964, President Johnson again advanced the proposal. And in April he announced that the USA was reducing production of fissionable material, and was putting one of the giant separation plants out of operation. Mr. Khrushchev, instead of repeating the previous Soviet line, said that the Soviet Union would respond to the American initiative by not proceeding with the construction of two large atomic reactors for producing plutonium, and that the USSR production of U 235 would be substantially cut.[11] Whether this decision has been adhered to, since Brezhnev-Kosygin replaced Khrushchev in the seat of power, has never been made public. In any case, there has been no indication that the

---

[10]U 235 is the isotope of uranium existing in very small proportions in natural deposits of the mineral. It and the artificial element, plutonium, alone have the property of being able to generate a nuclear explosion. Its separation from natural uranium is a very difficult and costly process.

[11]*United Nations and Disarmament*, 1945-65, page 128.

Soviet Union's accelerated programme of nuclear armament has been handicapped by a shortage of the explosive fissile material.

In the course of his address to the 1960 General Assembly, Prime Minister Diefenbaker mentioned some of the measures of disarmament and arms control in which Canada was particularly interested. After saying Canada was ready to open her Arctic regions to international inspection with the object of lessening West-East reciprocal fear of surprise attack (this was a contribution to President Eisenhower's "Open Skies" proposal),[12] he went on:

> I have frequently had occasion to urge publicly the end of nuclear weapons, the systematic control of missiles designed to deliver nuclear weapons of mass destruction, the designation and inspection of launching sites for missiles [space rockets?] the abolition of biological and chemical weapons, the outlawing of outer space for military purposes, and, especially, a ban on the mounting of armament on orbital satellites, an end to the production of fissionable materials for weapons and the conversion of existing stocks for peaceful purposes. Canada over and over again has advocated an end to nuclear testing.[13]

We see that here Mr. Diefenbaker gave priority to the need to control the vehicles which could deliver nuclear weapons, and to limit the possibility of using them in a surprise attack. As the narrative of the disarmament negotiations in the rest of the decade unwinds, we shall see the conflict of viewpoints and interests between the nuclear powers which prevented the achievement of these aims.

As mentioned at the beginning of this chapter, an account of the proceedings on disarmament items in the First Committee during the 1960 session of the UNGA goes to show that Canada's influence in international affairs is not as great as some of us once thought. The Canadian delegation, under the direction of Mr. Green, made strenuous efforts to push forward the resumption of substantive negotiations. By the time discussion on the subject had got under way, we had developed a draft resolution which was intended to promote this purpose. In its final form, the main provisions were the following.

It "expressed the hope . . . that every effort will be made to achieve

---

[12]*United Nations and Disarmament*, 1945-65, page 57.
[13]General Assembly Official Records, 871st plenary meeting, pages 110, 111. *Documents on Disarmament 1960*, pages 249, 250.

general and complete disarmament . . . by the earliest possible continuation of negotiations among the Powers principally concerned." It then "Requested the Disarmament Commission to examine and make recommendations of ways and means of facilitating the early resumption of negotiations, and the principles which should guide those negotiations." It also requested the Disarmament Commission to meet more frequently, to consider suggestions from member states, and reports from the negotiating powers. Finally it recommended that the Disarmament Commission should consider appointing subcommittees to study various disarmament questions.[14]

The reluctance of the superpowers to resume negotiations at an early date has been noted. This Canadian resolution, therefore, amounted to an attempt to drive the superpower horses to the disarmament water, and to make them drink. It did not work. The idea had been developed and the resolution drafted during a period when I was absent from the delegation in New York owing to a health problem. When I returned, early in November, the delegation was deep in the unrewarding process of trying to persuade other delegations to co-sponsor the resolution, or at least to vote for it. Sweden and Norway were with us from the beginning, but the non-aligned countries, on whose support we were counting, proved very wary of committing themselves. They knew that the Soviet Union objected to our resolution as inappropriate to the circumstances, and were saying so. Furthermore, the United States representatives were not pleased with the attempt to ginger them up. The Indian delegation, headed by Mr. Krishna Menon, was promoting a rival resolution. In fact they had been earlier in the field. Their resolution purported to set out the principles on which the negotiation of a treaty on general and complete disarmament should be based. The superpowers were not willing to have these principles laid down by other countries and consequently discouraged the initiative. But many of the non-aligned had in fact put themselves behind the Indians on this resolution, and so were not available to support our proposition, which was considered to be a competitor. There were a number of other resolutions on the table. The USSR set out its idea of what GCD should be, and tacked on to it the notion that the structure of the United Nations should be changed, so that the Socialist countries, the "members of the Western Powers' blocs," and the neutralist countries should be represented "on a basis of equality." This was the notorious troika scheme, a bombshell which had been hurled into the General Assembly plenary

---

[14]A/CI/L255 Rev. 1, December 8, 1960. Reprinted in *Documents on Disarmament, 1960.*

sessions by Mr. Khrushchev, who was displeased with the way Mr. Hammarskjöld had controlled the United Nations operations in the Congo. (The bomb turned out to be a dud.)

The United Kingdom, the United States and Italy presented a draft resolution which set out, generally, the principles contained in the later documents the Western Five had presented in the TNCD. The U.K. had a separate draft resolution calling for the creation of committees of experts to find solutions to the problems of control (verification) of the various measures of disarmament and arms control which had been discussed at Geneva. The Poles put out a resolution which called for the cessation of nuclear testing, and also for non-proliferation, and the removal of armed forces from foreign bases. The Ethiopians, with six other African nations, had a draft in which the use of nuclear weapons was alleged to be contrary to international law, and said that any nation using them ". . . would commit a crime against mankind and its civilization." The Secretary-General was to consult governments on whether it would be possible to convene a conference to negotiate a convention giving effect to these ideas.[15]

The Poles had a second resolution, calling on the establishment of a committee which would have the assistance of experts in various technical fields, to assess the consequences of the use of nuclear weapons. The purpose appeared to be to create support for "Ban-the-Bomb" types of declaratory agreements, by authoritatively describing the horrific potential consequences of the use of nuclear weapons.[16]

With this mass of drafts on the table, most of them controversial, and the end of the pre-Christmas session approaching, after consultation with other interested delegations, Canada introduced a procedural resolution which called for the non-dissemination and nuclear test ban resolutions

---

[15]The proposal, while not voted on at the 1960 UNGA session, was brought forward in slightly amended form, and passed as Resolution 1653/XVI, at the 1961 UNGA.

[16]This resolution was not voted upon in 1960. During the 1966 session Poland introduced one like it. After some negotiation the Canadian delegation, Poland and others sponsored Resolution 2162 A/XXI, which enabled the Secretary-General to set up a committee of twelve experts from different countries, which produced the report *Effects of the Possible Use of Nuclear Weapons and the Security and Economic Implications for States of the Acquisition and Further Development of these Weapons* (A/6858).

The main purpose of the report was to assemble arguments against the acquisition of nuclear weapons by non-possessing states, to be used by scientists, politicians, academics and others who supported adherence to the Non-proliferation Treaty.

to be voted upon, and also our own, while all the rest were not to be voted upon at the current session. Mr. Krishna Menon, for India, introduced an amendment which added the Canadian resolution to the list of those not to be voted upon. Incidentally, he had given us fair warning, a week before, that he did not think the Canadian resolution could be voted upon without opening the can of worms (that is, voting on all the others).

There was a recess in the First Committee meeting during which Mr. Wallace Nesbit, who, as Parliamentary Assistant to Mr. Green, was leading the delegation, got in touch with Mr. Green at Goose Bay by some marvel of electronic communication. He told Mr. Green that a canvass of key members of the committee had convinced us that our resolution would be shelved, and recommended that we withdraw it with what grace the circumstances allowed. However, Mr. Green was determined that the Indian amendment be put to the vote, which was done. The vote for "hoisting" our resolution along with the others was twenty-nine in favour, seventeen against, and twenty-six abstentions. Of the eighteen co-sponsors which the delegation had assembled with such difficulty, eleven did not vote with us on the Indian amendment. Those that voted with us (sixteen in all) were the NATO countries plus Australia, New Zealand, South Africa, Pakistan, China and two Latin American countries. None of the non-aligned whom we had hoped would follow our banner did so. When Mr. Green saw the list of how the nations had voted, he remarked pretty sourly that at any rate now we knew who our friends were.

I concluded from this debacle that it was an error to think that Canada had special prestige or charisma which would ensure a following in the UNGA for whatever resolution we chose to present, especially if the terms were such as to raise objections from either the Soviet Union or the United States. Certainly if both the superpowers objected to an idea, it was almost hopeless to promote it. In future sessions during the 1960's we were much more cautious in initiating any resolutions relating to disarmament.

CHAPTER 10

Preparations for negotiations, 1961

Those concerned with disarmament business in the Department of External Affairs were again engaged during 1961 in efforts to reactivate the negotiations on general disarmament, suspended when the Warsaw Pact representatives walked out of the TNCD. Eventually, the Eighteen-Nation Committee on Disarmament was set up, and began its meetings in 1962. Although Canadian efforts may have contributed to this result in some small measure, during 1961 they seemed to produce little but frustration.

When we reviewed our experience in the negotiations of 1960, and in particular the positions which the West had taken up in them, it seemed desirable that we should have a directive setting out the Canadian policy on disarmament. Accordingly, a memorandum was drawn up by the disarmament group, after consultations with other interested divisions of the department, and presented by the Minister to the Cabinet, which approved it on February 23, 1961. It has remained as the guideline of our policy since then. Its principal points may be summarized as follows.

The aim was to increase the security of Canada by moving towards a peaceful world, with armaments reduced to a minimum. Canada and our NATO partners had voted for the UN resolution calling for general and complete disarmament as a goal.

Negotiations on disarmament help to reduce international tensions and halt the arms race spiral. The first objective should be to initiate measures to reduce the danger of war breaking out through accident or miscalculation, or of minor hostilities developing into unlimited nuclear war.

Until substantial progress towards disarmament under effective international control was achieved, Canadian national security would depend primarily on collective defence within the NATO alliance. Open disagreement between NATO countries on disarmament policies could lead to weakening of the alliance, and so prejudice Canadian security. Canada should participate in NATO discussions of disarmament policies, taking the position that the security of all members would be increased through balanced and fully controlled disarmament agreements.

Reductions in manpower and conventional armaments in the first stage should be designed to bring approximate parity between the conventional forces of the Warsaw Pact and of NATO. The People's Republic of China must eventually be taken into account in disarmament negotiations. The reduction of conventional armament, not manpower, is decisive. It is not likely that Canadian forces would be subject to reductions until the second or third stage of disarmament.

The first stage of disarmament should include measures to prevent the dissemination of nuclear weapons, and risks of accidental war. Nuclear weapons should be reduced concurrently with manpower and conventional armament. The reduction of nuclear-weapons-carrying aircraft should begin in the first stage.

Ballistic missiles should be reduced in three stages. Within one or two years [this was written in January 1961] these will become the main deterrent of war and the principal guarantee that neither side could gain decisive advantage through evasion of disarmament provisions. Therefore it is unlikely that either West or East will be able entirely to give up this ultimate deterrent until the final stage of disarmament, when good faith has been proven.

There would be a need for development and modification of the organs of the United Nations to provide for effective means of keeping the peace in a disarmed world.

In the second stage, the development and stockpiling of chemical and biological weapons should be prohibited. The importance of these means of warfare might increase as nuclear weaponry was reduced. Therefore measures to prevent their use should be negotiated concurrently.

There were other points regarding the form which eventual disarmament agreements might take, and also regarding less important arms control measures.

In January and February Mr. Green had me make a tour of Washington, London, Paris and Rome to find out what our allies were intending to do about disarmament in the extended session of the 15th UN General Assembly. It had adjourned just before Christmas 1960, having decided to meet again in March 1961, to complete unfinished business, which had mainly to do with African problems, but also included the disarmament questions. Mr. Green still entertained some hope that the proposals in our draft resolution No. 455 might serve as a basis for resuming substantive disarmament negotiations.

A start had been made in organizing the United States Arms Control and Disarmament Agency, even before President Kennedy had been inaugurated. He had had this project in view for some time, no doubt partly inspired by the dovish in the Boston-Cambridge community of academics. Mr. John McCloy, distinguished in the world of finance, and as a government servant, had agreed to preside during the organizing period, until a permanent head could be appointed.[1] I had given Mr. McCloy a lift in the United Nations DC 3 from Beirut to Cairo, when he had come in 1957 to negotiate the terms of the financial assistance to be given to the Egyptian Government to cover the costs of reopening the Suez Canal. This previous acquaintance was a help in the occasional discussions I had with him during his leadership of ACDA.

When I visited Washington on the 18th and 19th of January 1961, I also saw several members of the ACDA organization, then being assembled. These were Mr. Edmond Gullion, who had headed the Disarmament Administration in the State Department, and who was shortly to depart, to become the American Ambassador in the Congo. Messrs. Spiers, Matteson and Sturgill were others who continued to occupy important positions in the organization for some years. Mr. Charles Bohlen, Assistant to the Secretary of State for Soviet Affairs, also took part in the talks. I was told that the Agency had been directed to give first priority to the preparation of a position for further test ban negotiations, which it hoped to recommence in early March. However, the administration would not be ready for substantive negotiations on general and complete disarmament until June.

Later, Mr. Saul Rae, acting as our Ambassador in Washington during Mr. Arnold Heeney's absence, had me to lunch to meet Mr. Paul Nitze.[2] Mr. Nitze said he had found the Pentagon willing to study disarmament proposals having regard to the national security, and assess their feasibility. Nitze also said that preparations for resuming test ban negotiations

---

[1]Mr. William C. Foster, who had a notable career as a businessman and in government service, was appointed Director of ACDA later in 1961.

[2]Paul Nitze was Assistant Secretary for International Security Affairs, Department of Defence, 1961-3.

were first on the list. He was concerned, too, with how an organization for verifying compliance with obligations in a disarmament treaty could be made strong enough to ensure the Russians would not block its working, which from past experience he feared might happen.

I tried to impress on all these people the Canadian view that the main disarmament negotiations should be picked up again at as early a date as possible. However, it was evident that they were not going to be hustled into a conference in the unorganized and badly prepared condition in which the Eisenhower administration had entered the TNCD.

The fifteenth session of the UNGA reopened on the 7th of March. I had desultory discussions with Signor Dainelli, the Italian disarmament expert, and Sir David Ormsby-Gore, about what form the Western position on GCD should take, and what the principles for negotiation should be. However, Mr. Sturgill, who was attached to the US mission as a liaison officer from ACDA, told me that Mr. McCloy was adamant against any discussion of principles until he had been able to examine the proposed new US disarmament position as a whole.

Mr. Adlai Stevenson, then leading the US Mission to the United Nations, had a series of talks with Mr. Gromyko about the date when negotiations should be resumed, and the composition of the body which should succeed the TNCD. They agreed that besides the five NATO and five Warsaw Pact members there should be some representatives of neutral nations. The problem was how many, and which.

The ACDA produced a paper on the principles for negotiations. On March 16 this was discussed with representatives of the other four NATO nations which had been members of the TNCD. We also examined a proposal on principles which the Russians had drawn up and which we found quite close to being acceptable. For the rest of the UNGA session, the representatives of the Western Five were occupied, off and on, in discussing drafts of principles and of a resolution calling for the resumption of negotiations.

We were soon informed by M. Michel Legendre, the representative of France in these inter-allied discussions, that his country could not accept having *any* neutrals to form part of the negotiating body. This was doubtless the decision of President de Gaulle, who had expressed his distaste for the United Nations as a forum for negotiation in the phrase: ". . . *instances tumulteuses et hétéroclites.*" The debates on Algeria had been very displeasing to him. Also, France had begun nuclear testing in the Sahara, and intended to continue. Nuclear tests were indispensable if France was to become a nuclear power. President de Gaulle must have foreseen that a French delegation to the projected conference would be under constant attack for this policy. A resolution was before the General Assembly, calling for a halt to testing in all parts of Africa. Consequently he must have judged that a conference whose membership would reflect that of the United Nations as a whole would be a very uncomfortable milieu for France. So, when the time came for the Eighteen-Nation Committee to assemble, we were informed that France would not take the place reserved for her. The chair and place at the table, with "France" on the sign in front, were kept there throughout the proceedings of the ENDC. Several appeals to the French Government to reconsider its decision were made, but without result. So there were only seventeen nations represented in the Eighteen-Nation Committee.

The Canadian delegation, in the resumed General Assembly, in accordance with Mr. Green's wishes, tried to insert in the resolution a reference to the idea in our rejected draft that the UN Disarmament Commission should have a role in the disarmament proceedings, and should set up subcommittees of experts to deal with the difficult technical problems. But while our allies patiently and politely listened to our suggestions, it was plain that they did not think much of them.

Finally, on March 29, Mr. Stevenson and Mr. Zorin, who was then heading the USSR mission to the UN, agreed on the text of a resolution which took note of statements and proposals relating to disarmament made during the fifteenth session, and put over discussion of them to the sixteenth General Assembly, in the autumn of 1961. Their resolution, No. 1617/xv, was passed unanimously on the 21st of April. The representatives of the superpowers made parallel declarations, stating that they would meet in order to reach agreement on the composition of the negotiating body, and the principles under which the negotiations would be carried on.

It was in 1961 that the term "Arms Control" came into general usage. This happened following a study group held during the summer of 1960 at Cambridge, Massachusetts under the auspices of the American Academy of Arts and Sciences, and supported by the Twentieth Century Fund. The subjects discussed were the problems of strategy in the nuclear age, and disarmament. Professor Bernard Feld was the general director, and among the nearly sixty participants were many of the scholars and writers who influenced the development of ideas on the subjects during the ensuing decade.

Three significant books which as a result came out in 1961 were: *Strategy and Arms Control*, by Thomas C. Schelling and Morton H. Halperin; *Arms Reduction – Program and Issues*, edited by D. H. Frisch; and *Arms Control, Disarmament and National Security*, edited by Donald G. Brennan (who had also assisted Schelling and Halperin in their book). In this year also Hedley Bull's *The Control of the Arms Race* was published in London for the Institute of Strategic Studies.

The ideas which emerged from these important studies came to be loosely grouped under the heading of "Arms Control." Until then the conferences convened under the auspices of the United Nations had been labelled "Disarmament," and they still are. But, as those readers who have followed the subject will know, the successes obtained in a quarter-century of negotiating – such as the Moscow Nuclear Test Ban Treaty, the Non-proliferation Treaty, the Treaty of Tlatelolco for the denuclearization of Latin America – come under the classification of arms control rather than disarmament.

What is the definition of Arms Control? Schelling and Halperin give the following:

> A conscious adjustment of our military forces and policies to take account of those of our potential enemies, in the common interest of restraining violence.[3]

Elsewhere they say:

> Arms control is essentially a means of supplementing unilateral military strategy by some kind of collaboration with the countries that are potential enemies.[4]

There is also a discussion of the definition of the term in my book *Megamurder*.[5]

When the bill to establish the US Arms Control and Disarmament Agency was going through Congress, the House of Representatives version proposed to call the organization the "United States Arms Control Agency." "Disarmament" was inserted in the title by the Senate.

It is not difficult to imagine why negotiating "arms control" is thought to be more feasible than negotiating disarmament. Under the arms control concept, a government can in a way have its cake and also eat it: opt for measures to limit the danger of an outbreak of nuclear war, while at the same time increasing its mass-destruction armaments. Thus it could conciliate those citizens who demand an anti-nuclear-war policy, and also satisfy the military who demanded more and costlier weaponry.

---

[3]Schelling, T. C. and Halperin, M. H., *Strategy and Arms Control* (New York: The Twentieth Century Fund, 1961), page 6.

[4]*Ibid.*, page 142.

[5]Burns, E. L. M., *Megamurder* (Toronto: Clarke Irwin, 1966 and New York: Pantheon, 1967), pages 6, 163.

A better reason for using the term, already discussed, has been the view held by Western governments and negotiators. They have concluded that if progress was to be made towards disarmament it had to be by getting agreement on less difficult and controversial measures, and not through a headlong assault on the citadels of armament, through a treaty which would disarm every nation in four years (the original USSR concept of GCD).

The basic arms control theory is that nuclear war should be prevented by the existence of a stable, balanced and invulnerable deterrent force in possession of both superpowers – or, at any rate, by the United States. Arms control measures should reinforce this basic preventative, and, it is to be hoped, lead towards an understanding between nations so that, in time, the threat of assured destruction would not be needed to prevent the outbreak of nuclear war.

Mr. McCloy and Mr. Zorin held a series of meetings in Washington, Moscow and New York during the months of June to September. On September 20, 1961, they placed before the United Nations General Assembly a statement of the principles they had agreed upon for the further conduct of negotiations on disarmament. Key clauses in this statement were the following:[6]

> The goal of negotiations is to achieve agreement on a programme which will ensure that disarmament is general and complete, and war is no longer an instrument for settling international problems. . . .
> . . . the programme shall contain the necessary provisions, with respect to the military establishment of every nation, for:
> a / Disbanding of armed forces, dismantling of military establishments, including bases, cessation of the production of armaments as well as their liquidation or conversion to peaceful uses;
> b / Elimination of all stockpiles of nuclear, chemical, bacteriological, and other weapons of mass destruction and cessation of the production of such weapons;
> c / Elimination of all means of delivery of weapons of mass destruction; . . . .
>
> The disarmament programme should be implemented in an agreed sequence, by stages until it is completed, with each measure and stage carried out within specified time-limits. . . .

---

[6]UN Doc. A/4879, September 20, 1961.

Note that it was *agreed* that *all* weapons of mass destruction and their means of delivery were to be eliminated.

What had not been agreed, of course, was in what sequence the weapons of mass destruction and their vehicles should be eliminated. This was one of the crucial points on which the subsequent negotiations in the Eighteen-Nation Committee on Disarmament proved fruitless, as will be described in the succeeding chapters.

> All measures of general and complete disarmament should be balanced so that at no stage of the implementation of the treaty could any State or group of States gain military advantage and that security is ensured equally for all. . . .

This was another principle which proved easier to enunciate than to apply. As we shall see, proposals which one side or the other put forward, nominally in accordance with this principle, appeared to the other side as likely, if implemented, to create a military advantage to the proposer, and hence to violate the principle and to upset the strategic balance.

> All disarmament measures should be implemented from beginning to end under such strict and effective international control as would provide firm assurance that all parties are honouring their obligations.

This control clause had been very difficult to negotiate and in fact it delayed agreement on the whole document. The final solution was that Mr. McCloy wrote a supplementary memorandum to Mr. Zorin which said that in order to come together on a document to submit to the United Nations the United States had agreed to omit the following clause from the paragraph about verification:

> Such verifications should ensure that not only agreed limitations or reductions take place but also that retained armed forces and armaments do not exceed agreed levels at any stage.

However, the clause was removed on the express understanding that the position of the United States as outlined in it remained unchanged.[7]

Mr. Zorin in his answering letter said in part:

> It appears from your letter that the United States is trying to establish control over the armed forces and armaments retained by States at any given stage of disarmament. However, such control, which in fact means control over armaments, would turn into an international system of legalized espionage, which would naturally be unacceptable to

---

[7]UN Doc. A/4880, September 20, 1961.

any State concerned for its security and the interests of preserving peace throughout the world.[8]

In these two statements was expressed another of the basic differences of viewpoint which prevented agreement or any real progress in dealing with the limitation of ICBM's and long-range bombers, the vehicles of the weapons of mass destruction.

President Kennedy spoke to the United Nations General Assembly on September 25, 1961. What he said about disarmament was a tonic to those of us who had been engaged in the dismal proceedings of 1960, which followed the fruitless meetings of the successive United Nations disarmament organs beginning in 1946. My diary records that I found the speech "very impressive." In it occurred the saying which was to become so well known: "Mankind must put an end to war, or war will put an end to mankind."[9] Perhaps his speech writer let rhetoric get the better of reality; the conclusion is too extreme. In any case, in the ensuing years neither the policy makers of the USA nor those of the USSR, in setting their disarmament negotiating positions, acted as if they really believed what Mr. Kennedy said.

Another eloquent passage was the following:

> Every man, woman and child lives under a nuclear sword of Damocles, hanging by the slenderest of threads, capable of being cut at any moment by accident or miscalculation or by madness.[10]

The "sword of Damocles" rapidly became a cliché in speeches about disarmament, to the discomfort of those who had to listen to many of them. The United States and the Soviet Union have since made progress in limiting the chances that nuclear war between them might begin through accident or miscalculation, even while the great nuclear armaments pile up. But when Mr. Kennedy spoke, the thread holding the sword was uncomfortably slender.

In a later part of his speech, Mr. Kennedy referred to the critical situations in Indochina (South Vietnam, Laos, Cambodia), and in Berlin. These conflicts were very serious, and, to the minds of some people concerned in international affairs, it would be unreasonable to consider disarmament negotiations while they were still unsettled. But the President said:

---

[8]UN Doc. A/4887, September 25, 1961.
[9]*Documents on Disarmament*, 1961, page 465.
[10]*Ibid.*, page 467.

Men no longer maintain that disarmament must await the settlement of all disputes, for disarmament must be a part of any permanent settlement. And men may no longer pretend that the quest for disarmament is a sign of weakness, for in a spiralling arms race a nation's security may well be shrinking even as its arms increase.[11]

Unfortunately the conclusion did not prevent a steep increase in long-range nuclear weapon vehicles (strategic armaments) during the administration of Mr. Kennedy and his successors.

The President then introduced the United States "Program for General and Complete Disarmament in a Peaceful World." As this document contained very much the same provisions as the proposal put before the Eighteen-Nation Committee on Disarmament in Geneva in April 1962, discussion of the measures it proposed for the limitation and reduction of mass destruction armaments will be left to the next chapter.

What remained to be settled in the 1961 General Assembly was which neutral nations should be added to the membership of the TNCD to compose the Eighteen-Nation Committee. On December 13, Ambassador Stevenson and Ambassador Zorin announced that agreement had been reached on this point, and on December 20, the General Assembly passed Resolution 1722/XVI welcoming the agreement on principles, and accepting the proposed composition of the negotiating body. It nominated the following non-aligned countries: Brazil, Burma, Ethiopia, India, Mexico, Nigeria, Sweden and the United Arab Republic. This group had been selected as representing the non-aligned countries in South America, Europe, Africa and Asia, balanced between those which generally tended to accept the viewpoint of the United States, and those which leaned more towards the Soviet Union's views.

Four months after President Kennedy had given the UN General Assembly his "Program for General and Complete Disarmament in a Peaceful World," Mr. Robert McNamara, Secretary for Defense, was expounding to the House of Representatives Appropriations Committee the preparations which the United States was making in case the world did not turn out to be peaceful. I shall set out in the following pages a few of the principal points in his statement, from which many passages were deleted in the published record. However, in spite of the deletions of particularly sensitive material, it is possible to get a good general idea of the strategic posture which the United States was intending to adopt over the next few years, and the production of armaments which it was programming in order to have the capabilities required. Presumably the

---

[11]*Ibid.*, page 467.

United States Government believed that this programme could be cut short if there should be an effective agreement with the Soviet Union, in the Geneva negotiations, to halt the arms race. But a comparison with what President Kennedy had put forward in his disarmament proposals certainly gives the impression that while the Government's left hand may have known what the right hand was doing, each hand was juggling a different variety of balls. Some cynics might say that while the right hand was juggling with nuclear bombs, the left hand was juggling with mere bubbles.

Mr. McNamara told the committee that what were described as "Strategic Retaliatory Forces" comprised heavy bombers, B 52, B 47 and B 58; the Minuteman, Atlas and Titan missiles, and the Polaris submarines. He said the requirement for this kind of force lent itself to reasonably precise calculation. First, the "aiming points in the target system" were determined; then the number and field of the nuclear weapons which would be required to destroy them; then what load each vehicle in the SRF could carry; its ability to penetrate enemy defences; its accuracy (circular error probability (CEP)); its reliability (what proportion of the missiles could be counted upon to take off on the required course); and, finally, the cost-effectiveness of each system (adopting a previous Secretary's phrase, how much bang on Soviet territory could be expected for each dollar (or rather millions of dollars) expended on manufacturing the system in question).

All this sounds an aseptic sort of engineering calculation. It was only a few years later that Mr. McNamara spelled out in terms of millions of human deaths what was really meant by "assured destruction," the strategic concept on which his policies of deterrence finally depended.

Through such calculations the Department of Defense had determined the size and character of the strategic retaliatory forces (SRF) required for the next five or six years – that is, the programme extended to 1967 – to assure that the United States would have at all times the capability to destroy any nation which might attack it, even after it had absorbed a first blow from that nation. There was no question that the US SRF had that capability at the time of the hearing.

Mr. McNamara announced that the build-up of the B 52 intercontinental bomber part of the force to 630 operational aircraft would be complete at the end of 1962. This strength would be maintained. Although funds had previously been provided for a greater number, it had been decided not to build them. Other means of retaliation would be less vulnerable to an enemy first strike, and less costly to construct and operate. Two wings (ninety aircraft?) of B 58 bombers would be operational by the end of the year. These were supersonic medium-range aircraft, nuclear weapon carriers. The B 47's, also medium-range nuclear weapon carriers, which had been located on bases around the periphery of the Soviet Union from which they could reach Soviet Union targets, would be phased out as the missile forces were built up.

Turning to the missile programme, Mr. McNamara said that the Atlas and Titan construction programme was provided for in the estimates. (There were probably fifty to sixty of each, although figures are not given in the record.) Through the year 1962, funds were provided for 600 Minuteman ICBM's, in hardened and dispersed sites, although when they would become operational was not stated. Development of a rail-mobile Minuteman had been suspended, because the benefits which might be gained would not be worth the cost.

Funds for constructing twenty-nine Polaris submarines were available through the fiscal year 1962 (which ended June 30). It was proposed to add six more Polaris in each of the fiscal years 1963 and 1964, bringing the total to forty-one. Then production would stop. (This programme was in fact achieved.)

For the period beyond the fiscal year 1967, there might be a requirement for more "advanced" strategic retaliatory systems. The B 70 bomber was still under development, and this would be continued, but its high cost would not be justified in terms of adding power to the strategic retaliatory forces. Funds were requested to initiate a study of a more advanced solid-fuelled ICBM. (Quite probably the MRV and MIRV[12] grew out of this study.)

A good start had been made on the construction of warning systems against ICBM attack. It was important to "do whatever was feasible" to develop, produce and deploy an effective system of active defence against ICBM attack. There were extensive development programmes on Nike-Zeus and on more advanced versions of terminal defence systems.[13]

So the arming was to go ahead, pretty well at full speed, so far as the United States was concerned, while getting ready to talk disarmament.

What was the Soviet Union doing to build up its comparable retaliatory force? The United States and its allies did not know, but later intelligence shows the following comparison of the United States and Soviet Union build-ups, from 1962 to 1965.

---

[12]MRV – Multiple Reentry Vehicle.
 MIRV – Multiple Independently-targetable Reentry Vehicle.
[13]Excerpts from report on hearings before the Committee on Armed Services, January 1962.

Growth of Strategic Missile Strength: 1962-1965

	1962	1963	1964	1965
USA ICBM	294	424	834	854
USSR ICBM	75	100	200	270
USA SLBM	144	224	416	496
USSR SLBM[14]	Some	100	120	120

From tables in *The Military Balance 1969-70*, ISS London, page 55.

---

[14]Soviet SLBM's include surface-launched ballistic and cruise missiles.

CHAPTER 11

Meeting of Eighteen-Nation Committee

During January and February, 1962, the Canadian disarmament group were engaged in preparing for the opening of the Conference of the Eighteen-Nation Committee on Disarmament, which had been tentatively set for mid-March in Geneva. This involved several visits to Washington, where we consulted with the US Arms Control and Disarmament officials, sometimes alone, and sometimes in a general conference with allies. The American disarmers were writing up position papers for all the several parts of the programme which had been placed before the UN General Assembly by President Kennedy on September 25, 1961.

Mr. McIlwraith was head of the Disarmament Division which had been set up in the Department of External Affairs, and was assisted by Mr. Max Yalden and Mr. Richard Tait. In the following pages I refer to the officers in the division and those in the delegation to the ENDC as the "Disarmament group." Canadian policies and positions were worked out in consultation by the two units. We made a tabular comparison of the American and the Russian programmes for general and complete disarmament, thinking that it would be good tactics for the Canadian delegation to stress the points where the two plans were not far apart, and to try to get the superpowers to concentrate negotiations on these. Our reasoning was that if agreement could be reached on a number of minor points, a momentum could be established which would make agreement on the knottier issues easier. The ENDC and its successor, the Conference of the Committee on Disarmament (CCD) have reached agreement on several arms control measures, but no agreements for the limitation and reduction of mass-destruction, or conventional armaments and armed forces have been achieved. Limitation of mass destruction weapons has, of course, been moved off the agenda of the CCD and now is under negotiation in the Strategic Arms Limitation Talks (SALT) between the superpowers.

Mr. Green, in consultation with the Prime Minister, had agreed that Canada should support the United States' GCD programme. The Cabinet decision in February 1961, on the general lines of a disarmament policy for Canada, has already been referred to. The USA plan was consistent with these principles, and the Prime Minister and Mr. Green felt that it was unnecessary to bring up the matter in Cabinet again.

The disarmament group also made a study of the USSR proposal for the elimination of all nuclear weapon vehicles in the first stage, and prepared arguments to show that it was not feasible. The Canadian policy was that the limitation and reduction of nuclear weapons vehicles, particularly those of intercontinental range, should start in the first stage of disarmament, and affect a large enough number of them to make a real impact. However, to abolish *all such armaments at once within the space of eighteen months*, as the Soviet Union plan proposed, would be impracticable for a number of reasons, which will be explained in the succeeding pages.

On a visit to Washington late in January, I emphasized to ACDA officials the Canadian view that it was very important to have a well-developed position on the reduction of nuclear weapon vehicles, conventional armaments and forces for the first stage of disarmament. They told me that they were working on this, but that it was difficult to get the Pentagon to agree to any numerical proposal. Another point I made in discussions in Washington was that it would be inadvisable in the early stages of negotiations to introduce provisions for the eventual world peace force to have nuclear armaments.

At the end of February there was a meeting in Washington of the heads of delegation of the Western members of the ENDC. Mr. William C. Foster was now presiding over ACDA, having been appointed Director by President Kennedy the previous September, when the act creating ACDA had been approved. As well as the programme for GCD, various arms control, or partial measures, were discussed. These included the non-dissemination of nuclear weapons, the prohibition of their testing, and the prohibition of chemical, biological and radiological means of warfare.

Some of the delegates thought that the USSR would be ready to discuss these and other partial measures – in spite of their insistence that the negotiations had to be on the basis of their plan for general and complete disarmament. One favourite partial measure of theirs was the Rapacki Plan. Adam Rapacki was the Foreign Minister of Poland, and in 1958 he had brought forward a plan for a denuclearized and partially demilitarized zone in Europe. This had never been the subject of serious negotiations, although suggestions for disengagement had been floated by Western spokesmen previously.[1] But from the NATO viewpoint, the Rapacki plan was heavily weighted in favour of the Warsaw Pact.

At a dinner given by Mr. Foster on February 28 I had two interesting conversations with American officials. Mr. Foy Kohler, later to be United States Ambassador to the Soviet Union, criticized the then current Canadian policy of refusing to have nuclear weapons on Canadian soil until war broke out. I pointed out that our politicians were reflecting a Canadian general aversion to nuclear weapons, at least as was indicated by the press and various organizations.

Of course, many Americans disliked the idea of nuclear war and weapons as much as Canadians did. It would be very difficult to measure the difference in public opinion on the subject in the two countries in specific terms. It might be that a majority of Americans thought that it was a good thing that they had nuclear weapons, and that their nuclear power was all that prevented a takeover of the world by communism. Canadians, not having nuclear weapons, and not wanting them, were in the middle between the two great powers, and certainly preferred Americans (the devil we knew) to the Russians (the devil we didn't know). But what we had most to fear was that the superpowers would escalate armaments and tensions until a nuclear war would come about, over our dead bodies.

Throughout 1962 the question of acquiring nuclear weapons for the Canadian forces was still unsettled. The Cabinet was split, and the ministers of External Affairs and of Defence were still on opposite sides. On January 5 I had a conversation with Air Marshal Frank Millar, the Chairman of the Chiefs of Staff Committee. He said the Department of National Defence was not hostile to disarmament, and regarded it as a necessary long-term object. But pending effective disarmament agreements, Canada had to do its part to maintain defensive power in NATO. I agreed to this, and also that to site defensive nuclear armaments (such as Bomarc) in Canada should not be of great concern. However, we and our respective

---

[1]See Howard, Michael, *Projects of Disengagement* (London: Penguin, 1958), Chapter 2.

ministers had different views in regard to the acquisition of nuclear weapons for our forces in Europe. In reply to my arguments that it would not be useful for our NATO contingents to have a nuclear role (see Appendix 1), he pressed the point that we were committed to play a part in NATO nuclear defensive arrangements, with the F 104 strike-reconnaissance aircraft, because of earlier decisions.

At the 1961 General Assembly Sweden and seven other countries had put forward a draft resolution (eventually passed as Res. 1664(XVI)) which requested the Secretary-General to inquire of all member states not possessing nuclear weapons whether they would be willing to enter into specific undertakings to refrain from manufacturing or otherwise acquiring them, and in future to refuse to receive them on their territory on behalf of any other country. This resolution was voted against by the United States, the United Kingdom and eight other NATO countries, as well as Spain and Nicaragua. What was objected to was the proposal that non-possessing countries should refuse to have nuclear weapons on their territory. This of course would have made it impossible to have nuclear weapons on the territory of European nations members of NATO, and we have seen that NATO had decided to rely on such weapons, by decisions taken in 1954 and 1957, to overcome the preponderance of the Warsaw Pact allies in conventional forces and armaments.

Canada voted for the resolution along with fifty-six other countries, including the Soviet Union bloc and an assortment of non-aligned states. However, we were kept company by Norway, Denmark, Iceland and Ireland. This is one of the very few occasions when we voted differently from our principal allies on disarmament resolutions.

In February, when a reply had to be made to the Secretary-General's inquiry, there was a dispute between Mr. Green and Mr. Harkness. It appears that Mr. Green had received the Prime Minister's approval of a draft reply which said that Canada would not acquire nuclear weapons unless the international situation deteriorated. This draft was not sent, and a more ambiguous reply replaced it, which, *inter alia*, stressed the need for an international agreement preventing further dissemination of nuclear weapons, to which nuclear powers and non-possessors would be parties.

My other conversation at Mr. Foster's dinner was with Mr. Paul Nitze,[2] about the reports that the United States would be orbiting intelligence-gathering satellites (Midas, Samos).[3] I said I hoped they would not

[2]See note 2, Chapter 10.
[3]Midas – Missile Alarm Defence System.
Samos – Satellite and Missile Observation System.

be put to photographing Soviet Union territory, because this might cause the breakdown of the ENDC, as the summit conference projected for May 1960 had broken down, and the TNCD with it because of the U 2 flights. Mr. Nitze gave me to understand that the United States was certainly going to go ahead with this intelligence-gathering project, which they considered vital for their security. And this they did, without too much outrage from the Soviet Union, which was busy building its own intelligence-gathering satellites, and soon brought them into operation. The result has been that since the mid-sixties the United States has been able to make a pretty accurate check of deployed USSR ballistic missiles. The USSR knew all about USA missile deployment through information given to the Congress and leaks to the media. The capacity to determine the adversary's array of ballistic missiles by satellites orbiting in space, where the general public is unaware of their presence, is now thought to be one of the most important factors which may make it possible to have an agreed limitation of weapons of mass-destruction, in the negotiations pursued in SALT.

Representatives of some of the non-aligned nations which were to take part in the ENDC called on me, to discuss the probable course of the negotiations and obtain our viewpoint. Canada had a somewhat special position having been in all the disarmament negotiations since 1946, and we probably appeared more approachable and ready to talk than the representatives of the great powers. The Yugoslav Ambassador to Canada, Mr. Belovsky, also came to see me. He told me that Mr. Khrushchev needed a success in the disarmament field at this time for reasons of internal politics. This seemed a hopeful factor. The Yugoslavs were much interested in disarmament, and in 1961 were disappointed that they had not been included among the eight non-aligned members of the ENDC. A year or so later they began to be critical of the lack of accomplishment of the negotiating body – as did other non-aligned nations outside the Eighteen. They were brought into the negotiations when in 1969 the body was renamed the Conference of the Committee on Disarmament, and was enlarged to twenty-six members. (France is still nominally a member but continues its boycott.)

Canada took an initiative at this time which was of considerable importance in the structure of the conference. In discussing how the ENDC should be set up, a good deal of attention was given to the chairmanship. The arrangements for the TNCD – chairmanship rotating each meeting between all members of the committee – had been patently unsatisfactory. There was some talk of having a neutral chairman, and Sr. Padillo Nervo, of Mexico, who was Chairman of the UN Disarmament Commission, was mentioned. But this idea was unacceptable to the Russians, and the Americans did not care for it either. It occurred to the Canadian disarmament group that an arrangement for a joint chairmanship, similar to that which had worked out successfully in the Laos conference, in which the USSR and the U.K. representatives had been joint chairmen, might work for the ENDC. An additional reason for our promotion of this idea was that the real problem in the disarmament negotiations was to get the superpowers to talk frankly with each other. A joint chairmanship would make frequent contacts obligatory in steering the work of the conference. In the eyes of the world the superpowers would become jointly responsible for the success of the proceedings.

After getting Mr. Green's approval I raised the subject with the other members of the Western Five during a visit to New York towards the end of January. The Americans were in favour but did not want to promote the idea themselves, for political reasons. The British and Italians agreed, after some hesitation, but the French did not like it, presumably because it would enhance the status of the Americans and the Russians, while leaving them out. After further discussions during February, with the agreement of our colleagues, I put the suggestion to Mr. Arutunian, the USSR ambassador in Ottawa. He was non-committal, but transmitted the proposal to Moscow. Finally the Russians agreed to the co-chairmanship, although with the provision that the chairmanship of meetings as they occurred, daily or at longer intervals, should rotate among all members of the conference. This meant that the USA and the USSR representatives would steer the conference; that is to say, decide on the general programme of discussion, after consultations with the rest of the delegations. This procedure was decided just a day or so before the conference opened, and was confirmed at the first meeting. The co-chairmen took care to keep the discussions as open and flexible as possible. Any delegation could raise any subject related to the disarmament plans or the partial measures, whether it was scheduled for that day's meeting or not.

Early in February, President Kennedy and Mr. Macmillan had proposed to Mr. Khrushchev that at the opening of the conference the delegations should be headed by the foreign ministers of the countries participating. Mr. Khrushchev countered by proposing that heads of government should lead the delegations. This was declined by President Kennedy and Mr. Macmillan, but they left the way open for a summit meeting later if sufficient progress should be made. The Berlin situation was still difficult, and no doubt this was one of the reasons why the suggestion was fended off. When the Conference did open, the following foreign ministers, among others, were present: Mr. Green, Canada; Mr.

V. David, Czechoslovakia; Mr. Krishna Menon, India; Signor Segni, Italy; Mr. Jaja Wachuko, Nigeria; Mr. Adam Rapacki, Poland; Mr. Manescu, Romania; Mr. Andrei Gromyko, USSR; Mr. Mahmoud Fawzi, UAR; Lord Home, U.K.; Mr. Dean Rusk, USA.

The first meeting of the ENDC was taken up in approving the procedural proposals which the co-chairmen had agreed upon. At the second meeting, on March 15, the series of position statements began. It happened, through the luck of the draw, that Mr. Green was in the chair on that day. The first speaker was Mr. Gromyko, who devoted himself mainly to introducing a Soviet Union draft treaty on GCD, and rehearsing once again the Russian arguments for this drastic solution to the threat of nuclear weapons. Perhaps to show that President Kennedy's speech writers had no monopoly of lofty imagery, he said:

> On fine days the snow-capped peak of Mont Blanc can be seen from Geneva. For a long time people thought it would remain unconquered. Yet the attack on that summit continued, and it was conquered. If disarmament is tackled properly then that summit too, on which the aspirations of the peoples have centred for ages, can be conquered in four years.

I suppose most of those seated around the conference table[4] liked the analogy, though probably none believed that general and complete disarmament would be achieved in four years. Writing nine years later, the goal seems even more distant, but we may hope that the superpowers in carrying on the Strategic Arms Limitation Talks now understand where the route lies which can lead to a more secure world.

The West was also encouraged by a later passage in his speech:

> While the Soviet Government considers . . . general and complete disarmament as the Committee's main task it would nevertheless consider it useful if a number of measures which could facilitate the relaxation of international tension, the strengthening of confidence among states and the creation of more favourable conditions for disarmament were taken forthwith, without awaiting the completion of the negotiations on general and complete disarmament.[5]

This meant that arms control measures could be negotiated, and, as it turned out, it was in this area that the conference eventually had a

---

[4]ENDC/PV.2, page 10.
[5]ENDC/PV.2, page 12.

degree of success. Mr. Gromyko, however, had salted his speech with dark sayings against powerful opponents of disarmament, and complained of the United States programme of nuclear testing which it had been announced would begin the later part of April.

At a lunch given a few days later by the Czechoslovak representative, I was seated next to Mr. Gromyko, who asked me when I thought our allies would be serious about disarmament. I said I thought President Kennedy and his entourage were serious about it, and that there was increased consciousness among academics and other writers of the need for disarmament, but that it had not spread to the American people generally. This would take time. Meanwhile militarists and armaments manufacturers were a strong influence against disarmament. The United States did not yet realize that in the world of today it could not enjoy unlimited sovereignty. Mr. Gromyko objected strongly to the idea of any limitation of the sovereignty of the great nations.

On another occasion when Mr. Zorin commented gloomily on the United States attitude to disarmament, I suggested that in the USA, as elsewhere, there were influential people who were for disarmament, and other influential people who were against it. It ought to be Soviet policy to avoid, in words and actions, giving ammunition to those who opposed disarmament, and, promoting instead better relations between the superpowers.

On March 16 I had a talk with Mr. Semyon K. Tsarapkin, who said the conference must not get entangled with technicalities which would happen if it resorted to subcommittee discussions. This was an early indication of the Soviet resistance to the idea of technical subcommittees, which persisted through the next few years, to the frustration of the Western group, and some non-aligned nations. They believed that progress might be made by having experts thrash out technical problems, such as the means required for verification of various measures of disarmament. The Soviet Union rejected this approach, doubtless on instructions from Moscow. They wanted to keep the negotiations political, rather than technical, and to keep them mainly in the framework of their draft treaty of general and complete disarmament.

The other speaker at the second meeting was Secretary of State Dean Rusk. He began by reading a message from President Kennedy, which contained the passage:

> . . . men now know that amassing of destructive power does not beget security; they know that polemics do not bring peace. Men's minds, men's hearts, and men's spiritual aspirations alike demand no less

than a reversal of the course of recent history – a replacement of ever-growing stockpiles of destruction by ever-growing opportunities for human achievement.[6]

I sometimes wonder if there is any other sphere of human activity in which so many fine words have been uttered, and so little actually achieved as in the pursuit of disarmament and a stable peace.

Mr. Rusk stated the objective of the conference, as the United States Government saw it, in the following terms:

> We must eliminate the instruments of destruction. We must prevent the outbreak of war by accident or by design. We must create the conditions for a secure and peaceful world. In so doing, we can turn the momentum of science exclusively to peaceful purposes, and we can lift the burden of the arms race, and thus increase our capacity to raise living standards everywhere.[7]

Mr. Rusk then referred to the United States programme for general and complete disarmament in a peaceful world, introduced by President Kennedy in the UNGA on September 25, 1961, and the Soviet Union draft treaty on GCD which Mr. Gromyko had presented. He said that a comparison of the two plans would show some areas of agreement. The US believed that it was the task of the conference to search for broader areas of accord leading to specific steps which all could take with confidence.

Mr. Rusk then announced that the United States would propose that a cut of thirty per cent. in nuclear delivery vehicles and major conventional armaments be included in the first stage of the disarmament programme. Strategic delivery vehicles would be reduced not only in numbers but in destructive capability. With faithful cooperation, this reduction could be carried out in three years, and there could be similar reductions in each of the later stages.[8]

This was a considerable advance towards the view held by Canada, France and other countries that the most important measure of disarmament was the limitation and reduction of long-range weapons of mass destruction; and that a beginning on this should be made in the first stage of any disarmament plan, if it was to be effective and acceptable.

Less helpful was Mr. Rusk's passage referring to the necessity of adequate verification of disarmament measures, concerning which, as we have seen, there had been a serious divergence of views. On this occasion Mr. Rusk said:

---

[6]ENDC/PV.2, page 15.
[7]ENDC/PV.2, page 17.
[8]ENDC/PV.2, page 21.

The United States proposes that . . . this conference undertake an urgent search for mutually acceptable methods of guaranteeing the fulfilment of obligations for arms reduction. . . .

We must not be diverted from this search by shop-worn efforts to equate verification with espionage. . . . No government, large or small, could be expected to enter into disarmament arrangements under which their peoples might become victims of the perfidy of others.[9]

One does not have to be an experienced diplomat to perceive that such a statement, on a very difficult point of the negotiations, would be, as the Americans say, counter-productive.

Towards the end of his statement Mr. Rusk referred to Mr. Gromyko's complaint that the US was intending to resume nuclear testing, and, as might have been expected, he used the *tu quoque* retort:

The Statement of Agreed Principles and this Conference were born among the echoing roars of more than forty Soviet explosions. A fifty-megaton bomb does not make the noise of a cooing dove.[10]

At this point it may be useful to digress briefly to note the status of negotiations to end nuclear testing.

When the conference opened, the non-aligned members, particularly Sweden, India and the United Arab Republic, were greatly concerned that negotiations for the cessation of nuclear weapon tests should be pursued vigorously. The United States, the United Kingdom and the Soviet Union had been meeting for this purpose since 1958, and testing had been suspended until 1961. At that date the Soviet Union resumed testing, and the three-nation conference recessed. The 1961 session of the UNGA passed resolutions calling for cessation of tests, and a resumption of negotiations. These recommenced at Geneva on November 28, 1961, and adjourned on January 29, 1962, no progress having been made. What prevented agreement was the difference of opinion between the West and the USSR on the requirements for verifying that no underground tests were carried out. The West maintained that it would be necessary to have a certain number of inspections on the ground in areas where seismography indicated that an event had taken place which might be either a nuclear explosion or an earthquake. The Soviet Union maintained that adequate verification was possible by seismological means alone, without on-site inspections.

---

[9]ENDC/PV.2, page 22.
[10]ENDC/PV.2, page 24.

On March 21, 1962, the ENDC established a subcommittee, consisting of the three nuclear powers, which was called upon to continue the consideration of a treaty to ban testing of nuclear weapons. On April 16 a joint memorandum by the eight non-aligned members of the ENDC was submitted, containing suggestions as to how the differences regarding verification might be resolved.[11] While the subcommittee continued to negotiate during the 1962 sessions of the ENDC, and during its recess, no progress on the difficult issue was made. The United States and the USSR both carried out heavy programmes of testing in the atmosphere. Further developments in the test ban issue will be referred to in later chapters.

At the fourth meeting on March 19, Mr. Green set out the Canadian viewpoint on GCD and partial measures. Among the more important passages were the following:

[Following] agreement on the basic principles of disarmament . . . we are in a position to move quickly from a general exchange of views to a detailed consideration of measures which will actually stop the competition in armaments, and bring about substantial reductions from present levels. In my opinion, the problem of stopping the development of more deadly weapons is perhaps more important than that of bringing about measures of disarmament.

Mr. Green later referred to the US programme of disarmament presented by President Kennedy on September 25, 1961, and said that Canada had participated in drafting the plan, and fully supported it.[12]

He suggested how the conference might approach the task of agreeing on a treaty on GCD as follows:

Starting from the joint statement of principles, we should search out specific problems on which the two sides are close to agreement, and try to settle these as quickly as possible. Having achieved this, we should then go on to study problems on which the two sides are farther apart – first to clarify differences and then to resolve them. In this way, my delegation believes we can systematically move toward a comprehensive system of disarmament and complete the fulfilment of the tasks which have been given us.[13]

Mr. Green then cited seven areas in which the positions of the two sides appeared to be relatively similar. These were mainly what we now

---

[11]ENDC/28. See *The United Nations and Disarmament*, 1945-1970, page 222.
[12]ENDC/PV.4, pages 12, 13.
[13]ENDC/PV.4, page 14.

call arms control measures, and among them were two on which agreement was eventually reached: the prohibition of mass destruction weapons in outer space, and the non-proliferation of nuclear weapons. The seventh area was the question of nuclear disarmament, in which he said that the positions of the two sides had been brought closer together by the proposal for a thirty per cent. first stage reduction in nuclear delivery vehicles, just made public by Mr. Rusk. He hoped that detailed negotiation would bring the two major military powers to agreement on phased reductions in this field. This, sadly, was a hope which has not been fulfilled.

CHAPTER 12

General and complete disarmament debate

The Soviet Union draft treaty on General and Complete Disarmament under Strict International Control, submitted by Mr. Gromyko to the Eighteen-Nation Disarmament Conference on March 15, 1962 is an extensive document.[1] I shall summarize those articles and clauses in it which relate to the limitation, reduction and elimination of the weapons of mass destruction, particularly the long-range vehicles for nuclear weapons. The programme was divided into three stages, as was that of the United States. This arrangement had been accepted in previous negotiations.

Article 5, paragraph 1, provided that all rockets capable of delivering nuclear weapons, of all calibres and ranges, and also pilotless aircraft were to be eliminated from the armed forces, and destroyed, together with the ground launching and guidance apparatus. Paragraph 2 provided that production of such vehicles and supporting apparatus should be discontinued, and factories, tools and equipment for their manufacture should be dismantled or destroyed. Strictly limited numbers of rockets for peaceful exploration of space could be retained, and the production of more rockets for this purpose under international control could also be permitted.

[1]ENDC/2, March 19, 1962.

Article 6, paragraph 1, provided that all military aircraft capable of delivering nuclear weapons were also to be destroyed, together with the ground installations serving them. Paragraph 2 provided that production of such aircraft would be completely discontinued.

Article 7, paragraph 1 provided that all surface warships which could be used as vehicles for nuclear weapons, and *submarines of any class or type* (italics added) should be destroyed. Paragraph 2 provided for the discontinuance of construction of such vessels, and the dismantling of shipyards specialized for their construction.

Article 8 contained provisions similar to those for rockets and aircraft, with respect to artillery systems capable of serving as a means of delivery for nuclear weapons.

The next section of the draft treaty dealt with foreign military bases and troops in alien territories. Article 9 provided that simultaneously with the measures for the destruction of nuclear weapon vehicles set out in the preceding articles, states which had military bases or depots of any kind in foreign territories should dismantle them, and evacuate the personnel to their national territory. All armaments and installations at such bases should be destroyed on the spot. These measures applied whether the bases were owned by the garrisoning state, or by the state on whose territory they were located, and included bases set up under military treaties or agreements for use.

Article 10 provided that simultaneously with the measures just described, troops of all states on foreign territories should be withdrawn. (This provision might seem redundant, in view of those of Article 9, but presumably was thought necessary to cover foreign troops which, technically, might not be located on or within specific bases.)

There were, of course, sections covering the reduction of conventional forces and armaments, and the reduction of military expenditure. Certain measures classifiable as arms control were set out, and some of these were later negotiated separately from the context of general and complete disarmament. Article 18 ("To ensure that the United Nations is capable of effectively protecting States against threats or breaches of the peace") called for all states party to the treaty to conclude agreements with the Security Council to make available armed forces, assistance and facilities as provided for in Article 43 of the Charter. Certain details regarding the location and command of such contingents were also specified.

Articles 5 to 10 each carried a paragraph stating that inspectors of the International Disarmament Organization (IDO) should verify the implementation of the measures described. Article 2 dealt with obligations thereto of the parties, and provided for the organization to be estab lished within the framework of the United Nations, with the duty of implementing control over disarmament. It was to begin operating as soon as disarmament measures were initiated. Articles 40 to 45 laid out a rather elaborate structure for it. Both sides included such an organization in their draft treaties, and the matter was discussed extensively during the TNCD and the early meetings of the ENDC. Interest in the question waned as it became obvious what the difficulties were in agreeing on concrete measures of disarmament, especially as concerned the weapons of mass destruction.

After the ENDC had been in progress about ten days the foreign ministers departed, one after another, and the negotiations were carried on by the diplomats designated as heads of delegation. The interventions of the foreign ministers in the debate as a rule had been confined to general themes. As they hoped to get the conference off to a good start, they avoided dwelling on the difficult questions which separated the positions of the two sides. Essentially, the problem of the conference was to bring the NATO countries and the Warsaw Pact countries to accept the maximum possible degree of disarmament, worked out in accordance with the McCloy-Zorin principles of negotiations. The non-aligned members of the conference were in the position of audience, assessors, referees sometimes, acting on behalf of those nations of the world which did not form part of the great armed alliances. This was their real role, although, from time to time, they made many sensible suggestions for compromise between the East and West positions; suggestions which, unfortunately, seldom had any immediate effect.

Criticism by the western countries of the provisions of the Soviet Union draft treaty did not really take form until the United States had laid before the conference its "Outline of Basic Provisions of a Treaty on General and Complete Disarmament in a Peaceful World" on April 18, 1962.[2] Before getting down to substantive discussion of the two programmes, the conference had to decide how exactly it should proceed to tackle the enormous problem facing it.

The question of procedure in such a conference is far from unimportant. The ordering of the agenda can give one side or the other a considerable advantage in achieving the result it wants, in adversary-type negotiations. The Soviet Union delegation, backed up by its Warsaw Pact allies, tried very hard to have its draft treaty adopted as the basis of discussion. They would have had the conference examine their draft,

---

[2]ENDC/30, April 18, 1962; and Corr. 1, April 25, 1962.

clause by clause, from start to finish, with the purpose of producing the text, agreed by both sides, of a treaty of general and complete disarmament. It does not require detailed argument to show the advantage which this procedure would have conferred on the Soviet Union. The West was somewhat inconvenienced, in this preliminary skirmishing, because the USA did not have its draft ready for presentation until the 18th of April. The Programme for GCD in a Peaceful World of September 25, 1961, on which it was based, was not in a form that would enable its provisions to be compared systematically with those of the Soviet Union draft treaty.

The West adopted the tactical position of arguing that it was necessary first to agree on the programme of general and complete disarmament, before beginning to produce a draft text in treaty language. The resolution of the UNGA, 1722 (XVI) of December 20, 1961 (which served as the mandate for the committee) recommended:

> ... that the Committee ... should undertake negotiations with a view to reaching, on the basis of the joint statement of agreed principles and taking into account, inter alia, paragraph 8 of those principles ... agreement on general and complete disarmament under effective international control.

Paragraph 8 of the agreed principles reads as follows:

> States participating in the negotiations should seek to achieve and implement the widest possible agreement at the earliest possible date. Efforts should continue without interruption until agreement upon the total programme had been achieved, and efforts to ensure early agreement on and implementation of measures of disarmament should be undertaken without prejudicing progress of agreement on the total programme and in such a way that these measures would facilitate and form part of the programme.[3]

It is clear, and the West so pointed out, that the resolution did not make a recommendation to *draft a treaty* of GCD, but to reach an *agreement* on what should go into the treaty. Paragraph 8 of the agreed principles quoted above, was a compromise to accommodate the USSR position (that priority should be given to agreement on a total programme), and the position of the USA and its allies (that if agreements could be reached on partial (arms control) measures, this would be valuable progress towards the declared goal of general and complete disarmament).

---

[3]UN Doc. A/4879; September 20, 1961. Reprinted *Docs. on Disarmament*, 1961, pages 440-1.

At the meeting on April 4, I argued against the USSR representative's insistence that their draft treaty should form the framework of our discussions, as follows:

> ... The order in which the different provisions of the eventual programme or treaty are considered is a matter of importance – of great importance. We have seen that there are differing views on what that order should be.

> If we take one or other of these documents [the Soviet Union draft treaty and the USA programme] and give it precedence as the framework of the agreement we are supposed to reach, we shall be in a sense prejudging the points which are really at issue, that is, the relations in time to each other of the various acts of disarmament, the duration of time required for their accomplishment, and so forth. ...

> Therefore, if one document is taken as the framework of our discussion, it puts those who are adhering to the formulation of the other document at a negotiating disadvantage. They would be put in the position of always having to offer amendments or objections, and thus would be shown, artificially, as being negative in their attitude.[4]

However, the co-chairmen did agree on one order of business, which was to draft a preamble to the eventual treaty. This was possible because most of the clauses in the preambles to the USSR draft treaty and the USA programme were not very different. So the American and Russian delegations got to work on this, with suggestions from other delegations, and after a week or so produced a draft. However, in this draft there were several areas where an agreed wording could not be reached. So the device of "bracketed" phrases, clauses or sentences was adopted. The alternative versions preferred by each side were shown in brackets, with the intention that the lack of consensus could be remedied later. This minimum of progress gave the conference some satisfaction at the time, but before long the disagreement on the difficult substantive points left this partially agreed preamble in limbo.

The reader unacquainted with diplomatic negotiation may regard the above account of procedural disagreement as tiresome squabbling, irrelevant or obstructive to the vital purpose of the negotiations, which was to agree on measures which would lessen the danger of nuclear war, if not eliminate it. However, it is inserted to show some of the difficulties in the course of the negotiation, which contributed to the delay in achieving any

---

[4]ENDC/PV.15, pages 44-6.

positive results, and indeed, in achieving any results on the problem of key importance, that is, the limitation of the long-range nuclear weapon vehicles (strategic arms).

Following up his statement of March 19, in which he had referred to areas common to the United States and the Soviet Union proposals, on March 27 Mr. Green proposed that a declaration be made by all of the members of the Committee prohibiting the orbiting or stationing in outer space of devices for delivering weapons of mass destruction; and requiring the Secretary-General of the UN to be notified of all launchings of space vehicles and missiles. He presented draft wording for such a declaration.

He observed that governments agreed that it was most important to ensure that the achievements in the field of space travel and satellite orbiting should not be diverted to destructive purposes. He also remarked that there were provisions similar to those he was proposing in both the United States and Soviet Union programmes for GCD. The specific language of the proposed draft declaration was only a suggestion. The proposal should be dealt with in the Committee of the Whole, which had been set up to discuss partial (or arms control) measures.[5]

The Minister was anxious that the ENDC should agree on something quickly. This particular proposal had been selected from the "areas" of which he had previously spoken, as the most likely to get through with not too much opposition from either side. The subject had been on the table for quite some time. However, it was not until the 1963 session of the UNGA that a resolution was passed, after consultations between the superpowers, in which the expressed intention of the USA and the USSR was not to station in outer space any objects carrying nuclear weapons or other weapons of mass destruction.[6] The resolution contained nothing regarding an obligation to notify launchings of missiles or space vehicles.

The declaration and the accompanying speech had been worked out by our delegation under the Minister's direction a few days before. Unfortunately there was a slip in our staff work, and the United States delegation was not informed beforehand of our intention to make this proposal. They were not a little annoyed at this, and George Ignatieff and I saw Mr. Dean and Mr. Stelle to apologize for the slip-up. We did not really understand the importance the US delegation attached to it. They told us it was

[5]ENDC/PV.10, pages 22-5.
[6]Res. 1884 (XVII) October 17, 1963.

because we were advocating a declaratory measure with no verification. However, it seems more likely that they feared that the Canadian delegation might be starting off on a course of independent initiatives, without consultation with them and the other NATO representatives – which, of course, we had no intention of doing.

The first criticism of the Soviet Union draft treaty by the United States delegate, Mr. Arthur Dean, was mild in tone. It was directed against the lack of provisions in the first stage for the halting of production and reduction in stocks of nuclear weapons – bombs and warheads. He asked why the Soviet Union draft treaty had no proposals for achieving this in the first stage, as the United States programme had. He pointed out that in the United States formulation, this measure could be negotiated separately, and made effective immediately, without waiting for a complete accord on GCD. Mr. Dean also asked why the Soviet Union had dropped from its most recent draft treaty the provision which had appeared in earlier ones, for a study of the means which could provide effective verification that nations agreeing to abolish all nuclear weapons did not clandestinely retain any.[7]

The Soviet Union had rejected the "Cut-off," as being practicable only as part of general and complete disarmament. Therefore the Russians were unlikely to agree to alter their formulation in response to the American criticisms. The real reason for Soviet Union rejection of this measure has already been speculated upon. In 1962 the Soviet Union was pushing ahead, though not very rapidly, with the construction of ICBM's, IRBM's, MRBM's, as well as a variety of tactical nuclear weapons. To put a check on the provision of these armaments, unless *all* nuclear armament production was halted under general and complete disarmament, was seen by the USSR as a one-sided measure, disadvantageous to them.

Mr. Dean also mentioned the provision in the USA programme which called for "an immediate stop to the spread of a nuclear weapons capability to nations not now having such capability." (This was the non-proliferation treaty in embryo.) This also was a "separable" measure, he said, which could be put into effect without waiting for agreement on GCD as a whole. And this is what eventually happened.

On April 18, Mr. Dean introduced the United States "Outline of Basic

---

[7]ENDC/PV.11, pages 11, 12.

Provisions of a Treaty on General and Complete Disarmament in a Peaceful World."[8] He said:

> Let me explain at the beginning that with respect to disarmament the scheme of the United States plan is a simple one. Fundamentally it is that the nations of the world should seize a moment in time to stop the arms race, to freeze the military situation as it then appears and to shrink it progressively to zero, always keeping the relative military positions of the parties to the treaty to as near as possible to what it was in the beginning.[9]

He went on to explain the articles of the "outline" in general terms. As had previously been indicated by Secretary Rusk, the United States proposed that in the first stage there should be a cut of thirty per cent. in all nuclear delivery vehicles and all major conventional armaments, to be applied in three yearly steps of ten per cent. each. The nuclear weapon vehicles and major armaments (including naval vessels) were divided up into categories and types, each of which would be cut by thirty per cent. in the first stage (Article A 1). Reduction by types was necessary, because otherwise a party to the treaty could eliminate the least effective armaments, and this might result in inequality in the overall reduction.

The reduction would be carried out in the first year, by putting one-third of the armaments to be eliminated in Stage I (that is, ten per cent. of the total of all armaments) in depots under the supervision of the IDO. During the second year, these would be destroyed under supervision of the IDO, "and assurance that retained armaments did not exceed the agreed levels would be provided by the IDO in accordance with arrangements to be worked out and set forth in an annex to the treaty."

This condition, the control over retained levels of armaments, was contrary to the Soviet Union position that control should be only over actual disarmament – that is, destruction or dismantling of armaments. We shall see how the dispute over control (verification) was one of the main reasons why it was impossible to reach agreement on the limitation and reduction of the long-range nuclear weapon vehicles, the carriers of the weapons of mass destruction.

Before further discussion of the problem of control over the elimina-

---

[8]See note 2 of this chapter. The reason for using this rather cumbrous title instead of calling it a draft treaty, as the Soviet Union called theirs, was explained to us by the American delegation. If they had called it a draft treaty, that would have probably obliged the Senate, under the terms of its "advise and consent" responsibility, to take a premature and perhaps embarrassing interest in the negotiation.
[9]ENDC/PV.23, page 6.

tion of long-range nuclear weapon vehicles, let us look at some of the other important provisions of the US Outline.

In Stage I, the United States and the Soviet Union were each to reduce their armed forces to 2,100,000 men. Other "specified parties" (The People's Republic of China?) would have their manpower levels fixed at a figure not exceeding that for the USA and the USSR. All other parties to the treaty would, with certain agreed exceptions, reduce their force levels to 100,000, or one per cent. of their population, whichever was the greater.

Other partial, or arms control measures proposed for Stage I included non-proliferation, prohibiting the testing of nuclear weapons, prohibiting the orbiting of weapons of mass destruction, measures to limit the risk of war by accident, miscalculation, failure of communications or surprise attack. As we shall see, in one way or another, agreement or partial agreement was reached on all of these measures during the next six years.

In Stage II (to be of three years duration) the parties would reduce their remaining armaments of the categories specified in Article A 1 by half, that is, by another thirty-five per cent. This would apply to the means of delivery of nuclear weapons, of course. The remaining armed forces of the USA and the USSR would also be reduced by half, that is, to 1,050,000 men each. Those of other parties would be reduced by agreed percentages. Production of new armaments would be stopped.

In Stage III "the parties would continue the disarmament process which had been started in Stages I and II until they achieved the goal of "general and complete disarmament in a peaceful world."[10]

At the end of Stage III, which would be completed within an agreed period of time, as promptly as possible, states would have at their disposal only such non-nuclear armaments, forces, facilities and establishments as were agreed to be necessary to maintain internal order and protect the personal security of citizens. States would also provide agreed manpower for a United Nations peace force.

Mr. Dean then went on to give the United States view on how verifying obligation to reduce the most important categories to specified levels might be carried out. He quoted the United States interpretation of the agreed principle relating to "strict and effective international control" as follows:

> The extent of inspection during any step or stage would be related to the amount of disarmament being undertaken and to the degree of risk to the parties to the treaty of possible violations.

He then gave an outline of the United States idea of progressive zonal

---

[10]ENDC/PV.23, page 13.

inspections, a proposal which had been elaborated by Mr. Louis Sohn.[11] The territory of each party would be divided into an agreed number of zones. Each party would declare the total level, but not the precise location of the armaments, forces and installations subject to inspection within each zone. These zones would be progressively inspected, starting when disarmament started. Zones would be added as disarmament progressed until, when disarmament was complete, all territory would be open to inspection.[12] The procedure for selecting the zones to be inspected would be such that the state being inspected would have no advance notice of which zone would be chosen, and there would be arrangements to prevent clandestine movements of armament in or out of the zone being inspected.

It was hoped by this ingenious system, which was based on sampling techniques, to allay Soviet Union suspicions of inspection intended to verify allowable remainders of armaments. It was later explained in more detail by the United States delegation, but to no avail, as the Soviet Union representatives refused to consider it, alleging that it would be nothing but an elaborate camouflage for spying.

The Soviet objection to "control over armaments" is made clear by the following extract from the proceedings. At the meeting on April 16 Mr. Zorin read a letter from Mr. Khrushchev to Mr. Macmillan, in reply to one in which the Prime Minister had proposed a nuclear test ban treaty, the provisions of which included on-site inspections. But the objections to inspection which Mr. Khrushchev vigorously raised in this connection were also applicable to the kind of inspection which the Western nations – not only just the United States – felt would be necessary to verify that reductions and limitations of major armaments, particularly long-range NWV's were implemented in an agreement on general and complete disarmament. Mr. Khrushchev wrote:

> I wish to express a few considerations concerning the United States and United Kingdom proposal that the Soviet Union should sign an agreement on the discontinuance of nuclear tests which would give the intelligence organs of NATO an opportunity to have its agents in our territory under the pretext of international control.
>
> We have told you clearly that we cannot agree to this, and I think you understand us correctly. How can we accept your proposal if we have no reason to trust you? You have surrounded the Soviet Union and other socialist countries with your military bases, you threaten us with all kinds of disasters, practically total annihilation, and boast that you have superiority over the USSR in means of annihilation.

[11]Louis B. Sohn (Professor of International Law, Harvard Law School).
[12]ENDC/PV.23, page 15.

You would like . . . to secure our permission to carry on intelligence work in our country without hindrances. . . .

[There followed a passage relating to disappointing negotiations with President Eisenhower relating to his "open skies" proposal.]

Now the Western powers . . . want to establish intelligence centres in our country so as to find out the vulnerable places, the location of our rocket troops and of vitally important targets . . . they now want to plant nests of spies in our country under the guise of international inspectors. And what, it may be asked, is all this for. For choosing the moment to attack the Soviet Union; there can be no other explanation.[13]

What justification, from the USSR viewpoint, could there be for this violent reaction by Mr. Khrushchev? It has to be remembered that in 1958 a conference of experts representing the Soviet Union, the United Kingdom, the United States and five other countries (including Canada) had agreed upon an elaborate system for verifying that nuclear tests were not taking place, and there were to be a very large number of posts on Soviet territory for this purpose.[14] The three nations had been negotiating from 1958 to 1961 on this basis, and it was only after 1961 that the Soviet Union had taken up the position that international inspection on its territory was completely unacceptable.[15] What had caused this change?

If we look at the balance of forces, especially of vehicles capable of carrying nuclear weapons to the territories of the United States and the Soviet Union respectively, as it appeared or was projected in 1962, we shall see, I think, that the Soviet Union had some cause for apprehension. The following figures are taken from *The Military Balance, 1962-1963*, published by the Institute of Strategic Studies, London, in November 1962.

	USSR	USA
ICBM'S	75	630[16]
IRBM'S and MRBM'S	700	250
Intercontinental-range Bombers	190	630
Intermediate-range Bombers[17]	1,400	1,630 (USA AND NATO)

[13]ENDC/PV.21, pages 11, 12.

[14]*The United Nations and Disarmament; 1945-1965*, page 144.

[15]*Ibid.*, page 165.

[16]Projected to July 1963.

[17]Many of the US intermediate-range bombers were on foreign bases from which they could reach USSR vital points.

The Soviet Union strategists could hardly have come to any other conclusion from these figures than that the USA was capable of wiping out their ICBM's (which at the time apparently were nearly all "soft")[18] and their intercontinental bombers by a preemptive strike. But could the government of the Soviet Union believe that the United States would initiate a nuclear war by a surprise attack? To judge by Mr. Khrushchev's tirade, they certainly could believe it possible, and there were quite a few statements by American hawks which they could quote to substantiate their apprehensions. We have also to remember that after the good relations Mr. Khrushchev thought he had established with President Eisenhower (the "Camp David spirit") in 1959, that the President had authorized the systematic reconnaissance of Soviet territory by the U 2 aircraft.

So, in this matter of inspection to verify the fulfilment of disarmament obligations, we find the two superpowers with deep suspicions of the other's good faith. The USA feared the USSR would cheat on disarmament, unless tight inspection procedures were written into the treaty, and the USSR feared that the USA wanted inspection so that they could secure the intelligence for targetting a possible preemptive strike. With this deep mutual suspicion is it surprising that the superpowers could not agree on limiting the armament for delivering nuclear weapons during the disarmament negotiations in the 1960's?

At the meeting which took place on April 24, 1961 I commented on Mr. Zorin's statement at the twenty-first meeting, in regard to the verification question. He had said:

> It is disarmament measures that are controlled and verified, and not the armed forces and armaments remaining at the disposal of States at a particular stage.

I said this was an amplification of the frequently reiterated position of the Soviet Union, which was sometimes abbreviated as "control over disarmament." I said that I did not think that this position and the explanations which Mr. Zorin had given of it corresponded with what he had also said: "We are not prepared to take anyone at their word. . . . We ourselves do not ask that we should be taken at our word."[19] I then referred to the US proposals, pointing out that while there was some risk of failure to fulfil obligations, even if these were put into effect, yet such a risk

---

[18]*The Military Balance, 1962-1963* (London: ISS, 1962), page 3.
[19]ENDC/PV.21, page 27.

would be acceptable if disarmament proceeded in relatively small increments, when there would be little danger of upsetting the balance of forces even if the declared quantities of armaments on which the reduction was to be based had not been correct. But if there were to be total abolition of certain kinds of armaments in a single step (as proposed in the Soviet Union draft treaty) the danger of relying on the unsupported word of the other side would be considerable. I gave a hypothetical case, to put the proposition in simple terms, as follows:

> Let us consider that State "A" and State "B," under the disarmament treaty, are obliged to destroy all their tanks in one step. State "A" has 2,000 tanks, and so declares to the international disarmament organization. State "B" has 3,000 tanks, but only declares 2,000. Pursuant to the principle of verifying the destruction of armaments, the inspectors of the international disarmament organization supervise the destruction of 2,000 tanks of each side. So at the end of this process, State "B" has 1,000 tanks concealed somewhere which could give it considerable military advantage from that time forward. I have used tanks in my illustration, but members of the Committee will appreciate the applicability of the point illustrated to more important armaments – for example, to intercontinental ballistic missiles.[20]

Earlier in this meeting, on April 24, Mr. Dean had also criticized the USSR position on verification, in somewhat different terms. He had also criticized the Soviet Union proposal to eliminate all vehicles for nuclear weapons in Stage I. His points were as follows.

In the first stage there would be only a small change in conventional armaments in which the Soviet Union and its allies were stronger, while all nuclear weapon vehicles were to be eliminated, doing away with the armaments on which the West mainly relied. Thus the Soviet proposition would not conform to the agreed principle that the existing balance of forces and armaments was not to be upset through the process of disarmament. Although the Soviet Union proposal had the appearance of great simplicity, Mr. Dean said, it was just not realistic. If it was to be considered, it was up to the Soviet Union to show how their proposal could be implemented consistently with the principle of balanced reduction.[21]

---

[20]ENDC/PV.26, page 18.
[21]ENDC/PV.26, page 12.

CHAPTER 13

Nuclear weapon vehicles debate

At the twenty-sixth meeting of the ENDC on April 24, Mr. Zorin advanced criticisms of a number of the elements of the United States Outline, but I shall refer only to those which bore on the problem of limiting nuclear weapon vehicles. He welcomed, in rather dry terms, the United States step forward in presenting its proposals in a more complete form than they had been in the document of September 25, 1961. His delegation would give them detailed consideration.

But he complained of the lack of balance in the United States proposals, as Mr. Dean had complained of the lack of balance in the USSR draft treaty. He said that while the new USA plan called for some reduction, in the first stage, of the means of delivering nuclear weapons, it said nothing about eliminating foreign bases.

> Behind this was the obvious intention to weaken the Soviet Union in respect of a number of types of weapons essential for its defence, and at the same time to leave intact the widespread network of foreign military bases placed by the United States in the vicinity of Soviet frontiers.[1]

In proposing very limited disarmament measures for the first stage,

[1]ENDC/PV.26, page 21.

namely the reduction of the armed forces of the USSR and the United States to 2.1 million and some reduction of the means of delivery, the United States at the same time put forward a demand for the establishment of a comprehensive control which in reality would result in a legalized system of international espionage.

Mr. Zorin went on to say that averting danger of a nuclear war – the main task – could only be achieved if all means of delivering nuclear weapons were completely eliminated. The Soviet Union draft treaty provided for this to be done within eighteen months, whereupon the threat that any state would be attacked by nuclear weapons would disappear. But under the United States plan, the threat of nuclear war would hang over the world for an indefinitely long time. Even after three years, the nuclear powers would still have seventy per cent. of their nuclear weapon vehicles, nor would the threat even disappear at the end of the second stage of the USA plan. There was no unequivocal provision for the elimination of the nuclear weapons (warheads, bombs) as distinct from their vehicles – only a proposal that they would be done away with if a commission of experts could find a satisfactory means of verifying that an obligation to get rid of all of them would be carried out.

Mr. Zorin also pointed out that the USA plan left it to be understood that the eventual United Nations peace force, which it would seem would be a large one, might be equipped with nuclear weapons. Thus the United States did not want nuclear weapons to be finally and completely abolished. In a later intervention, he said that the United States wanted nuclear weapons to be retained so they could be used as "a deterrent against the peoples," and for its own political purposes keep the world on the brink of nuclear war.[2]

At the forty-ninth meeting, on June 5, Mr. Dean said that the USSR draft treaty would prohibit nuclear weapons for the future United Nations peace force "categorically, right now"; whereas the USA plan would leave the matter open for later decision, after broader agreement on the details of the treaty was reached, and taking account of the views of all the nations which might become a party to it. Then it would be possible to decide whether the force should have nuclear weapons or not, taking account of the possibility that after the last stage of disarmament had been completed it might be discovered that some nation had retained or secretly produced arms of mass destruction.[3]

[2]ENDC/PV.47, page 33.
[3]ENDC/PV.49, page 19. For the Canadian position on this question see Chapters VIII and XI.

Mr. Arthur Lall stated at this meeting, and on other occasions that the Government of India could never agree to the United Nations peace force being armed with weapons of mass destruction.[4] None of the non-aligned nations, so far as I know, ever accepted the idea of a nuclear-armed UN force which would keep order in a disarmed and peaceful world. It is certainly a dilemma. Even supposing the present nuclear powers were to eliminate all their nuclear weapons and their vehicles, it must be taken into account that the knowledge of how to make a nuclear bomb and the technical and industrial ability to do so is spreading more and more widely. Some nation, under the control of a new Hitler, might make a bomb, and, as the expression is, hold the world to ransom. That idea is alarming, but the safeguard proposed, that is, to equip a force under the control of the United Nations (becoming less and less predictable in its actions) would alarm other nations as well as the USSR. But the goal of general and complete disarmament, or even general and complete elimination of nuclear weapons is now seen to be so far in the future that perhaps the problem is now more of philosophical than practical interest.

Mr. Zorin had other criticisms of the provisions in the United States Outline concerning "a peaceful world" which required (and he quoted from an interpretation given in the *New York World Telegram*):

The establishment of international institutions which would encourage countries to give up the greater part of their national sovereignty; the undoubted and unconditional recognition of the jurisdiction of the International Court of Justice; the acceptance of supranational inspection and verification; willingness to make national security dependent on an international peace force under a greatly changed and strengthened United Nations.[5]

At the thirtieth meeting on May 3, I explained the criticism of the Soviet Union first stage proposals which I had previously offered, and I shall quote this criticism at some length. It shows that at this early stage in the negotiations, it was already clear that there was a great gulf between what the Soviet Union would accept, and what the United States would accept, in regard to the limitation and reduction of long-range nuclear weapon vehicles. This conflict, and the consequent lack of any progress in disarmament (as opposed to arms control) was to continue through the negotiations in the 1960's, and indeed continues at the time of writing. I said:

4ENDC/PV.49, page 19.
5ENDC/PV.26, page 29.

. . . the most important difference between the United States and the Soviet Union plans for disarmament . . . lies in the respective provisions for the reduction and elimination of the means of delivering nuclear weapons. This is a difference which must be resolved if we are to have general and complete disarmament. It therefore becomes the most urgent task of this committee to explore these differences fully, examine the viewpoints and difficulties of each side, and compare possible solutions, if we are to make serious progress in our task of drafting an agreement.[6]

I then asked for an amplification and explanation of the provisions in the Soviet draft treaty concerning control over the elimination of nuclear weapon vehicles. I said that these were very general in character, and that we found it difficult to conceive how the Soviet Union proposed to have the 100 per cent. elimination of nuclear weapon vehicles carried out in fifteen months and controlled in a manner which would satisfy all parties to the treaty that in fact no vehicles for delivering nuclear weapons were being retained anywhere. It would be necessary, in any agreement, to be completely specific and concrete about the methods to be used to prove that every agreed disarmament measure which was put into execution was actually carried out honestly by both sides, without the need to depend on any party's good faith or unverified assurances.

I said we understood the Soviet Union's concern that until they actually knew that the West was in the process of abolishing its nuclear weapon carriers, the international disarmament organization should not put into effect control measures of a kind which would give the West full information on all the Soviet Union's ballistic missile sites and other bases for delivery systems, which was information which would lay the Soviet Union open to surprise attack. On the other hand, the location of a large proportion of the nuclear carriers on which the West relied as a deterrent was public knowledge, so that the West might be said to be already subject to the danger of a surprise attack on its deterrent capability by intercontinental ballistic missiles. The secrecy which the Soviet Union maintained about the locations and numbers of its nuclear striking force obliged the West to contemplate this possibility.

The provisions in the Soviet Union draft treaty, and the explanations so far given by their delegation indicated that the nuclear powers should provide the IDO with full information regarding their NWV's and their bases, so that the inspectors could go there to verify the information provided them. Then all this inspected armament and associated facilities

[6]ENDC/PV.30, page 7.

would be dismantled or destroyed which, I said, could not be done instantaneously, but would require a considerable time.

Then would arise the major difficulty: when the IDO had been notified as above, how would either side know that undeclared rockets or other long-range nuclear weapon vehicles were not hidden somewhere in the vast territories of the Soviet Union, or of the United States? Would the Soviet Union be willing to let international inspectors visit every part of its territory to ensure that no NWV's existed except those on the declared sites, and, if so, when would this be done? Obviously, the inspection of all territory to determine that nothing was concealed must precede and not follow the destruction of declared NWV's. Otherwise one side might pretend to collect and destroy all its nuclear vehicles while hiding a number of them in uninspected territory. If the other side honestly collected and destroyed all its nuclear vehicles, it would find itself at a considerable military disadvantage – to put it in the mildest possible language.[7]

Furthermore, I observed, suppose the Soviet Union should collect all its NWV's at specified sites, and declare location and numbers to the IDO, would not this be known to the West, and create the situation which the Soviet Union professed to fear, which was that the West would possess intelligence which would enable it to carry out a surprise nuclear assault to destroy the Soviet Union's deterrent capacity? How could the Soviet Union accept such a condition? This seemed to the Canadian delegation to be an insuperable obstacle to the Soviet Union's plan for the elimination of *all* NWV's in Stage I, and, instead, would make a programme of more gradual reduction and elimination necessary, as the United States Outline proposed. Such a programme would conform to the agreed principles of maintaining security and balance between the powers while disarmament was in process.

I then went on to say that even if the problem just discussed could be solved there would still remain the possibility that nuclear weapons could be delivered by improvised means, since under the Soviet plan nuclear weapons (bombs, warheads) would not be eliminated until Stage II. Some rockets built for space exploration would remain in existence, and it would not be too difficult to fit nuclear warheads on these. Civil aircraft, such as the Boeing 707 and similar Soviet models could be converted to carry nuclear weapons, though doubtless they would not be very efficient in that role. So I asked whether any nuclear power could eliminate all its means of retaliation, the deterrent on which it primarily relied, in the early stages of disarmament, when very many nuclear weapons still existed, and

[7]ENDC/PV.30, page 11.

confidence in good intentions in regard to disarmament and the creating of a peaceful world had yet to be established and consolidated. This seemed to me a very strong and perhaps a decisive argument that reduction in nuclear weapon vehicles had to take place in stages, and to be completed – reduction to zero – in the final stage.

This last argument was pretty summarily dismissed by Mr. Zorin and other Warsaw Pact spokesmen as inconsequential. At the forty-second meeting on May 25, Mr. Dean supported my contention, saying that almost all types of commercial aircraft could be modified to carry nuclear weapons. With the wide area of devastation which multi-megaton bombs would produce, lessened accuracy in dropping them would not be greatly significant. He observed that the Soviet Union long-range turbo-prop aircraft which had brought Mr. Khrushchev to the United States in 1959 was the civilian version of a Soviet long-range bomber. These comments were doubtless based on expert advice.[8]

I concluded my May 30 statement by saying:

Canada is not a nuclear power; nor are the majority of the members of this Committee; but we all realize the vital importance of establishing with all clarity what the problem of eliminating nuclear vehicles really is and of exploring the proposals for a solution which must conform to the agreed principles of balance and effective international control. At this stage of our negotiations we may not be able to find an answer to this problem which can be accepted by all the nuclear Powers and their allies. But we can and must face the issue squarely, realizing that agreement on this point is the prime essential if the whole programme of general and complete disarmament is to become a reality.

Other Western delegations made the same points in criticism of the Soviet Union proposals for abolition of nuclear weapon vehicles in the first stage of disarmament. However, I have set down the Canadian statement to show our public stand in the matter, and to show that the Canadian authorities realized clearly the crucial character of the provisions for limiting and reducing the long-range nuclear weapon vehicles in any plan for general disarmament. We shall see that the Soviet Union, after vigorously defending its proposal for abolishing all nuclear weapon vehicles in Stage I during the sessions of the ENDC from March to September, modified it in the 1962 UN General Assembly, although not sufficiently to permit the West to accept it.

---

[8]ENDC/PV.42, page 13.

Was all this argument as to the relative feasibility of the Soviet Union and the United States programmes for eliminating nuclear weapon vehicles only an exercise in unreality – shadowboxing? Refer back to the table on page 106 and also to the testimony given in the January 1962 House of Representatives Appropriations Hearings (Chapter 10). These figures and statements show what the policies of the superpowers were really based upon. The Soviet Union could not accept a solution which would keep it inferior in means of delivering nuclear weapons to the territory of its adversary, nor could the United States accept a solution which in a year or so would have reduced its nuclear deterrent to nullity.

At the thirty-first meeting, on May 4, Mr. Zorin resumed his attempt to rebut the Western representatives' criticism of the Soviet Union proposal for elimination of all NWV's in Stage I. In particular, he undertook to give an explanation of what was meant by Mr. Khrushchev's statement, which he had quoted, that, "The Soviet Union is prepared to accept any proposal on control over disarmament that the Western powers may put forward if they will accept the Soviet proposals on general and complete disarmament." I had suggested that this could be interpreted in at least three different ways. Mr. Zorin gave an explanation of Mr. Khrushchev's meaning, but he concluded by stipulating that the West's measures must be "control over disarmament and not control over armaments."[9] So we were exactly where we were before.

At the thirty-fifth meeting on May 11, I returned to the same argument. The only additional points which I made and which seem worth setting down here are the following:

> Let us consider in realistic terms what prevents any kind of nuclear attack in the world today. It is the knowledge of each side that if it unleashed a nuclear war it would bring upon itself a terrible retaliation by the other side. The problem we have before us is to escape from the balance of terror, as it is called, and reach a climate of international relations such that the two sides have so much confidence in each other's good intentions that they do not believe that there is any likelihood of their attempting to use nuclear weapons against each other in any circumstances; and then the last nuclear weapon vehicles can be eliminated. In other words, we have an exercise in confidence-building, which must accompany disarmament.[10]

I then quoted from what Mr. Atta, the representative of Nigeria, had said at an earlier meeting:

---

[9]ENDC/PV.30, page 13.
[10]ENDC/PV.35, page 41.

. . . my delegation believes that verification, confidence-building measures and disarmament are one and the same thing. These three elements must rise or fall together.[11]

I concluded my statement on this day with the following remarks:

Some delegations have contrasted unfavourably the United States proposal for a 30 per cent. reduction in the first stage with the Soviet proposal for a 100 per cent. reduction. I have asked some questions that, in the view of the Canadian delegation, must be answered satisfactorily if we are to believe that a 100 per cent. reduction in the first stage is practicable. Let us think, on the other hand, what the effect would be if there could be an agreement between the two sides here on a staged reduction, with 30 per cent. of nuclear weapon vehicles to be eliminated in about three years and the rest in a few years more. Such an agreement, although it does not sound as big as the 100 per cent. reduction, would announce the end of the arms race, and it would begin the building of confidence between the two sides which is essential if the goal of 100 per cent. reduction on nuclear weapon vehicles and the other measures constituting general and complete disarmament is to be reached.

The argument on the respective merits (or demerits) of the United States and Soviet Union plans for limiting and eventually eliminating the nuclear weapon vehicles went on until the conference recessed on the 15th of June. Mr. Zorin's clearest statement of why the United States plan was unacceptable to the USSR was made on May 14, at the thirty-sixth meeting of the Committee, when he said:

Under the Soviet draft treaty, States would have to submit information on their armed forces and armaments that are subject to reduction. But we cannot submit information *on the location* [italics added] of armed forces and military installations, and we do not demand that other States should do so. It is self-evident that so long as nuclear weapons and the means of delivering them exist, it might be extremely dangerous for States to disclose their vital centres. In order to avoid controversy, I shall not quote statements by United States military men about the present importance of specifying targets for bombing. I would merely like to say that the United States proposals for a so-called percentage reduction of delivery vehicles, accompanied by control for the purpose of detecting concealed weapons,

[11]ENDC/PV.31, page 6.

would lead to a situation where, before the completion of general and complete disarmament – if this ever takes place at all under the United States plan – the danger of a nuclear blow would not only remain, but would become infinitely greater, because the United States proposals on control mean providing opportunities to locate targets for attack. It is precisely for this reason that the United States proposals cannot provide a basis for the solution of the disarmament problem.[12]

After a few more meetings devoted mainly to the problem of what should be done about reducing (or eliminating) long-range nuclear weapon vehicles in Stage I, which saw a repetition of previous positions and arguments, the conference moved on to a discussion of the measures proposed for Stage II in the Soviet Union and United States programmes. But at this point a curious contretemps occurred, in connection with one of the partial or preliminary measures proposed by the Soviet Union for the reduction of international tension, and to smooth the way towards disarmament. A short account may throw some light on the way the general climate of relations between the USSR and the USA affected negotiations at Geneva.

To provide for discussion of the partial disarmament or arms control measures which had been proposed, in the early days the ENDC had set up what it called a "Committee of the Whole," borrowing from British parliamentary terminology. The proceedings of this committee were less formal than those of the plenary, and no verbatim record of its proceedings was issued. The co-chairmen (Mr. Arthur Dean and Mr. Zorin) had a good deal of difficulty in agreeing on the agenda of this committee. Eventually it was decided to select one item from each superpower's list, and discuss these alternately. The item agreed upon from the Soviet Union list was a declaration against war propaganda. Its substance would be that governments would undertake to suppress or at least discourage any publication in the media of material which could be classified as incitement to warlike action. This idea obviously presented difficulties to the United States and other Western countries with longstanding traditions of freedom of speech, and especially for the United States where an article of the constitution guaranteed it. For the Soviet Union, with its censorship of everything, it was merely a minor administrative problem.

It seemed an unlikely measure on which to reach agreement, but surprisingly, on May 25, 1962 the co-chairmen presented to the plenary

[12]ENDC/PV.36, page 36.

meeting a draft "Declaration against War Propaganda,"[13] which had been adopted unanimously in the committee of the whole. However, the representatives would have to get instructions from their governments before formally indicating their country's acceptance. So it was decided that there should be a plenary meeting on May 29, at which the formalities should be completed. Mr. Zorin said that the position was that the governments were to consider the document and it would be finally approved.

But on May 29 Mr. Zorin opened the plenary meeting not with the expected acceptance by the Soviet Government, but a tirade against recent United States actions and public statements by important figures. The Soviet Government, in the light of these facts, had concluded that the draft declaration required considerable strengthening.

Some of the facts complained of were: the publication of an article by F. J. Strauss, Minister of Defence of the Federal German Republic, in which, Mr. Zorin alleged, he called for the immediate arming of the Bundeswehr with atomic weapons for war against the Soviet Union; the occupation of Thailand by the forces of the United States and its allies of the "aggressive SEATO bloc" which might lead to a large-scale conflict with disastrous consequences; pronouncements by a "top-ranking United States statesman" to the effect that in certain circumstances the United States might take the initiative in a nuclear conflict with the Soviet Union; numerous books and articles published in the United States urging the need for the early use of nuclear weapons for the solution of international problems; "universal public indignation" which had been aroused by Edward Teller's book *The Legacy of Hiroshima.*

It turned out that the "top-ranking statesman" had been none other than President Kennedy. In the March 31, 1962 issue of the *Saturday Evening Post*, Mr. Stewart Alsop had published an article entitled "Kennedy's Grand Strategy." He had quoted President Kennedy to the effect that the United States might in some circumstances, where its vital interests were concerned, have to take the initiative in a nuclear war with the USSR.

Considerably later, on July 25, Mr. Dean read into the proceedings the explanation given by Mr. Pierre Salinger, the Presidential Secretary, who had said:

The President's statement represents no change in American policy. It has always been clear that in such a context as a massive conventional attack on Europe by the Soviet Union, which would put

---

[13]ENDC/C1/20 of May 25, 1962.

Europe in danger of being overrun, the West would have to prevent such an event by all available means.

This has been United States policy since the late nineteen-forties, and it represents no change. The real change, as Mr. Alsop points out elsewhere in the article, is in the strengthening of our defensive alternatives to nuclear warfare.[14]

Mr. Zorin proposed a series of amendments to the draft declaration, the last of which called for parties to the declaration to enact, within six months, legislation declaring war propaganda in any form a grave crime against peace and humanity, and providing for removal from all official posts, the loss of all ranks and titles, and criminal prosecution for all persons guilty of it.[15]

The immediate result of Mr. Zorin's bombshell was that most Western delegations attacked him with some heat. On the previous Friday he had implied that there would be no difficulty in formal acceptance of the agreed draft in plenary session. How could negotiations be conducted if the Soviet Union made abrupt changes of position when agreement had been reached after considerable difficulty? The amendments he suggested were, of course, completely unacceptable to the United States and its Western allies.

It was pretty clear that Mr. Zorin had received peremptory orders to change his position between Friday and Tuesday. He had an established reputation as a cautious and tough negotiator. No one in the Committee ever thought that he would have agreed to the original terms of the declaration unless he had cleared them with Moscow. What had caused the change in instructions? One can only surmise that it came from the top, quite probably from Khrushchev himself, inspired indeed by the several matters cited by Mr. Zorin. But other political factors may have contributed to the veto of the negotiated draft declaration. Khrushchev was in political difficulties at home. A faction within the Communist Party was opposing some aspects of his foreign policy, particularly those leading towards better relations with the United States. In a meeting of the central committee in early March, he had been obliged to agree to giving priority to defence requirements in the allocation of funds, contrary to his previous policy. In the USSR's relations with world communism, the

---

[14]ENDC/PV.61, page 15.
[15]ENDC/PV.44, pages 6, 7.

People's Republic of China was making trouble, with its strong opposition to his attempts to seek better relations with the United States, and generally to forward the policy of peaceful coexistence.[16]
At the forty-third meeting on May 28, I quoted Mr. Zorin's remarks:

> It is our duty to find a solution to the differences which have arisen. Can we find a way out of the situation if we limit our discussion to the first stage only, and we delay the discussion of the two remaining stages of disarmament? Of course not. In this connection I should like to remind you of the considerations concerning the possibility of transferring measures from one stage to another, which have been expressed by several delegations. What follows from this? It follows that between the various stages there are deep inner links and therefore that in order to elucidate the possibilities of overcoming the differences which have arisen, we must take a look at the second and third stages of disarmament.[17]

He went on to suggest that the committee might ask the co-chairmen to try to bring closer the positions of the two sides relating to the first stage of disarmament. The Soviet delegation was ready to enter into such negotiations.

I said this was encouraging. However, the talks – and I do not know whether in fact they were pursued – failed to produce any significant bringing together of incompatible positions.

At the fiftieth meeting on June 6 The Hon. J. B. Godber, Minister of State representing the United Kingdom, made an interesting statement. It threw light on the fact which has been referred to many times in this book, that there would be no practicable means of verifying that all *nuclear weapons* – as distinct from the large aircraft and rockets which were their long-range vehicles – were eliminated from the arsenals and territories of the nuclear powers. He told the conference that a strategic nuclear warhead, which would be capable of destroying a whole city, could be contained in a cylinder five feet long with a diameter of two feet. To dramatize the point further, he observed that enough of such warheads to destroy all the capital cities of the nations represented at the conference could be concealed in the Council Chambers of the UN Head-

---

[16]See the article "America, China and the Hydra-Headed Opposition", by Robert M. Slusser, in *Soviet Policy-Making*, Ed. Juviler and Morton (New York: Praeger, 1967), pages 214-16.
[17]ENDC/PV.39, page 38.

quarters in Geneva, in which the meeting was being held, in the walls, or the ceiling, or the banks of seats surrounding the conference table.[18]

The conference recessed for a month, from June 15 to the 16th of July. At the last (fifty-sixth) meeting on June 14, Mr. Zorin gave a very negative summing-up of the results of our three months of negotiation. I gave my impression of what he said, as follows:

> . . . it would seem that the discussions of the past three months have not effected the slightest change in the outlook of the Soviet Union. The Canadian delegation came here hoping that there would be negotiations, which implies a readiness on both sides to change their positions in order to accommodate themselves to views expressed and to the interests of the other side in reaching some agreement. We regret to say that what we have heard in the speech of the representative of the Soviet Union is not at all encouraging. We hope, however, that his last sentence, to the effect that we should all reflect on what we have heard, and the positions expressed here, may perhaps indicate that the statement made previously is not the very last word, and that we may be entitled to expect, when we return here, . . . some flexibility in attempting to get agreement on how to achieve the final result of general and complete disarmament, which both sides are agreed upon, and which is expressed in the Agreed Principles.[19]

When the conference resumed on July 16, Mr. Dean and Mr. Zorin both spoke. Mr. Dean did not announce any changes in the proposals in the Outline of Basic Provisions. Mr. Zorin had some unkind words for Mr. McNamara's Ann Arbour, Michigan, speech on June 16, and alleged that he was proposing that rules for the use of nuclear weapons in war should be set up, ignoring the UN General Assembly resolution No. 1653 (XVI) which declared that nuclear war would be a crime against mankind and civilization. Mr. McNamara also ignored the fact that the United States representatives in Geneva were declaring that their country wished to reach an agreement on disarmament.[20]

On the credit side, Mr. Zorin mentioned the agreement reached by the conference on Laos, also sitting in Geneva, in the Palais des Nations.[21] He went on to say that the Soviet Government had decided to make cer-

[18]ENDC/PV.50, page 8.

[19]ENDC/PV.56, page 36.

[20]U.S. *Documents on Disarmament*, 1962, Volume 1, page 626. This was the notable speech in which Mr. McNamara outlined the United States intention to evolve a strategy of controlled response.

[21]ENDC/PV.57, page 19.

tain modifications and additions to its draft treaty. The most important of these was in accepting the US proposal for reducing *conventional armaments* by thirty and thirty-five per cent. in the first and second stages of the disarmament programme, and in the last stage to the minimum required for internal security and furnishing contingents to the proposed UN peace force.

He also said that in consideration of the views expressed by many delegations, the Soviet Union would negotiate on the USA proposals for reducing the risk of accidental outbreak of war, by exchanging military missions, and by establishing rapid and reliable communication between the heads of government and the Secretary-General of the United Nations. (This was to become the "Hot Line.")[22] However, it seemed from his statement that these measures were not to take place until the first stage of disarmament. In a speech a couple of days later, I urged that they should be agreed to and put into effect even before disarmament began. That is, they should become one of the preliminary arms control measures.

The Soviet Union offer to reduce conventional armaments by percentages, in accord with the American plan, was gratifying, as any adjustment of differences between the programmes had to be. However, as was quickly pointed out by Western representatives, it had the same defect from their viewpoint as the reduction of nuclear weapon vehicles by percentages had for the Soviet Union. The Warsaw Pact forces in Europe had a very considerable superiority over those of NATO in these conventional armaments – tanks, artillery, strike aircraft. So if the reductions were by percentages, they would retain this advantage throughout the process – while, according to the Soviet plan, all the nuclear armament of deterrence in which the United States was superior, would disappear in the first stage. Nevertheless, the Soviet delegation's move was an encouragement. It followed a usual pattern of Soviet Union negotiation; that is, after maintaining positions unacceptable to the West throughout long sessions, after a recess they would come back with some changes in their stand intended to meet Western positions part way. But the changes were seldom of enough substance to produce agreement. Also, in the melancholy chronicle of disarmament parleys in the fifties there had been occasions when the West had backed away from its own proposals when the Soviet Union had seemed ready to accept them.

At the fifty-ninth meeting on July 18, Mr. Zorin returned to his usual

---

[22]The expression does not refer to the possibly vehement character of the messages which might pass over it, but is a borrowing of the electricians' term for a circuit which has a current flowing through it – as is comparable to the link between government heads.

polemical style. He criticized the United States authorities for not having made any change in their plan, for appearing not to be as ready for compromise as the Soviet Union had shown itself. He quoted John Finney's report to *The New York Times* on the resumption of the ENDC sessions:

> I believe at the present time the United States Government is attempting to have a double policy, striving to give the impression of movement while in fact standing pat.[23]

It is the main argument of this book that this obvious ambivalence in the American position was produced by the conflict between the recommendations of the US Government's responsible advisers; between the advice to maintain security through great armaments, and the advice that eventual security could only be achieved by dismantling the enormous arsenals of destruction which both superpowers possessed. And, of course, the same kind of conflict was going on in the Soviet Union, screened by the dense mists of its secret governmental processes.

On July 24, five foreign ministers who had come to Geneva to sign the Laos Treaty spoke at the sixtieth ENDC meeting: Mr. Dean Rusk, Lord Home, Mr. Gromyko, Mr. Krishna Menon and Mr. Green. They did not break any new ground, but their presence helped to reassure the regular delegations of the importance which the home governments attached to their deliberations.

Mr. Green mainly stressed the step forward which had been taken in deciding to discuss non-dissemination, and the measures to reduce the risk of accidental war. In this he urged action on two of the arms control measures on which success eventually was to be attained. Mr. Krishna Menon also spoke in favour of pursuing the non-dissemination discussions, and argued strongly for agreement to stop nuclear weapon tests. Lord Home reviewed the field of the Conference's proceedings, and laid particular emphasis on the need for progress in the matter of verification. He also hoped that the non-dissemination issue would be pursued, and that some agreement would be reached.

Mr. Gromyko began in a gloomy vein:

> Some of the members of the Committee assert that, although negotiations on disarmament may not bring us closer to solution of this problem, nevertheless such negotiations are better than none at all. We do not agree with this view. . . .

No progress has as yet been achieved in any of the major issues of

---

[23]ENDC/PV.59, page 39.

disarmament, neither on the banning and destruction of nuclear weapons, nor on the liquidation of means of delivery, nor on the dismantling of foreign military bases and the withdrawal of troops from abroad.

He went on to place the blame on the intransigence of the Western nations, of course, and to reiterate many of the points which Mr. Zorin had been trying to make during the previous months, especially on the question of control. He took a shot at Mr. McNamara's new strategy of controlled response:

> . . . the announcement of ever new strategic doctrines, each more aggressive than the last. Almost every NATO general, the more so the higher the rank, puts forward his own strategic doctrine, which becomes the subject of wide discussion. The main concern seems to be not how to exclude nuclear war from the life of society, how to prevent it, but how virtually to legalize it under the guise of drafting "rules" for waging it or of reaching agreement on what targets should be made the objective of the first nuclear strike.[24]

Mr. Rusk gave a more hopeful assessment, welcoming the signing of the Laos Treaty as proof that with some give and take agreement could be reached on a difficult problem. However, he did not disregard the difficulties in disarmament negotiations caused by suspicion and conflicting political objectives of the superpowers and their allies.

During the rest of the meetings in July, there was nothing new on the limitation of nuclear weapon vehicles. Mr. Zorin argued at one meeting that, even if the claimed superiority in nuclear force of the United States were eliminated in the first stage, the assertion that NATO forces would be very inferior to the remaining conventional forces and armaments of the Warsaw Pact had no foundation. He quoted figures from the annual *Military Balance* of the Institute of Strategic Studies. At a later meeting I undertook to point out that a crude adding up of manpower on each side and finding the totals were about the same did not mean that there was equality in the strategic position. Geography, communications and other factors of military importance had also to be taken into account. I did not succeed in convincing Mr. Zorin, even after a couple of exchanges, but what I said was backed up by other speakers on the Western side, while the non-aligned preserved a discreet silence.[25]

At the sixty-seventh meeting on August 8, Mr. Dean introduced some

---

[24]ENDC/PV.60, page 38.
[25]ENDC/PV.63, pages 13-20.

amendments to the USA Outline. They modified the conditions which had previously been set for the transition from one stage of disarmament to the next. These had been criticized by the Warsaw Pact delegates as leaving open the possibility of the disarmament process being halted by unilateral action on insufficient grounds, allowing one side to get an advantage by doing so. The matter is not of sufficient importance to the central theme of this book to be worth discussing in further detail here, and has only been mentioned to show that the United States had made a change in its plan as well as the Soviet Union.

When the sixty-ninth meeting was held on August 14, Mr. Zorin had left the Soviet Union delegation, on being appointed Permanent Representative of the USSR to the United Nations, in New York. He was replaced by Mr. Vasily Kuznetzov, a senior Deputy Foreign Minister. Years before, Mr. Kuznetzov had spent some time in the United States, working in the foundry of the Ford Company in Detroit, and attending the Carnegie Technical Institute. He spoke English better than any of the other senior Russian representatives, and it was generally believed that, when the Soviet Government wanted to take a forthcoming position, Mr. Kuznetzov was appointed to represent them. When they wanted to follow a hard line, Mr. Zorin was the delegate. No one would be likely to maintain that Mr. Zorin possessed an ingratiating personality. During the TNCD and at the start of the ENDC he had a habit of replying each day to any points which the West had brought up which he thought important. These replies would usually start about 1 p.m., and might go on for nearly an hour, causing the other delegates, who usually had lunch appointments, to become very impatient. Hints were dropped to more junior members of the Soviet delegation that Mr. Zorin's arguments would get a better hearing if he did not always insist on giving them at length at that time of day. One of the Soviet diplomats remarked that Mr. Zorin, prior to entering diplomacy, had been a professor of Marxism-Leninism, and had acquired the ability to talk for a very long time without stopping.

In spite of his polemical approach, I had a kind of liking for him. He was not very lucky as a negotiator in those years. First, there was the abrupt exit from the TNCD, which I am sure he was not prepared for and which was probably executed on peremptory orders from above. Then there was the episode of the declaration on war propaganda, described earlier in this chapter. Then in October, during the Cuban crisis, he would be trying to defend a very equivocal Russian position, obviously not being kept fully informed of what was going on by the Kremlin. In short, he repeatedly had the bad luck of having the rug pulled out from under his feet, and one could feel a certain sympathy for him.

Apart from the negotiations on the cessation of nuclear weapons tests, which will be discussed in the next chapter, there was only one departure from the positions previously held by the two sides. The Soviet Union's draft treaty had been criticized because it said nothing about reducing nuclear arms (bombs and warheads) in the first stage of disarmament. At the eighty-first meeting on September 5, Mr. Kuznetzov announced that the Soviet Union would be willing, if the Western powers agreed, to transfer all the measures for elimination of nuclear weapons, including destruction of stockpiles and cessation of production, which had been in later stages of its programme, to the first stage.[26]

Mr. Dean, in a brief reply at the same meeting said that the United States delegation would of course examine this proposal, and then went on to say, rather testily, that the Soviet Union in the past had shifted disarmament obligations from one stage to another, but that had not enabled the West to engage in meaningful discussion. The Soviet Union would not discuss details, and specific obligations. "The Soviet Delegation loves to engage in those circus propaganda stunts."[27]

At the eighty-second meeting, on September 7, I commented on this new proposal, saying that the Soviet Union delegation had failed to explain how the 100 per cent. elimination of nuclear weapon vehicles in the first stage could be verified, and now it was suggesting compounding the problem by steps which would require as well the verification of the elimination of 100 per cent. of nuclear weapons in the first stage.[28]

I also quoted at this time what Señor Padilla Nervo, the leader of the Mexican delegation had said:

One of the principles agreed on by the Great Powers . . . is that disarmament should be implemented by stages. . . . That is a wise and indeed indispensable principle, since the difficulty of the task demands that it be carried out by stages. Only God himself could say "Let there be light, and there was light"; but there are no leaps in nature. The greatest achievements of man and his science have been made by small steps.[29]

That such an impracticable suggestion as to eliminate all nuclear weapons and their vehicles in Stage I was made causes one to wonder how some of the proposals which the Soviet Union delegation laid before the

---

[26]ENDC/PV.81, page 15.
[27]ENDC/PV.81, page 27.
[28]ENDC/PV.82, page 10.
[29]ENDC/PV.80, page 31.

conference were formulated. American students of Soviet Union disarmament policy have observed that Mr. Khrushchev took great personal interest in propagating Moscow's disarmament policy. The main lines probably followed his preferences, although the details may have been left to functionaries.[30]

The authors of one book tried to get diplomats from the Soviet bloc to comment on it, but without much success. The major specific criticism offered by a communist official was that the Soviet approach had been too rationalistic, looking for complicated explanations where a more elementary one would have sufficed, and seeking to associate top leaders' motives with proposals prepared perfunctorily by foreign office staff.[31]

At the same meeting, Mr. Dean had sounded a philosophical note:

> Disarmament is a substitute way for maintaining the national security of a State. It is a radical substitute for a national security system based on armaments which have taken years to acquire and to which, unfortunately, nations have become accustomed. My first appeal, therefore, is that our Soviet colleagues should join with us to change the deep-rooted idea that armaments today can bring security. . . . Steps to halt the arms race must be taken soon before the will to do so degenerates into despair.[32]

Mr. Dean did not say so explicitly, but he was probably thinking that he and Mr. Kuznetzov should try to persuade the hard-nosed in both their countries that disarmament could lead to a safer world than the continuation of the nuclear arms race, and that to win this security a price had to be paid in compromise. No doubt such arguments have been advanced many times by the doves to the hawks, but as the rising tide of strategic armaments shows, the hawks up to 1971 have had the last word.

The September 7 meeting was the last before the Eighteen-Nation Disarmament Committee recessed, to take up the debate in the UN General Assembly.

[30]*Khrushchev and the Arms Race*, page 170.
[31]*Ibid.*, page 300.
[32]ENDC/PV.32, page 23.

CHAPTER 14

Test ban/Cuban crisis/"Gromyko umbrella"

For the last month of its session prior to recessing for the UNGA in September, the ENDC had devoted most of its attention to the question of the cessation of nuclear testing. It has been mentioned that the eight non-aligned members of the conference had submitted a joint memorandum, proposing a solution to the problem of verifying that no nuclear weapons were being tested underground.[1] The memorandum suggested it should be possible to agree on a system for continuous observation and effective control on a purely scientific and non-political basis. This system could be built up using existing seismographic and other means of observation, plus perhaps some more posts in locations to be agreed. An international commission of highly-qualified scientists, possibly from non-aligned countries, could be set up. It would have the responsibility of evaluating data received from the observation posts, and of reporting on any nuclear explosion or "suspicious event." Parties to the treaty would be obliged to furnish the information necessary to establish the nature of such events. The parties, in fulfilment of this obligation, "could invite" the commission to visit the site of an ambiguous event.

The nuclear powers accepted the memorandum as a basis for further negotiation. They disagreed as to whether it called for obligatory inspec-

[1]See note 1, Chapter 11.

tion. While the ENDC was debating these proposals, the United States carried out a heavy programme of testing, from April to November, as did the Soviet Union, from August to December.

At the twenty-eighth meeting of the ENDC, on the 26th of April, Canada's position was made clear by placing on the record the following statement by Prime Minister Diefenbaker:

> In view of the position consistently taken by Canada on the question of nuclear weapon tests, it is a matter of deep regret to the Canadian Government that no solution has been found at Geneva to enable the nuclear powers to dispense with further testing under reasonable safeguards against the possibility of clandestine evasion of an agreement.
>
> The Canadian Government has always been concerned not only with hazards to human health but also with the implications of such tests in terms of continuation of the nuclear weapons race and the prospects for disarmament. The new situation makes it even more imperative to persist in the efforts now being made at Geneva to bring about a test ban agreement which could provide for some acceptable international system of verification. The proposals put forward by the eight non-aligned members of the Disarmament Committee constitute a constructive effort to find a compromise solution. . . . The whole matter is of such consequence to the future of the human race that the search for a solution must be pressed with the utmost determination.[2]

On August 27, 1962 the United States and the United Kingdom submitted two alternative draft treaties.[3] One would prohibit all testing, whether in the atmosphere, under water, in outer space or underground, and provided for a quota of on-site inspections. The other draft prohibited tests in the first three environments, without international verification. The USA and the U.K. favoured a total – and inspected – ban, but if the USSR would not accept compulsory on-site inspection, the three-environment treaty was proposed as a first step. The Soviet Union, in accordance with its previous position, rejected the total prohibition draft, and said it would accept the three-environment draft, if there were also an *uninspected* moratorium on underground tests, until a final solution of the verification problem in this environment could be attained.

---

[2]ENDC/PV.28, page 37.
[3]ENDC/58 and ENDC/59. See *Documents on Disarmament*, 1962, Volume II, pages 792, 804.

The cessation of nuclear testing was the first item of business on the agenda of the First Committee, at the seventeenth (1962) United Nations General Assembly. Brazil had taken the initiative in producing what eventually became a draft resolution sponsored by thirty-seven member nations. The eight non-aligned nations represented on the ENDC had been largely responsible for the draft, which would have had the General Assembly condemn all nuclear weapon tests, and ask that they cease immediately, and in any case not later than January 1, 1963. It endorsed the eight-nation joint memorandum of April 16 as a basis for negotiation.[4]

A draft was also tabled by the United Kingdom and the United States, advocating that the ENDC should agree on a treaty on the lines of one or other of the drafts which they had submitted on the 27th of August.[5]

The USSR supported the provision in the thirty-seven-nation draft for cessation of all tests by January 1, 1963. The United States and the United Kingdom objected to it because it implied an uninspected moratorium for underground testing. In general, the terms of the thirty-seven-nation draft were acceptable to Canada, in view of our position set out in Mr. Diefenbaker's statement. Mr. Green's stand, which conditioned the delegation's tactics in the rather complicated negotiations which followed, was "No testing! Period!" Nevertheless, we had to try to avoid what would look like an open break with the United States and the United Kingdom on the question.

On October 11 I stated the Canadian position in a speech which had been approved after much consultation with Ottawa. I said that while arguments were heard that continued testing was necessary to ensure national security, in the long run it could only maintain the momentum of the arms race. Cessation of tests would confer no special advantage on any country. It would reduce the radiation hazard, inhibit development of more destructive nuclear weapons and the spread of nuclear weapons to more countries, and would be a start towards disarmament.

I went on to say that it remained to devise a practical formula for resolving the difference between the nuclear powers on the question of verification. Canada considered that the eight-nation proposals offered a sound basis for agreement. The risk alleged by the Soviet Union, that on-site inspection would permit espionage, was a remote one, and should not be compared with the risk inherent in continued testing. The risk of a state evading its obligations under a test ban agreement, which concerned the Western nuclear powers, while significant, should be balanced against

---

[4] A/C1/L310.
[5] A/C1/L311.

the dangers hanging over mankind if there were no agreement. Canada endorsed the Mexican proposal to end all testing by January 1, 1963.[6]

Shortly after this statement had been made we noticed a distinct coolness in the United States delegation, with whom we had been on very friendly terms during the Geneva sessions. This lasted about a week, until we found out that the root of the trouble was that one of the non-aligned group's leaders had given Mr. Dean a misleading impression of Canada's position, going so far as to suggest that we wanted to become a co-sponsor of the thirty-seven-nation draft. In fact, we had been trying to work out amendments to the draft which would make it more acceptable to the Americans and British. Mr. Green had decided, at the beginning of the session, doubtless remembering the difficulties we had encountered in 1960, that we should not rush in with a draft resolution, but should wait and see how the situation developed. This was a wise decision, for after some two weeks of discussions with the representatives of the eight non-aligned ENDC members, consultations with the British, Americans and Russians, explanations to representatives of other NATO countries, we succeeded in getting amendments to the thirty-seven-nation draft which took away its rather peremptory tone, and removed what the British and Americans had felt to be a bias towards the USSR position.

The thirty-seven-nation draft had no less than twelve preambular paragraphs. We added one more, by amendment, which referred to letters exchanged between Chairman Khrushchev, President Kennedy and Prime Minister Macmillan on October 27 and 28, welcoming their declarations that they intended to find a speedy settlement of the remaining differences on the cessation of nuclear tests. This placatory paragraph had been suggested by Mr. Peter Dobell, then on the permanent Canadian delegation to the United Nations.

The first amendment to the operative paragraphs followed the first two of the original thirty-seven-nation draft, which were:

1. *Condemns* all nuclear weapons tests;
2. *Asks* that such tests should cease immediately and not later than 1 January 1963;

Our amendment which became operative paragraph three ran:

3. *Urges* the Governments of the United States, the Union of Soviet Socialist Republics and the United Kingdom to settle the remaining differences between them in order to achieve agreement on the cessa-

---

[6]See summary report of Proceedings of First Committee, General Assembly, Seventeenth Session, page 962.

tion of nuclear testing by 1 January 1963 and to issue instructions to their representatives on the Sub-Committee of the Eighteen-Nation Committee on Disarmament to achieve this end;

(In the eventual voting on November 5, this paragraph was adopted unanimously.)

Another amendment ran, as we originally proposed it:

6. *Recommends* that if against all hope the parties concerned do not reach agreement on the cessation of all tests by 1 January 1963, they enter into an immediate agreement prohibiting nuclear tests in the atmosphere, under water and in outer space;

A sub-amendment by Ghana added:

. . . accompanied by an interim arrangement limited in time suspending all underground tests, taking as a basis the eight-nation joint memorandum and taking into consideration other proposals presented at the seventeenth session of the General Assembly.

Finally, the United Kingdom and the United States added a further sub-amendment to the end of the paragraph:

Such interim agreement shall include adequate assurances for effective detection and identification of seismic events by an international scientific commission.

The Canadian amendment, as sub-amended, passed by a vote of sixty-two to eleven, with thirty-one abstentions. The Warsaw Pact bloc, plus Cuba and Mongolia, voted against. The non-aligned were divided between approval and abstention. On November 3, 1962, the final resolution on nuclear testing was passed as General Assembly Resolution 1762A (XVII). Part A of it, the thirty-seven-nation resolution, was passed by a vote of seventy-five in favour, none against, with twenty-one abstentions. The USA-U.K. draft, which became Part B, was passed by fifty-one for, ten against, and forty abstentions.[7]

The Canadian efforts in this series of manoeuvres were thus successful, in contrast to our vain labours in the 1960 session. I suppose this might be said to be evidence that our representatives can do better in a kind of brokerage job (in this case between the non-aligned and the Americans) than if we try to take a lead ourselves. It might also be said that the resolution with our amendments as passed helped towards the

---

[7]*Documents on Disarmament*, 1962, Volume II, pages 1002-3, 1029-33.

first substantial success in arms control, the Moscow Test Ban Treaty, concluded in August 1963.

In the midst of our debate on the cessation of nuclear weapon tests, the Cuban crisis suddenly confronted us with the reality of the threat of mass destruction. Imagining the sequence of events which might follow President Kennedy's broadcast of October 22, and the warlike preparations which it implied, what had been the horror of a distant nuclear Armageddon came very close – as close as next week. But still it did not seem that nuclear war could really erupt.

According to Robert Kennedy's Book, *Thirteen Days*, it was on Tuesday, October 16 that the crisis began, with the report to the President by the US Intelligence Community that photographic reconnaissance and other information had convinced it that the Soviet Union was placing missiles and atomic weapons in Cuba. On that date, and for the remainder of the week, the attention of the disarmament negotiators at the United Nations was absorbed by resolutions on the cessation of nuclear weapon tests.

On October 22 President Kennedy announced on television the blockade to prevent the build-up of offensive weapons in Cuba. He declared that the United States would defend the West's rights in Berlin. He said that meetings of the Organization of American States and the UN Security Council would be called to deal with the situation. I concluded my diary for that day with the words:

> This probably puts *finis* to any hopeful disarmament negotiations for an indefinite period – if it does not result in anything worse.

Although I did not think there would be a nuclear war, I was too pessimistic as to the aftereffects of the crisis.

The following morning the First Committee resumed its debate on the prohibition of nuclear testing. In the afternoon I attended the Security Council meeting on the Cuban crisis. On the 24th, the scheduled morning meeting of the First Committee was cancelled, because the Security Council was meeting again. It was UN Day, and in the afternoon delegations and guests were entertained in the General Assembly hall by a concert by the Leningrad Philharmonic Orchestra and the famous Russian violinist David Oistrakh – a somewhat singular divorce of culture from politics. On the next day I had a lunch for disarmament colleagues, mainly non-aligned. I recorded that Mrs. Myrdal and Arthur Lall would have liked to get back to negotiating at Geneva, so they too must have felt that the Cuban crisis would be solved without nuclear explosions.

On October 27, Mr. Green arrived from Ottawa. My diary records mainly his attitude towards what our delegation should do about the nuclear test cessation resolution. The only entry indicating that he was concerned about the Cuba crisis was for Sunday, October 28:

> The Cuban trouble seems on the way to solution with Khrushchev's letter to President Kennedy, saying that weapons and technicians would be withdrawn from Cuba. The SSEA, Mr. Green, wants Canada to get in the act by sending observers.

It had been proposed that the UN Secretary-General should send an observer team to Cuba to make sure that the nuclear weapon vehicles were indeed removed. Although U Thant made preparations for this, Cuba balked at having UN observers on her soil. No doubt Castro had been considerably piqued because the arrangements for the withdrawal of the armaments, including the UN observation of it, had been made without giving him a part in the negotiations.

The First Committee went on with its discussion of a nuclear test ban. The achievement of the Moscow Test Ban Treaty in August 1963 was, it seems to me, largely due to the wise decision which President Kennedy made when the crisis was over. He instructed all members of the government to give no interview nor make any statement which would claim any kind of victory for the United States. As Robert Kennedy wrote: "If it was a triumph, it was a triumph for the next generation and not for any particular government or people."

Robert Kennedy also reported that the President had read Barbara Tuchman's book *The Guns of August* not long before the crisis. At one point he had remarked:

> I am not going to follow a course which will allow someone to write a comparable book about this time, *The Missiles of October* . . . if anyone is around to write after this.

The main point of *The Guns of August* is that the rulers of Europe stumbled into a war none of them wanted, as though fatally deprived of the ability to see the inevitable results of the decisions they were taking. The influence which Mrs. Tuchman's book had on President Kennedy must be an encouragement to those who write on historical themes. For so long it has been easy to believe Hegel's dictum "that experience and history teach this – that people and government never have learned anything from history."

Two other points made in *Thirteen Days* are worth mentioning here:

"One of the Joint Chiefs of Staff once said to me he believed in a preventive attack against the Soviet Union."[8]

This view held by a man in the top row of the United States military hierarchy – and by not a few other senior officers as well – could not have been a secret from the Soviet Union intelligence apparatus. So it is no wonder that the Soviet Union rejected inspection which might compromise the secrecy which they hoped gave security to their nuclear deterrent missiles.

Another matter reported in *Thirteen Days* is relevant as we consider the balance of forces, the facts of life under which the disarmament negotiations were carried on. This was the presence of Jupiter IRBM's in Turkey and Italy. In the early exchanges during the crisis, Chairman Khrushchev had suggested to the President that these should be withdrawn as a *quid pro quo* for the withdrawal of the Soviet nuclear weapon vehicles from Cuba. This proposal was rejected. On October 28, when the terms under which the crisis would be liquidated were practically decided upon, Ambassador Dobrynin asked Robert Kennedy whether the missiles in Italy and Turkey could not be withdrawn as part of the bargain. Mr. Kennedy said that no such arrangement was possible as it would seem to be made under pressure. However, he went on to tell the Soviet Ambassador that the President had been anxious to take these missiles out for a long time, and in fact had already ordered their removal. They would probably be gone soon after the crisis was over.[9]

This did happen, and for some time there was no publicity about it. From the United States viewpoint, there were valid military reasons for their removal. They were liquid-fuelled, standing in the open, and hence very vulnerable to a first strike. Also, it must have been a cause for concern that such powerful nuclear weapon delivery systems were in a situation where, in a crisis, despite the double-key system, they might be started on their way without American authorization, and thus touch off irretrievable disaster. One can see that the American authorities would have felt happier if the Jupiters were repatriated. With the increasing numbers of ICBM's in the territorial United States, IRBM's in bases abroad had become dispensable.

In the general debate which began the proceedings of each annual session of the UN General Assembly, speakers generally gave the views of their country about the international state of affairs, and what the Assembly

---

[8]Kennedy, Robert, *Thirteen Days* (New York: Norton, 1969), page 119.
[9]*Ibid.*, page 108.

should do about it. Mr. Gromyko spoke for the Soviet Union, on the 21st of September. This was a month before the Cuban crisis became known to the world, but the first portion of his speech was devoted to castigating the United States for its aggressive policy towards the neighbouring island, and elsewhere in the world. He then turned to the theme of disarmament, and complained of the lack of progress in the ENDC sessions, which, he explained, was due to the wrong attitudes and lack of flexibility of the United States and the other Western countries there. He pointed out that the Soviet Union had made several changes in its draft treaty, in an attempt to meet objections raised by the West, but the United States had only amended its Outline in one respect, and that not very important.

After giving the usual argument for the Soviet Union proposal to eliminate all nuclear weapon vehicles in the first stage, he said that the United States had categorically objected to this:

> . . . declaring that States embarking on disarmament would for some time allegedly need some sort of protective umbrella. We do not believe such arguments to be justified, but in order to make a genuine move forward we are ready to make yet another effort.

> Taking account of the stand of the Western Powers the Soviet Government agrees that in the process of destroying vehicles for the delivery of nuclear weapons in the first stage exception be made for a strictly limited and agreed number of global intercontinental missiles, anti-missile missiles, and anti-aircraft missiles of the ground-to-air type which would remain at the disposal of the Union of Soviet Socialist Republics and the United States alone. Thus for a definite period the means of defence would remain in case someone, as certain Western representatives fear, ventures to violate the treaty and conceal missiles or combat aircraft.[10]

The Soviet Union submitted a revision of its draft Treaty (ENDC/2/ Rev. 1), embodying this new proposal and the changes previously announced. This seemed a hopeful step indeed, but, as will be seen from the record of discussions on this subject in the meetings of the ENDC on its return to Geneva, the Western delegations were unsuccessful in their attempts to find out what precisely the Soviet Union had in mind when it spoke of "a strictly limited and agreed number." The hoped-for reconciliation of the new Soviet stand with the United

---

[10]*Documents on Disarmament*, 1962, Volume II, pages 904-5.

States plan of percentage reduction through three stages came to nothing, after many months of discussion.

The General Assembly also passed Resolution 1767 (XVII) which called upon the ENDC to resume its negotiations for an agreement on general and complete disarmament, "expeditiously and in a spirit of constructive compromise." The co-chairmen, after consulting the rest of the members, arranged for the ENDC to resume its meetings on the 26th of November.

At the first meeting Mr. Dean referred to the proposal announced by Mr. Gromyko. He said that as the problem of disposing of nuclear delivery vehicles was the most acute of those facing the conference, any new approach deserved careful explanation, clarification and exploration in depth. The U.S. delegation hoped to participate in this, in the plenaries and in discussion with the Soviet Union co-chairman.[11]

Mr. Tsarapkin, then leading the Soviet delegation, said at the same meeting that the gist of the Soviet Union's amendment to its treaty was that the United States and the Soviet Union would retain an agreed and strictly limited number of intercontinental missiles, anti-missile missiles and anti-aircraft missiles in the "ground-to-air" category, exclusively on their own territories, until the end of the second stage of disarmament. This, he said, clearly went toward meeting the point of view of the Western powers in regard to what was called a "protective umbrella." (So far, he had said nothing Mr. Gromyko had not said.) However, he went on, he had misgivings because the West were asking for details. The principle had to be accepted before details could be discussed.[12]

The Canadian Delegation's first statement at the resumed session was made at the eighty-fifth meeting on the 30th of November. In it I welcomed the "Gromyko umbrella" (as we came to call this initiative), and referred to what Mr. Green had said at the General Assembly, to the effect that the proposal would have to be carefully studied and considered in order to find out its true meaning. The rest of the speech was devoted to argument that the Committee should devote itself mainly to trying to get agreement on the nuclear test cessation, in accordance with the expressed wishes of the UN General Assembly. The difference between the two sides was narrow, and every effort should be made to get agreement by the date called for in the General Assembly resolutions – January 1, 1963.

---

[11]ENDC/PV.83, page 13.
[12]*Ibid.*, page 21.

I supported the proposals of the Swedish delegation for setting up an international commission to evaluate the data received from seismological stations. Mr. Edberg, the Swedish representative, had said that the question of inspection had not been solved by achievements in seismology. I went on to say that we had heard statements from the socialist countries that the problem was really a political one, and that intervention by scientists would be unnecessary. I said that, looked at rightly, the problem of whether on-site inspections were necessary required both scientific advice and political decision.

The question scientists should answer was this: What was the probability of "x" nuclear underground explosions of "y" kilotons over a period of "z" months *not* being detected and identified by extra-territorial instrumentation only? If the answer should be that the probability of the explosions *not* being detected and identified was negligible, governments could take the decision to disregard this limited risk. If the possibility that the explosions would not be detected was considerable, then another means of assurance must be provided; that is, on-site inspection. Another political decision would then be required. If a few on-site inspections were required, would there be a serious risk that the inspecting organization would acquire important military information, reducing the security of the country being inspected?[13]

The Defence Research Board advised the Canadian disarmament delegation on the feasibility of detecting underground nuclear explosions using seismological means, based on information from the experts in the Department of Mines and Resources. In 1962 the Department had set up a number of new seismographic stations which would improve capacity for detecting underground events, and discriminating between nuclear explosions and earthquakes. Some years later, after British seismologists had developed a system of improving identification by placing seismographs in groups or arrays, spread out over an extended area, they set up one such array near Yellowknife. Later, the Canadian authorities took over the responsibility for operating this post. Canadian scientists acquired expertise in this field which was internationally acknowledged. Our policy was to develop, in cooperation with the scientists of other interested nations, the ability to detect underground nuclear weapon tests, in terms of the size of the explosion and the certainty of identification, which would make it very improbable that any country could carry out underground tests which would be significant in terms of weapon development

---

[13]ENDC/PV.85.

without a very high probability of being detected. But in spite of the considerable progress achieved in this branch of applied science, no agreement had been reached until 1971. The Canadian seismologists had never been able to tell our disarmament negotiators flatly that all significant underground nuclear explosions could be detected and identified by the means currently available. Their position was that there would always be some residue of unidentifiable events, perhaps of low magnitude, and a political decision would have to be taken as to how much risk of evasion could be accepted, in the light of the gains to be had from a cessation of all testing of nuclear weapons.

The Americans still maintain that on-site inspections are necessary. The Russians refuse to accept even a minimum number of these, and both superpowers have been deaf to the ingenious compromises suggested by non-aligned countries. Since 1967 the non-aligned have been saying, more or less bluntly, that the superpowers go on testing and refusing to work out an agreement for a ban, because they want to continue developing nuclear weapons, and not because they really believe that the verification problem is insoluble except on their own terms. But all this takes us ahead of the year 1962, the point which the narrative has reached.

At the ninetieth meeting on December 10, Mr. Tsarapkin discussed the Gromyko proposal a little further, but without enlightening us much as to its intended scope. He stressed that the reduction of long-range nuclear weapon vehicles in the USSR proposal was tied firmly to the removal of all "foreign bases," as the great rockets with their warheads were the Soviet Union's means of defence against this encircling threat. All he would say as to the number of vehicles to be retained under the Gromyko proposal was that it would be "strictly limited," and that there should be an agreement "in principle" before any details could be discussed usefully.[14]

It seems quite probable that the Soviet Union proposal had never been worked out in detail. Nor had their military authorities been consulted and agreed to it – as the American Outline proposals for percentage reductions of all armaments and forces throughout the disarmament process had been agreed to with their military authorities. It could be another example of the rather uncoordinated, not to say amateur, approach to disarmament which the Soviet Government had shown from time to time during the Khrushchev régime.

At the same meeting Mr. Charles Stelle, temporarily leading the US delegation, also spoke. He said he hoped the requisite clarifications of the

[14]ENDC/PV.90, pages 25-6.

Gromyko proposal could be given primarily in discussions between the co-chairmen (a foretaste of SALT?). The question was, how far away, quantitatively speaking, would the Gromyko proposal be from the US thirty per cent. reduction? In other words, what was the dimension of the gap to be bridged if the USA and the USSR proposals on the reduction and eventual elimination of nuclear weapon vehicles were to be reconciled?[15]

At the ninety-second meeting, Mr. Dean made a speech with some pretty tough morsels in it.

> It should by now be clear to one and all that no amount of debate and casuistry will be able to convince the United States to abandon its allies in the west and elsewhere to the mercies of the Soviet military machine. Let me be very clear: we will not allow NATO to be fragmented, as would be the case under the Soviet proposals.[16]

And later he said:

> The slight encouragement which we in the west received from the introduction of Mr. Gromyko's proposal on nuclear delivery vehicles at the General Assembly last September did not stem from the substance of that proposal, which is still not clear to us. Our encouragement was caused by the fact that this was the first sign that the Soviet Government had begun to face military-strategic realities. We were most anxious to discover how far this evolution in Soviet disarmament policy had gone, what it means in specific terms, and how and when it would be carried out.[17]

At the ninety-third meeting on December 17 I commented on the Soviet Union delegation's refusal to go into details of the Gromyko proposal.

> We hope that there is not to be a repetition of the Soviet Union stand in this conference in regard to other subjects, a stand which can be summed up as saying: "You must agree to accept our idea in principle, before we will discuss any details of it with you," because that, of course, is an impossible demand; it is impossible to conduct our business in that way. Our Soviet Union colleagues frequently say that what they want is a "businesslike discussion." Well, to Western minds, at least, it is not realistic or business-like to accept a proposition before you know what you are accepting. The old proverb about not buying a pig in a poke has been quoted here several times.[18]

---

15 *Ibid.*, pages 30-1.
16 ENDC/PV.92, page 15.
17 *Ibid.*, page 17.
18 ENDC/PV.93, page 18.

At the ninety-fourth meeting, on December 19, Mr. Tsarapkin complained, with some justice one must admit now, that the Western proposals applied one yardstick and one principle to reducing those elements of the war machine in which they had a particular interest, and another principle and a completely different yardstick to reducing the other elements. He went on to say that while the US Outline proposed reductions by a certain percentage of nuclear weapon vehicles in which the West considered itself strongest, there were much sharper cuts in conventional forces and armaments, in which the West was saying that the Warsaw Pact powers were stronger. This was not in accord with the principle of balance.[19]

From the United States viewpoint, the Gromyko proposal appeared almost as disadvantageous as the prior Soviet proposition that all nuclear weapons should be eliminated in the first stage of disarmament. The Americans had the lead in the megaton vehicles, which accepting the Gromyko proposal would oblige them to surrender. However, it should be remembered that some groups in the United States concerned in disarmament questions were discussing the idea of a minimum nuclear deterrent at this time. This idea was that the superpowers, or even the United States unilaterally, should decide that 50, 100, 200, or x megaton vehicles would be enough as a deterrent, and when they had that number of them they would stop building. So the United States delegation and the ACDA had to feel out the Russians, to find out what figure they envisioned when they spoke of a "strictly limited and agreed number."

From December 20, 1962 until February 12, 1963 the conference took a recess, during which delegations were to consult with their governments and review their positions, to see where any advance towards agreement could be made.

---

[19]ENDC/PV.94, page 25.

CHAPTER 15

Moscow Test Ban Treaty/
Canada's nuclear weapon policy

When the ENDC met again on February 12, Mr. Arthur Dean had retired as leader of the United States delegation, and his place was taken
by Mr. William C. Foster, the Director of ACDA. For the next five years
he continued to head the delegation, alternating from time to time with
Mr. Adrian S. Fisher, his Deputy Director. Mr. Charles Stelle also led the
delegation during the spring of 1963.

For the first weeks the conference devoted its efforts mainly to the
cessation of nuclear tests. Later our time was divided between this issue
and the effect of the change in position on elimination of nuclear weapon
vehicles announced by Mr. Gromyko at the recent UN General Assembly.

The negotiations on the nuclear test ban eventually resulted in a partial success, the Moscow Treaty of August 5, 1963 which prohibited
testing in the atmosphere, under water and in outer space. But *if one takes
at face value* what was set out in published documents, including the letters exchanged between President Kennedy and Chairman Khrushchev,
the positions of the two sides, as of late 1962 and early 1963, were very
close together, and it should have been possible to reach agreement for
the total prohibition of the tests, including those underground.

Chairman Khrushchev said in his letter of December 19, 1962:

You and I agree that national means of detection are adequate for the control of a ban on nuclear testing in outer space, in the atmosphere, and under water. However we have not yet been able to find a mutually acceptable solution to the problem of the cessation of underground tests. The main obstacle in the way of an agreement is the insistence of the United States on international control and inspection of the cessation of underground testing in the territories of the nuclear powers.

There followed several paragraphs on the use and location of the so-called "black boxes," automatic seismological stations which could be placed on the territory of nuclear powers, and would reduce, if not eliminate, the need for manned stations allegedly capable of facilitating espionage. This idea had come out in a recent meeting of the Pugwash group[1] in London, and had been considered promising by scientists of the three nuclear powers. Much discussion about the "black boxes" went on in late 1962 and early 1963, but on the signature of the Moscow Treaty, the idea seems to have dropped from view. Mr. Khrushchev's letter went on:

You and your representatives, Mr. President, refer to the fact that, without a minimum number of on-site inspections, it would be impossible for you to persuade the United States Senate to ratify an agreement on the cessation of testing. . . . Very well; if this is the only obstacle to agreement, we are prepared to meet you on this point in the interests of the noble and humane cause of ending nuclear weapons tests.

We have noted that on October 30, 1962, in discussions held in New York with Mr. V. V. Kuznetzov . . . your representative, Ambassador Dean, said that in the opinion of the United States Government 2-4 on-site inspections a year in the territory of the Soviet Union would be sufficient. At the same time, according to Ambassador Dean's statement, the United States would be ready to work out measures to rule out any possibility of espionage being carried out under cover of these inspection visits. . . .

We have given consideration to all these points, and with a view to overcoming the deadlock and reaching a mutually acceptable agreement at last we would be prepared to agree to 2-3 inspections a year

---

[1]The "Pugwash" conferences were attended by scientists from both sides of the Iron Curtain, who sought to find means for resolving disarmament and other problems. The name comes from its first meeting having been held at Pugwash Nova Scotia, the birthplace of Mr. Cyrus Eaton, the steel and railroad magnate who financed it.

being carried out in the territory of each of the nuclear powers, when it was considered necessary, in seismic regions where any suspicious earth tremors occurred.[2]

President Kennedy's reply, dated December 28, 1962, while forth-coming in tone, denied that the US official representative had agreed on two or three inspections, and this dissipated hopes which the previous correspondence might have aroused.

> With respect to the number of on-site inspections, there appears to have been some misunderstanding. Your impression seems to be that Ambassador Dean told Deputy Minister Kuznetzov that the United States might be prepared to accept an annual number of on-site inspections between two and four. Ambassador Dean advises me that the only number which he mentioned in his discussions with Deputy Minister Kuznetzov was a number between eight and ten. This represented a substantial decrease in the request of the United States, as we had previously been insisting upon a number between twelve and twenty.[3]

The question of who misunderstood whom will probably never be cleared up satisfactorily. Mr. Dean sticks to what he told President Kennedy, as set out in the extract above. Mr. Kuznetzov seemed to be sure that he had not misunderstood what was proposed at the time. He remarked some time later that he had "got hell" from Mr. Khrushchev over the incident. This seems to be a prime example of how a simple misunderstanding between honest representatives can wreck a promising diplomatic negotiation.

The reports to Mr. Khrushchev perhaps also were influenced by a discussion which Dr. Jerome Wiesner, then Special Assistant to the President for Science and Technology, had with Mr. Fedorov, a Russian scientist with whom he had become acquainted at Pugwash meetings. Dr. Wiesner may have contributed to the impression that the United States would be content with considerably fewer on-site inspections than the figure of eight to twelve annually, which was at that time the official US requirement.[4]

Mr. Khrushchev, acting on the advice he received from his negotiator, with some difficulty had persuaded the Council of Ministers to agree to

---

[2]ENDC/73, January 31, 1963.

[3]ENDC/74, January 31, 1963.

[4]Jacobson and Stein, *Diplomats, Scientists and Politicians* (Ann Arbor: University of Michigan Press, 1967), page 426.

reinstate the acceptance of two to three annual on-site inspections, which had been their position about two years earlier. When he discovered that this figure would not be accepted by the Americans, he felt that he had been led up the garden path, as the British say. Because of the domestic opposition to his policy of seeking détente with the West, and criticism from the Chinese People's Republic, he concluded that it would be impossible for him to go back to the Council of Ministers and get them to agree to raise the quota. They would probably tell him that if he made this concession, the Americans would increase their demands again. So the result was that the Soviet Union position became "no on-site inspections."

In my diary for February 5, 1963, I noted a conversation with Mr. Arthur Lall, the Indian delegate, who said he had been meeting with Messrs. Padillo Nervo, Samir Ahmed, Mello Franco and von Platen, representatives of Mexico, the UAR, Brazil and Sweden respectively, trying to get them to make a combined statement on behalf of the eight non-aligned members of the ENDC pressing the nuclear powers to take the final step to agreement. He had hopes of being able to act as a broker between the United States and the Soviet Union, to settle on a "magic number" of on-site inspections. In his book *Negotiating Disarmament*[5] he described the efforts of the other non-aligned delegates to help the nuclear powers achieve a compromise. These efforts were eventually frustrated, in part because of pressure applied to the non-aligned home governments by both the USA and the USSR, who alleged that they would be "seriously embarrassed" if the plan non-aligned were presented in the conference.

Until March 15, the nuclear test ban took up nearly the whole of every meeting. Then, with no immediate prospect of a favourable outcome to the "numbers game" (that is, a number of on-site inspections which the USA considered adequate and which the USSR would find acceptable), the conference decided to turn to other questions on the agenda, although it was agreed that any delegation was free to raise the test ban question or any other it might wish at any of the meetings.

I had seen Mr. Green on December 12, 1962 in Paris, where he was attending the semi-annual conference of NATO foreign ministers. After approving the line which I suggested the delegation should take at the ENDC, he told me that pressure for Canada to accept nuclear weapons was growing. The situation was critical. In previous communications he had expressed the hope that some substantial success would be achieved

[5]Lall, A. S., *Negotiating Disarmament* (Ithaca: Center for International Studies, Cornell University, 1964), pages 24-8.

in the disarmament negotiations. This could strengthen his argument that it was not the time for Canada to seem to reverse the trend by joining the ranks of the nuclear armed.

The dispute in the Cabinet as to whether Canada should accept nuclear warheads and bombs for the delivery vehicles we were acquiring had continued on through the latter part of 1962. Indecision in the matter seemed greater after the Conservatives had lost their overall majority in the June election. During the Cuban crisis, the delay in deciding to place the Canadian elements of NORAD on the same state of alert as were their American counterparts brought it home to members of Parliament, if not to the voting public, that the Conservative Government did not have a consistent and solid defence policy. Its failure to complete the equipment of the nuclear weapon vehicles it had agreed to put into service for NATO and NORAD alienated those who believed that Canada should play a proper part in the alliance and live up to her commitments. And the failure to declare firmly and finally that it would not enter into arrangements for using nuclear weapons in Europe or in North America left it open to attack by neutralists and those espousing unilateral disarmament.[6]

The controversy became acute following a speech which Mr. Diefenbaker made in the House of Commons on January 25, 1963. In the course of this he had said, regarding the CF 104 fighters that were being delivered to the RCAF contingent in Europe, that their ". . . strike-reconnaissance role has been placed in doubt by the recent Nassau declaration concerning nuclear arms, as well as other developments both technical and political in the defence field."[7] Mr. Diefenbaker had been at Nassau, and had seen the President and the Prime Minister after the conclusion of their discussions. It might be presumed that what he said could reflect decisions which might not have been set out in the communiqué.

This statement considerably disturbed the US State Department, which felt that unless the impression which Mr. Diefenbaker's remarks might leave with the European NATO allies were corrected, they might believe that President Kennedy and Prime Minister Macmillan had made new decisions about NATO strategy without consulting them.

So the State Department took the unusual step of issuing a press release, in which it was said: "The agreements made in Nassau have been fully published. They raise no question of the appropriateness of nuclear

---

[6]Newman, Peter C., *Renegade in Power* (Toronto: McClelland and Stewart, 1963), pages 333, 340. McLin, Jon, *Canada's Changing Defense Policy: 1957-1963* (Baltimore: Johns Hopkins, 1967), page 145. Lyon, Peyton, *Canada in World Affairs, 1961-63* (Toronto: Oxford, 1968), pages 121-3.

[7]McLin, *op. cit.*, page 161. Newman, *op. cit.*, page 361. Lyon, *op. cit.*, page 180.

weapons for Canadian forces in fulfilling their NATO or NORAD roles." And other parts of the release contradicted assertions in the Prime Minister's January 25 speech that negotiations for the nuclear arming of the Canadian forces, if necessary, were going forward satisfactorily.[8]

On February 4, Mr. Douglas Harkness, the Minister of National Defence, resigned. This was after a stormy Cabinet meeting[9] in which he and some other ministers had tried to get the Prime Minister to promise to issue a clear statement on defence policy. On February 4 Mr. Pearson, the Liberal leader introduced a non-confidence motion in the House of Commons, which was supplemented by an amendment by the Social Credit party saying, *inter alia*, "This government had failed up to this time to give a clear statement of policy respecting Canada's defence." In the vote, the Government was defeated and soon thereafter a general election was called for the 8th of April.[10]

On February 10, the disarmament delegation received a message from Mr. Green, urging that we make great efforts to promote agreement on the nuclear test ban. The delegation duly put together a statement, which I delivered on the 14th of February. It was mainly hortatory, and I concluded by saying:

> What is needed is a final effort to overcome the few outstanding differences which separate the two sides. Those differences are small indeed compared to the obstacles which existed when the nuclear test ban was last discussed in this Committee. Any disadvantage which either side might possibly suffer by making a compromise is of small significance when compared to the benefits which would flow from a nuclear weapon test ban agreement.[11]

Several delegations expressed appreciation of this address, but of course it had no discernible effect on the stand of the nuclear powers. Some days later I saw Mr. Foster and Mr. Godber, to represent Mr. Green's unhappiness over lack of progress towards a nuclear test ban. Mr. Godber, a politician himself, was rather quick to relate Mr. Green's concern to the forthcoming election.

At the ninety-sixth meeting on February 12, which reopened the conference, Mr. Kuznetsov attacked what he called "measures taken by the Western powers to intensify the arms race and the further spread of nuclear weapons." Among these were "the plans for a so-called multi-

---

[8]McLin, *op. cit.*, page 162. Lyon, *op. cit.*, pages 157-8.

[9]Newman, *op. cit.*, page 364. Lyon, *op. cit.*, page 174.

[10]Newman, *op. cit.*, page 374. Lyon, *op. cit.*, pages 180-5.

[11]ENDC/PV.97, page 21.

lateral nuclear force for NATO" (briefly referred to in the communiqué issued after the Nassau meeting) and ". . . the steps taken by the United States to impose nuclear weapons on Canada."

I cabled Ottawa asking for instructions on whether to reply correcting this distortion of the situation and was told that I should say nothing.

The position of the Liberal party on the nuclear weapons for the Canadian forces controversy had been set by Mr. Pearson in his noted speech at Scarborough on January 12, 1963. The key sentence was:

> The Ottawa government should end its evasion of responsibility by discharging its commitments. It can only do this by accepting nuclear warheads.[12]

This decision had been taken after much thought, in which considerable weight was given to the memorandum written by Mr. Paul Hellyer, the Liberal defence critic, after a visit to the Canadian forces in Europe.

After the voting on April 8, the Liberals had won 129 seats, against some 90 held by the Conservatives. Although the Liberals did not have a clear majority, they were entitled to the opportunity to form a government. Mr. Green, with other Conservative ministers, had lost his seat. I was sorry for this. I had a high regard for him; for his honesty and dedication to the idea of disarmament. We had started off, in 1960, with something in common: in World War I he had been an officer in the 54th Battalion in the 11th Canadian Infantry Brigade, of which I was brigade signal officer. While I was working for him we had always got on well together, although his tendency to overestimate the degree of influence which Canada could exert in negotiations sometimes put Canadian diplomats in the position of being asked to make bricks without straw. But the minority of votes he received seemed a poor reward for his many years of honorable service to his constituents. Perhaps it reflected the fact that the Canadian voting public did not care much about being protected from nuclear holocaust, but were more concerned with bread and butter and other matters close to home.

After Mr. Pearson had put his Cabinet together, and taken over the government, he visited England. It was said he did this to repair the cracks in British-Canadian governmental understanding, caused by some ineptitudes of the previous administration.

On May 1 I saw the new Prime Minister in London. He told me that there would be no change in disarmament policy under the Liberal Government. He said they believed in the necessity for disarmament as much

---

12Newman, *op. cit.*, page 396. McLin, *op. cit.*, pages 159-60. Lyon, *op. cit.*, pages 139-40.

as the previous government, but were "not so optimistic about it as How-ard [Green]." So I could go back to Geneva and answer the discreet inquiries of some of my colleagues by saying that there would be no change in Canadian disarmament positions.

The communiqué on the meeting at Nassau between President Kennedy and Prime Minister Macmillan carried an attached statement on nuclear defence systems. It set forth the arrangements under which the United Kingdom would obtain Polaris missiles from the United States, as a sub-stitute for the Skybolt air-to-ground missile. It had been intended to install these on the British nuclear-weapon carrying v-bombers, hoping thereby to prolong their usefulness as a deterrent force. But Mr. McNamara had cancelled the programme, because of technical difficulties in its develop-ment, and its great cost, and because the United States did not really need it, in view of the extensive force of Minuteman missiles and Polaris sub-marines existing and provided for.

> . . . the president and the Prime Minister agreed that the purpose of their two governments with respect to the provision of the Polaris missiles must be the development of a multilateral NATO nuclear force in the closest consultation with other NATO allies. They will use their best endeavours to this end.

It was also agreed that allocations from the United States Strategic Forces, the United Kingdom Bomber Command and from tactical nuclear forces now in Europe would be assigned as part of a NATO nuclear force and targeted in accordance with NATO plans.[13]

In the ninety-sixth meeting of the ENDC on February 12, Mr. Kuznet-zov expressed the very hostile reaction of the Soviet Union to the plans thus announced. He said:

> Recent measures taken by the Western Powers to intensify the arms race and the further spread of nuclear weapons are arousing particu-lar anxiety amongst all those who cherish peace. We are referring to the United Kingdom-United States agreement at Nassau concerning atomic submarines carrying Polaris rockets with nuclear warheads, the plans for a so-called multilateral nuclear force for NATO, the mili-tary treaty between France and Germany. . . .

> If we take, for instance, the plan for a multilateral nuclear force for NATO or the conclusion of a military treaty between France and Ger-

---

[13]Department of State Bulletin, January 14, 1963, pages 43-5.

many, it becomes obvious that in taking these steps the Western Powers are raising the nuclear arms race to a new level and are leading up to giving access to nuclear weapons, in one form or another, to other Western countries, especially Western Germany, where revanchist military circles are in power. Statements to the effect that, for instance, the plan for establishing a multilateral nuclear force for NATO does not provide for putting nuclear weapons directly into the hands of the West German revanchists, are intended only to confuse world public opinion.[14]

This theme was repeated by the Soviet Union representatives in the ENDC during the next three years, with few variations. This went on until in 1965 President Johnson decided to allow the multilateral force idea to lapse into oblivion. Until then its existence had blocked all progress towards the agreement on a non-proliferation treaty, which was to become the principal measure under negotiation in 1964 and the succeeding years.

Later in the same speech Mr. Kuznetzov announced:

On instructions from the Soviet Government, we are submitting to the Eighteen-Nation Committee on Disarmament a draft declaration on renunciation of the use of foreign territory for stationing strategical means of delivery of nuclear weapons (ENDC/75). This draft provides that within a short period . . . the States concerned will renounce the use of foreign ports for basing submarines with nuclear missiles and aircraft carriers carrying on board aircraft with atomic and thermonuclear bombs; they will renounce the stationing on foreign territory of intermediate and long-range missiles with nuclear warheads and strategic bombers armed with nuclear weapons. The implementation of these measures would be a great contribution to the prevention of war.[15]

Some meetings later, Mr. Joseph Godber, representing the United Kingdom, pointed out that these measures would be entirely one-sided, to the advantage of the USSR. That nation did not have any aircraft-carriers, nor any need to base missile-carrying submarines in foreign ports, but what it did have was some 700 MRBM's and IRBM's stationed in its territory (near the Baltic) which were targeted on every part of NATO Europe. The Soviet Union declaration would do nothing about removing the menace to the European nations which these constituted.[16]

---

[14]ENDC/PV.96, pages 15, 16.
[15]ENDC/PV.96, page 20.
[16]ENDC/PV.115, page 41.

This is a characteristic example of how the superpowers put forward proposals, ostensibly for disarmament or measures leading towards it, but which if executed would create a more favourable strategic situation for themselves, without compensating advantage to the other party.

At the ninety-ninth meeting on February 18, Mr. Foster countered Mr. Kuznetzov's criticisms as follows:

> Certain attacks on United States policy made by the Soviet Union . . . have centred on the creation of a NATO multilateral nuclear force and alleged transfer of control over nuclear weapons to non-nuclear powers. . . .

> United States policy is firmly against the transfer of nuclear weapons into the national control of States which do not possess them. This policy is expressed in our internal legislation, in our support of the Irish resolution (1665 (xvi)) in the General Assembly. . . .

> No arrangement for a NATO multilateral nuclear force proposed at Nassau or elsewhere would violate this long-standing United States policy. Instead, it would serve this policy by giving our allies a voice in nuclear strategy. It would thereby remove whatever incentive might conceivably exist for those who do not now have nuclear weapons to seek to acquire an independent nuclear capability.

> Nor is the recent Franco-German treaty of co-operation concerned with nuclear weapons. As President Kennedy remarked at his press conference on 7 February, Germany would remain bound by its 1954 treaty obligation renouncing nuclear weapons.[17]

These arguments did not then persuade the Soviet Government that MLF would be a good thing; nor was it ever persuaded.

At the 114th meeting, on March 27, Mr. Tsarapkin, who had assumed leadership of the USSR delegation, returned to strong criticism of the US programme for disarmament. He said that effective disarmament measures to eliminate the threat of nuclear war must begin with the great powers which possessed nuclear weapons. But if the US plan were implemented, he said, the militarily strong nuclear powers would become even stronger, while the smaller and militarily weaker powers would go on disarming. And under the US plan the danger of nuclear war would constantly increase. At the end of the second stage, the armed forces and conventional armaments of all states would be reduced by sixty-five per cent., while the nuclear arsenal and military bases on foreign territory,

---

[17]ENDC/PV.99, pages 19-20.

now available to the USA and NATO, would remain intact. The nuclear arsenal might even grow, as under the US programme the manufacture of nuclear weapons in the first and second stages would not be prohibited. Would such provisions not open the possibility of political blackmail and pressure on other states? The United States plan for "disarmament in a peaceful world" looked like preparing the conditions for the undisputed dictatorship and military and political domination by the nuclear powers.

Mr. Tsarapkin's interpretation of the USA plan was tendentious, of course, but it did reflect the point that its provisions for the reduction of nuclear weapon vehicles would keep the Soviet Union in a position of inferiority in numbers of nuclear weapon vehicles usable in a contra-superpower nuclear exchange. And so it could not be accepted.

Mr. Tsarapkin also referred to discussions being held in the West about a revised strategy for NATO if a MLF were created, and quoted reports of Lord Home's speech in the North Atlantic Council on March 20 referring to the increased influence the European members of NATO would have on targeting policy. And this, of course, Mr. Tsarapkin suggested, would explain why the Western powers were so interested in putting disarmament inspectors on Soviet Union territory (to collect information on suitable targets, he implied).[18]

At the next meeting, on March 29, he continued to denounce the MLF suggesting that what the West intended was to find the best way to provide the West German militarists and revanchists with nuclear armaments. The Soviet Union did not fear this for herself. If the revanchists started a war, "within the first few hours . . . everything there will literally be burned up; everything will be reduced to dust by thermonuclear explosions. The Soviet Union was concerned for the fate of the world, to prevent a nuclear missile war with all its monstrous and catastrophic consequences to mankind."[19]

A more hopeful development surfaced at this meeting. Mr. Charles Stelle, acting leader of the USA delegation, went into some detail as to how more direct and secure communication between governments of the superpowers might be established. This preliminary measure was common to the USA and the USSR disarmament programmes. To bring it into effect was particularly to be desired, as the experience of the Cuban crisis had shown. Mr. Stelle said that negotiations would probably be more fruitful if carried on initially in informal discussions between the representatives of "those states possessing the most modern weapons."[20]

---

[18]ENDC/PV.114, pages 37, 40.
[19]ENDC/PV.115, page 22.
[20]ENDC/PV.115, page 19.

At the 118th meeting, on April 5, Mr. Tsarapkin, at the conclusion of a lengthy speech in which he denounced NATO and all its works, and most of the United States proposals for arms control measures, produced a spoonful of jam which for the West took away part of the bitter taste. He said that the Soviet Union was ready to agree immediately, without waiting for general and complete disarmament, to the establishment of a direct telephone or teletype communications line between the Governments of the Soviet Union and the United States. Mr. Stelle welcomed this announcement.[21] The two delegations then entered into private technical discussions, and on June 20, 1963 Mr. Stelle and Mr. Tsarapkin initialed the "Hot Line" agreement, as it is generally called. This was the first success of the ENDC in negotiating an arms control measure, and it was an encouragement to hope that the tide of rejection and negation was beginning to ebb.

At the 117th meeting, on April 3, I tried to smoke out the Soviet Union on the details of the Gromyko umbrella proposal, by a somewhat general discussion of the problem of deterrence.

> Soviet Representatives have insisted that the reduction of nuclear weapon vehicles by including them in equal across-the-board percentage cuts of all categories of major armaments, as suggested in the United States outline of provisions of a treaty (ENDC/30/Add.1,2) is not a satisfactory method. . . . The Soviet Union . . . obviously has in mind a method of reducing nuclear weapon vehicles involving unequal percentage reductions of the vehicles possessed by the several parties. Although it has never been clearly stated, we have to assume that those unequal reductions under the Gromyko proposal would result in approximate parity between the Soviet Union and the United States in either the number or the destructive capacity of the weapons systems which they would retain until the end of the second stage. . . .

> The Canadian delegation believes that the Soviet Union should . . . explain how the reduction of nuclear weapon vehicles from present levels to the levels it proposes is to be staged and phased. That implies, of course, that the Soviet Union must be more specific about the number of vehicles which it believes should be retained if its proposal is implemented; also there should be more details about the categories and types of armaments which would be retained and those which would be destroyed. . . .

> What the Soviet Union is proposing, in effect, is that the great nuclear

---

[21]ENDC/PV.118, page 52.

powers should reduce their means of delivery from their present high levels to what would be required for "minimum deterrence". That theory of minimum deterrence has been extensively discussed in the West by scientists, political experts and others interested in disarmament. The essence of the idea is that each side should keep a sufficient number of vehicles, all or mainly intercontinental ballistic missiles, in protected launching sites to ensure that if a nuclear attack were launched by the other side a retaliatory attack of devastating power could still be launched. A mutual "minimum deterrence" would require approximate equality of the vehicles to be kept by each side. Such a system of deterrence would be stable, provided there were simultanously a cut-off of development of new armaments, testing and production. The stability would be due to the fact that if Nuclear Power "A" wanted to destroy an intercontinental missile of Nuclear Power "B", it would probably have to fire three or four of its own intercontinental ballistic missiles to be sure of knocking out the other. But as both sides are approximately equal in those great missiles neither would have the additional numbers to enable such an aggressive first strike to be launched with any prospect of success. Possibly it would clarify the Gromyko proposal for the Conference if the Soviet delegation were to discuss it in terms of the minimum deterrence theory.

Later I made the point that a balance of nuclear armaments existed, citing figures for all kinds of nuclear weapon vehicles from the ISS tabulations. This was sometimes described as a balance of terror. I also cited part of a speech of Marshal Malinovsky, published by the *Journal de Genève* of February 23-4, which, translated, read as follows:

I affirm categorically that, faced with the 344 rockets with which Mr. McNamara threatens us, we should be able to reply by a simultaneous strike many times heavier, by rockets whose nuclear load would be of such power that they would sweep from the surface of the earth all objectives and all industrial administrative and political centres of the United States, and that they would destroy totally those countries which have allowed the establishment of American military bases on their territory.

I remarked that this extract, and the Marshal's speech as a whole, could not be described as more than somewhat peace-loving.[22]

---

[22]ENDC/PV.117, pages 9, 10.

At the 120th meeting and again at the 124th meeting Mr. Tsarapkin rejected the suggestion that the Soviet Union proposal was based on "some far-fetched concept of minimum deterrence." He also disputed the arguments I had advanced based on the figures for ICBM's given by the ISS, which showed a very large USA superiority in numbers. He extended the quotation from Marshal Malinovsky's speech, in which it was implied that no imbalance of this kind existed. But careful reading of the text[23] shows that the Marshal was referring to a total of USSR ICBM's, IRBM's, and MRBM's; not just ICBM's – and the Gromyko proposal was that each side should eliminate all but "a strictly limited and agreed number of global intercontinental missiles, anti-missile missiles and anti-aircraft missiles."

Towards the end of my speech, I had suggested it could be concluded that it was becoming increasingly probable that the great nuclear powers would never use their enormous armament unless the other side was about to attack them. However, as Mr. Cavalletti, the representative of Italy had pointed out shortly before, if a war began with the opposing forces using only conventional weapons, it would soon escalate into a nuclear conflict. There existed a position of balanced deterrence, but on an extremely high level. Furthermore, the balance was unstable, because of the continuing arms race.

I have inserted the rather long quotation above, and Mr. Tsarapkin's line in answering it, because these exchanges touch on the questions, "How much deterrence?" and "What kind of armaments and how many of them are necessary to maintain this deterrence?" The ENDC found no answer to these questions in the years which followed 1963, and the same problems face the superpowers in SALT today.

In spite of Mr. Tsarapkin's refusal to admit that the Gromyko proposal was to reach a situation of minimum deterrence during the first two stages of the general and complete disarmament programme, that is indeed what it was. It seemed to me at the time that to consider the theory and reasoning back of the concept (which incidentally had been discussed at Pugwash meetings) our military-diplomatic fencing match might permit some progress. But Mr. Tsarapkin wanted none of it. And the US Government, advised by Mr. McNamara and the Chiefs of Staff, could hardly be expected to welcome the idea of an early reduction to a minimum, on the basis of equality with the USSR, of the retaliatory nuclear arsenal they were building. It has to be remembered that the Cuban crisis was only five months past, and the Soviet Union's deception and duplicity which had attended the attempted build-up of IRBM's in Cuba was not

---

[23]ENDC/PV.120, page 37.

forgotten – and still is not forgotten. Hence the United States insisted on a high degree of assurance, through effective means of verification, that any obligations to reduce important weapons systems were actually carried out, and that no undisclosed stocks existed. It is difficult to see how, in the circumstances, President Kennedy's administration could have agreed to more generous, or more trustful proposals than were contained in the provisions in the Outline for percentage reductions of all kinds of armaments through the three stages of disarmament.

The month of April saw the continuation of the sterile wrangling over the Gromyko proposal. The representatives of the United States and of the United Kingdom had offered much the same criticisms of the Soviet Union disarmament plan as amended by Gromyko as I did. They tried to extract fuller information on the modalities which the Soviet Union had in mind for its phasing, and particularly for verification procedures, but without success. Mr. Tsarapkin refused to budge from his position that the proposal must be accepted in principle first. Negotiation of details could follow. I believe now that he could not enlighten us further because the Soviet Union planners in Moscow themselves had not worked out any details.

On one point Mr. Tsarapkin was very definite: there would be no extensive inspection of Soviet Union territory before the completion of the massive reductions of ICBM's and other NWV's which their disarmament programme provided for in the first stage. And of course neither the United States nor its allies could accept such conditions. Put crudely, the United States was not going to be the sucker in an international confidence game, played with ICBM's as counters. Since the ENDC had returned to the table in Geneva, after the 1962 General Assembly, it had become pretty clear that the Gromyko proposal had not altered the unacceptability of the original Soviet Draft Treaty proposals for the elimination of NWV's.

As we have seen, the Soviet Union's refusal to agree to any effective inspection to verify that no undeclared armaments existed was probably due to a fear that the considerable superiority of the USA in intercontinental means of delivery of the nuclear weapon could mean an option for a first strike – and indiscreet utterances of some highly-placed American officers about preemptive strikes had given cause for apprehension, not only to the Russians. Furthermore, the Soviet Union, knowing its inferiority in long-range delivery systems (in spite of Marshal Malinovsky's bluster), would not disclose actual numbers, or engage in any "numbers game" bargaining, for disclosure of their actual strength would be injurious to their prestige, and contradictory of some of Chairman Khrushchev's claims of the Soviet lead in nuclear weaponry.

The United States, too, had at various times been fearful of a first strike. These were the bomber and missile gap scares. Also, the United States had made the commitment to its NATO allies that it would intervene with nuclear arms if there were a danger of an overwhelming attack by conventional forces of the Warsaw Pact. To make it credible to themselves that this commitment would be fulfilled, the United States authorities had to preserve a substantial margin of superiority.

Previous chapters include short accounts of the United States military posture, as given in hearings before congressional committees. On January 30, 1963 Secretary McNamara made a statement to the House of Representatives Armed Services Committee on the American strategy, as it then was. It illustrates the reasons for the impasse in disarmament negotiations. Mr. McNamara began by citing good reasons why the superpowers should halt the arms race, as follows:

> As the events of last October have so forcefully demonstrated, the expanding arsenals of nuclear weapons on both sides of the Iron Curtain have created an extremely dangerous situation not only for their possessors but for the entire world. As the arms race continues and the weapons multiply and become more swift and deadly, the possibility of a global catastrophe, either by miscalculation or design, becomes ever more real.

> More armaments, whether offensive or defensive, cannot solve this dilemma. We are approaching an era when it will become increasingly improbable that either side could destroy a sufficiently large portion of the other's strategic nuclear force, either by surprise or otherwise, to preclude a devastating retaliatory blow. This may result in mutual deterrence, but it is a grim prospect. It underscores the need for a renewed effort to find some way, if not to eliminate these deadly weapons completely, then at least to slow down or halt their further accumulation, and to create institutional arrangements which would reduce the need for either side to resort to their immediate use in moments of acute international tension. . . . But until we can find a safe and sure road to disarmament, we must continue to build our own defenses.[24]

Up to the last sentence, disarmers could applaud. But then came the fateful dichotomy in policy. Curiously, the Secretary did not seem to recognize, or his position did not allow him to say, that the great and growing pile of armaments blocked the "safe and sure road" to disarmament.

---

[24]Hearings on Military Posture and Appropriations during Fiscal Year 1964, pages 306, 308.

Mr. McNamara went on:

Last year I told this committee: "There is no question but that, today, our Strategic Retaliatory Forces are fully capable of destroying the Soviet target system, even after absorbing an initial surprise attack". This statement is still true.

After giving an estimate of the Soviet Union's probable build-up of intercontinental NWV's, Mr. McNamara went on:

It will become increasingly difficult, regardless of the form of the attack, to destroy a sufficiently large proportion of the Soviet's strategic nuclear forces to preclude major damage to the United States, regardless of how large or what kind of strategic forces we build.

Even if we were to double and triple our forces we would not be able to destroy quickly all or almost all of the hardened ICBM sites. And even if we could do that, we know of no way to destroy the enemy's missile launching submarines at the same time. We do not anticipate that either the United States or the Soviet Union will acquire that capability in the foreseeable future. . . .

What we are proposing is a capability to strike back after absorbing the first blow. This means we have to build and maintain a second strike force. Such a force should have sufficient flexibility to permit a choice of strategies, particularly an ability to (1) strike back at the entire Soviet target system simultaneously, or (2) strike back first at the Soviet bomber bases, missile sites, and other military installations associated with their long-range nuclear forces to reduce the power of any follow-on attack – and then, if necessary, strike back at the Soviet urban and industrial complex in a controlled and deliberate way. . . .

In talking about global nuclear war, the Soviet leaders always say that they would strike at the entire complex of our military power including government and production centers, meaning our cities. If they were to do so, we would, of course, have no alternative but to retaliate in kind. But we have no way of knowing whether they would actually do so. It would certainly be in their interest as well as ours to try to limit the terrible consequences of a nuclear exchange. By building into our forces a flexible capability, we at least eliminate the prospect that we could strike back in only one way; namely, against the entire Soviet target system including their cities. Such a prospect would give the Soviet Union no incentive to withhold attack against our cities in a first strike. We want to give them a better alternative. Whether they would accept it in the crisis of a global nuclear war, no one can say. Considering what is at stake, we believe it is worth the additional effort on our part to have this option.[25]

The question one has to ask, in considering Mr. McNamara's argument, is: Who is going to strike first? He rules out the possibility of an effective disarming preventive or preemptive strike by either American or Russian counter-superpower nuclear forces. Then, in the second paragraph as set out above, he speaks of American alternatives for second strikes – which assumes the Soviet Union had struck first. Why should the Soviet Union strike first? There was, however, a reason why the United States might have to strike first – the NATO commitment.

One can read into the statement an underlying suggestion to the Soviet Union that if a nuclear exchange should somehow begin, it should be carried on as a duel between intercontinental or counter-superpower nuclear forces – leaving cities aside. This proposition, looked at from the Soviet side was not very attractive, as the table in Chapter 12 indicates.

If there had been an exchange of intercontinental missiles in 1963, the probabilities were that the United States, having many times more, would have some left at the end, while the Soviet Union would have none, and its cities would be forfeit unless the United States terms for ending the war were met. Marshal Malinovsky's statement can be taken as a reply to what Mr. McNamara said on this occasion.

Was Secretary McNamara, in making public the strategy of "controlled response," trying to put into practice the theory advanced by Schelling and Halperin in *Strategy and Arms Control*?

> . . . arms control might help to limit damage in general war. . . . One possibility is to create *expectations* that even a major strategic war might be susceptible of limitation. The main motivation for restraint would be to induce reciprocation; . . . Creating a shared expectation of the possibility may therefore be a prerequisite to restraint, and any understandings, even tacit ones, that can be reached, however informal they are, deserve to be considered.[26]

The early Russian reaction to the strategy of controlled response was a pretty contumelious rejection of the idea that nuclear war, once begun, could be conducted according to agreed rules, like a soccer game, and that destruction of cities and industry could be averted.

---

[25]*Ibid.*, pages 308, 309.
[26]Schelling, T. C. and Halperin, M. H., *Strategy and Arms Control* (New York: Twentieth Century Fund, 1961), pages 21, 22.

CHAPTER 16

Eighteen-Nation Committee, 1963-1964

Many statements in the desultory debate on the "Gromyko umbrella" modification of the Soviet programme for eliminating NWV's showed the close connection between military thinking and policies and the proposals for disarmament. For example, at the 132nd meeting on May 15, Mr. Tsarapkin argued that the clandestine retention of missiles by any party to the treaty – presumably one of the superpowers – would not really be a threat to world peace. He said if a country retained nuclear weapon vehicles secretly for the purpose of carrying out aggressive plans, this would require the military defeat of the opposing state. However, this could not be accomplished by a few retained ICBM's and bombers alone. Victory would require invasion and occupation of the entire territory of the country attacked, and this in turn would require immense armed forces and quantities of the most modern weapons. And therefore a state which concealed a certain number of missiles or bombers would not gain anything, since it could not wage a war, much less win it, with such limited means. If the provisions of Stage I of the Soviet draft treaty were put into effect, no nation would have the immense forces for such an aggression.

Here we see the reflection of the Soviet military thinking of that time. Their intercontinental rockets were all very fine, but to win a war between great powers, armies and armaments as great as those with which World

War II was fought would be needed. Victory would be finally won by occupying the enemy's territory and totally subjugating him.

The Western countries, however, were apprehensive of what might happen if even a few of the great number of long-range nuclear weapon vehicles then built or building were retained in an otherwise disarmed world. The NATO countries did not forget the threats of President Bulganin to Britain and France in 1956 at the time of the Suez crisis, when the Soviet Union may have thought it had a monopoly of long-range nuclear ballistic missiles. And more recently Soviet diplomats had practised deception, denying the intention to place offensive missiles in Cuba. It is hard to say, in the light of these experiences, that the Western fear that intercontinental nuclear weapon vehicles might be clandestinely retained was irrational.

Typical of Mr. Tsarapkin's "explanations" of the Gromyko proposal was part of his statement at the same meeting:

> ... the words "agreed and strictly limited number of missiles" are not pure coincidence. They mean first of all that the number of missiles to be retained must be strictly limited, that is, minimal; and secondly that this strictly limited number must be agreed upon between us. This means that the figures for the missiles to be retained by each side are by no means purely arbitrary quantities; these figures must be the subject of an agreement.[1]

It would be unfair to leave the impression that this extract was representative of Mr. Tsarapkin's usual negotiating style. On matters other than the Gromyko umbrella he was clear enough, and expounded the Moscow line with force, if not very persuasively.

Attacks on the concept of the Multilateral Force for NATO (MLF) constituted a material part of the Warsaw Pact statements during this period. These were usually coupled with denunciations of West German "revanchism and militarism." The Western delegations replied to the unjustified attacks on West Germany, pointing out that that country, by an annex to the treaty which governed their entry into the North Atlantic Alliance, had renounced the right to possess nuclear weapons, which no other country had done.

Arguments by the Western side that the Soviet Union proposals on the whole were not in accord with the principle of balance – one of those agreed upon between Mr. McCloy and Mr. Zorin for the negotiation of general and complete disarmament – were met by a somewhat mixed-up

---

[1]ENDC/PV.132, page 16.

argument by the Warsaw Pact members. They said the West was basing its attitude towards disarmament on an obsolete political conception of "balance of forces," which they confused with the pre-World War I political concept of a balance of power. The idea of a balance of power, which had produced the alliances before both world wars, had not prevented the outbreak of either one, but had rather contributed to it, they said. However, this line of argument was presently dropped after painstaking explanations that it was the current approximate balance of forces between West and East which prevented any great power from taking the horrid risks of war. This emphasized the importance of the fifth of the agreed principles:

> All measures of general and complete disarmament should be balanced so that at no stage of the implementation of the treaty could any State or group of States gain military advantage, and their security is ensured equally for all.

The Soviet Union delegation's habitual references to the "aggressive NATO alliance" were replied to, after repetition of the phrase became too tiresome, by Western statements of the reasons for NATO's creation – the apparent threat of the extension of the communist empire from the already dominated Eastern European States to the States of Western Europe.

In reply, Mr. Tsarapkin gave the Soviet Union version of why NATO was established:

> The whole world knows that what led the Western Powers to establish the aggressive NATO bloc was the course, taken by them at the end of the second world war, of the cold war policy, the policy "from a position of strength", the main provisions of which were formulated by Winston Churchill in his Fulton speech, at which very significantly, the then President of the United States was present.

> This openly-aggressive course of the foreign policy of the Western Powers was devised and worked out in the fumes of intoxication from the United States' atomic monopoly.[2]

At the 137th meeting, on May 27, the Soviet Union delegate levelled a further accusation of militaristic aggression against the NATO countries. He read into the proceedings a note sent by the Soviet Union to the United States and a group of Mediterranean states, the first paragraphs of which read as follows:

---

[2]ENDC/PV.135, page 35.

Quite recently the Soviet Government was compelled to utter a warning against the plans for the creation of a NATO nuclear force which would give the West German *Bundeswehr* access to atomic weapons and unleash a nuclear armaments race knowing neither State nor geographical bounds. Today . . . the governments of the United States and certain other NATO members are taking further steps in the same direction.

The point in question is the already started implementation of plans for the deployment of United States nuclear submarines equipped with Polaris nuclear missiles in the Mediterranean area. . . .

Thus the United States and some of its allies are demonstrating once again that concern for the prevention of a thermonuclear war or at least for the reduction of the danger of its outbreak is alien to their policy. . . .

Further on in the lengthy note, the following passage occurred:

Further light on the intentions of the United States is shed by the statements of United States military leaders who recently justified the need to station United States nuclear weapons in Canada by saying that in the event of war this would make it possible to draw part of a nuclear counter-blow away from the United States and divert it to Canada. . . .

Some people may consider it almost the summit of military thinking to hide their nuclear missile bases as far away as possible from their own vital centres and closer to the borders of other countries. But can the millions of people living in the Mediterranean area be content with the positions of hostages in which the leading Powers of NATO are trying to place them?[3]

The British and United States representatives replied by quoting Soviet threats of nuclear attack on the territories of those states which had the temerity to engage in a defensive alliance, instead of trusting to the well-known peace-loving character of the USSR. When the array of Soviet MRBM's and IRBM's was considered, the Soviet note took on something of the accents of the wolf sympathizing with the sheep that liked the protection of the sheepdogs and the shepherd.

In more sober style, at the 138th meeting on May 29, Mr. Tsarapkin gave his delegation's view on the position which the negotiations had

---

[3]ENDC/PV.137, pages 9, 10, 13.

reached, and his observations merit some analysis. He said that if the conference could reach agreement on the main issues, which were the destruction of all means of delivery of nuclear weapons (except for a small, strictly limited and agreed number of delivery vehicles to be retained by the Soviet Union and the United States until the end of the second stage), and on the simultaneous elimination of all foreign military bases on the territories of other states, and the withdrawal of foreign troops from those territories, then the relatively minor differences still remaining between the Socialist States and the Western powers, in regard to the reduction of conventional armaments and their production, would undoubtedly be overcome.[4]

He rightly pointed out that limiting and then eliminating nuclear weapon vehicles was the main issue. I believe he was also correct in asserting that if agreement could be reached on this, it would be relatively easy to come to terms on the dismantlement of conventional arms and forces. Then he inserted the vexing problem of "military bases on foreign territory."

What stood in the way of agreement or even understanding of the basic problem was that the two sides looked at it in completely different ways. The Soviet Union saw the bases as facilities which the United States had established for launching nuclear attacks on the Soviet Union with medium-range vehicles – bombers and missiles. This represented to them a crowding-in of the United States to their boundaries – encirclement – and it can be understood that they should regard it as a menace. The NATO partners, on the other hand, feared a Soviet Union aggressive urge to extend communist rule, and felt that to be able to resist it they would need the armed support of the United States. And that support required that bases for the US forces should be created on the territories of the NATO allies, and in a few other locations. These, apart from the airfields and the short-lived Thor and Jupiter installations, were required for normal logistic reasons.

The Russians continued, all through the discussions of general and complete disarmament in the ENDC, to link elimination of US bases on foreign territories with the reduction of intercontinental nuclear weapon vehicles. This was not unjustifiable, in my view. The Western position was that the bases would be dismantled, or lose their armament throughout the three stages of disarmament. What did not seem reasonable in the Soviet Union position was the contention that all foreign bases had to be removed in the first stage.

---

[4]ENDC/PV.138, page 34.

The same problem, in essence, appears to have faced the SALT negotiators. It was reported in the press that one of the difficult points in the discussions was to define "Strategic Arms." It was said that the Soviet side wanted to apply the term to any vehicle which can carry a nuclear weapon to the territory of one of the superpowers. This would mean that medium-range US and allied bombers or IRBM's on bases in Europe would be included in the definition, while the Soviet Union IRBM's and MRBM's (which threaten the European NATO countries) would not.

It would therefore seem that the negotiators have the problem, not only of working out some kind of parity between the superpowers' holdings of ICBM's and SLBM's, but also between the Europe-based NWV's that can strike at Soviet territory, and the Soviet-based vehicles of medium-range that can hit Western and Southern Europe. This is not a matter that affects the United States and the Soviet Union alone, but more vitally concerns the European NATO partners. From this, it might appear that it will be necessary to get agreement on limitation of the European-range nuclear armament, in a European security conference of some kind, before SALT can reach any useful conclusion.

By the spring of 1963 the Eighteen-Nation Committee on Disarmament had arrived at an impasse on the limitation and reduction of nuclear weapon vehicles, and consequently on general and complete disarmament, although we did not fully realize this at the time. But then two events brightened the arms control outlook. On April 29, 1963, the Presidents of Bolivia, Brazil, Chile, Ecuador and Mexico announced that their Governments were prepared to sign a multilateral agreement whereby they would undertake not to manufacture, receive, store or test nuclear weapons or nuclear launching devices. It took several years of difficult negotiation before the Treaty of Tlatelolco came into effect, but it was encouraging that one continent had statesmen who recognized that keeping it free of nuclear weapons and vehicles would be the best way to achieve security against the danger of nuclear war.[5]

The other element of hope came from the speech of President Kennedy at the American University on June 10, which was welcomed by both sides and the non-aligned at the 143rd meeting on the 12th of June. The President said:

> Chairman Khrushchev, Prime Minister Macmillan and I have agreed that high-level discussions will shortly begin in Moscow looking towards agreement on a comprehensive test-ban treaty.

[5]UN and Disarmament, 1945-1965, page 216.

On June 21, the ENDC recessed until July 30, and during this period the partial test ban treaty was signed in Moscow.

The signing of the Moscow Test Ban Treaty produced an euphoria in the disarmament community. We thought that a real break in the dreary years of fruitless negotiations had been achieved. The danger of radioactive waste in the atmosphere had been removed, except for the then relatively unimportant testing activities of France and China, which did not adhere to the treaty. Furthermore, the preamble to the treaty declared that the original parties – the United States, the United Kingdom and the Soviet Union – were "seeking to achieve the discontinuance of all test explosions of nuclear weapons for all time, determined to continue negotiations to this end, and desiring to put an end to the contamination of man's environment by radioactive substances."

Although negotiations have indeed continued for a comprehensive test ban, no real progress up to now has been made in resolving the point of difference between the USSR and the USA over the necessity of on-site inspection, to verify that no underground tests have taken place. Before and after its signature considerable opposition to the treaty developed in the United States among some Republican politicians and other hawkish individuals. In order to be sure of the necessary two-thirds of Senate votes required for ratification, President Kennedy had to give the following assurances in a letter to Senators Mansfield and Dirksen, respectively Democratic and Republican leaders in the Senate.

1. An underground testing programme would be vigorously carried forward.
2. The USA would maintain readiness to test in three environments and would test if the Soviet Union violated the treaty.
3. The treaty did not limit authority of the President to order use of nuclear weapons for defence of itself or allies.
4. The Government would maintain strong weapons laboratories and maintain strategic forces capable of destroying aggressors after absorbing a first strike.
5. The USA would continue to pursue the development of peaceful nuclear explosions.[6]

All these promises of President Kennedy have been fulfilled by his and succeeding administrations. The question of prohibiting underground testing and thus making the Moscow treaty "comprehensive" remains on the agenda of the Conference of the Committee on Disarmament (CCD)

---

[6]Congressional Record, Volume CIX, Part 12, pages 16790-1.

and continues to be debated in their sessions and at the General Assembly. Large improvements in the means of detecting and identifying under-ground nuclear explosions have been made, but still the United States claims that in order to ensure that none take place some on-site inspec-tions are necessary. The non-aligned members of the negotiating bodies have been openly asserting for several years that neither of the super-powers wants to stop underground testing; and that they put on the comedy of disagreeing over the means of verification in order to protect their right to go on with the development of more and worse nuclear weapons.

At a meeting of the CCD on May 3, 1971, Señor Castaneda, repre-sentative of Mexico, attacked the superpowers' leadership of the confer-ence for practically shelving the matters of a combined ban on chemical and biological warfare, and the prohibition of underground testing.[7] Mrs. Myrdal of Sweden in a previous meeting had implied that the real reason the superpowers need underground tests is to perfect the missiles that SALT are intended to do away with. Mrs. Myrdal has in fact been "im-plying" this out loud for several years.

The ENDC began its meetings again on July 30, 1963 and continued through to August 29, when it recessed, preparatory to going to the UNGA for the disarmament discussions there. The glow of the Moscow Treaty persisted for a while, but there was no new ground broken on any im-portant aspect of disarmament, and certainly no progress was made on the solution of the deadlock about how the great NWV's should be reduced and finally eliminated. At some meetings we made statements about such measures of arms control as reduction of the troop levels in Europe, a freeze on military budgets, and the international manning of control posts at strategic points on both sides of the Iron Curtain, to lessen the danger of surprise attacks, but there seemed to be little purpose or direction in the ENDC's proceedings at this point.

At this time I noted in my diary some doubts as to the future of the ENDC. After nearly two years, progress towards general disarmament was *nil*. And while the agreement on the "Hot Line" and the Moscow Treaty were gratifying, and we could hope that they would lead to further accommodations, they had been worked out, in the final stages, by the great powers alone. This might presage the exclusion of non-aligned and allies from the most significant disarmament negotiations, which would be continued as a dialogue between the superpowers. And that indeed is

---

[7]N.Y. Times service in *Globe and Mail*, May 5, 1971.

what has happened, with the establishment of the Strategic Arms Limitation Talks in late 1969.

Later, at the UN General Assembly, Charles Stelle told me that Tsarapkin had suggested to him that the ENDC was not useful any more, and that negotiations should be between the great powers. That the Russians should suggest this was somewhat surprising. In their disarmament performance there was a large element of playing to the gallery. Perhaps some of them realized that their efforts to be the heroes of the fight to avert the danger of nuclear war, while casting the Americans as the villains, were not being altogether successful. Some of the boos and jeers from the gallery seemed to be directed impartially towards both protagonists. However, these forebodings as to the continuance of the ENDC proved unfounded, and it went on meeting through the next five years, finally to become expanded by new membership, and to be renamed the Conference of the Committee on Disarmament (CCD).

At the eighteenth UN General Assembly, there was a further small step taken towards limiting the environments in which the means of waging nuclear war could be present. Mr. Gromyko on September 19, 1963, making the Soviet Union statement in the general debate, said: "The Soviet Government deems it necessary to reach agreement with the United States Government to ban the placing into orbit of objects with nuclear weapons on board." This was welcomed by President Kennedy, who spoke the next day, and after negotiations between representatives of the United States and the Soviet Union, Mexico submitted a draft resolution on behalf of the seven participating members of the ENDC which called upon all states:

> To refrain from placing in orbit around the earth any objects carrying nuclear weapons or any other kinds of weapons of mass destruction, installing such weapons on celestial bodies, or stationing such weapons in outer space in any other manner.[8]

The resolution also welcomed the expressed intention of the United States and the Soviet Union not to do any of these things.

Some three years later, on January 27, 1967, the "Treaty on principles governing the activities of States in their exploration and use of outer space, including the moon and other celestial bodies," was signed. Article 4 of this treaty repeated the obligation contained in the above resolution, with some further restrictions on military uses of outer space.

To the reader unacquainted with the history of the flowering of arma-

---

[8]UNGA Resolution 1884 (XVIII), October 17, 1963.

ments in the last two decades, the prohibition of the cited activities might seem like a municipal ordinance prohibiting pigs from flying. However, some of the proposals for military activities in outer space which found their way into print occasionally make one wonder if the creators of Buck Rogers and Flash Gordon were now generals in the Pentagon.[9]

Mr. Gromyko mentioned his umbrella proposal of the previous year, regretting that the Western members of the ENDC had refused to negotiate on it in a serious way. He said that as a further concession on the part of the Soviet Union they were ready to extend the period over which the Soviet Union and the United States might retain the "strictly limited" number of ICBM's, etc. (all other nuclear weapon vehicles having been destroyed in the first stage of the disarmament programme) from the end of the second stage to the end of the third stage – when all other measures of disarmament would be completed. So far as it went, this was a step in the right direction; but it was a very small step indeed. After this, there were no further real negotiations or serious discussion of the problem of reducing and finally eliminating the carriers of the weapons of mass destruction – nuclear weapon vehicles.

At a meeting of the Western members of the ENDC on November 4,

---

[9]That there was some need for an agreement to close off outer space to the expensive adventurings of the geniuses of rocket-cum-nuclear warfare is shown by the following short accounts of ideas which were apparently seriously considered at one time.

"The war of the world, carried into outer space, would involve far more, however, than the mere detection and tracking of bomb-orbiting satellites. It would involve, of necessity, their pursuit and destruction, and the Air Force is already financing a project to think through the infinite possibilities. It is called deceptively Project BAMBI [Ballistic Missile Booster Interceptor].

"The object would be to put so many orbiting, nuclear-armed BAMBIS into outer space that some of them would always be in position to keep watch on what the Russians were doing; and if the Russians sent up a bombloaded BAMBI of their own, our own defending spaceships would hurtle in for the kill." (Cook, Fred J., *The Warfare State* (New York: Macmillan, 1962), page 348.)

"General Putt, in evidence before the House Committee on Armed Services, explained that the United States Air Force aims at establishing a missile base on the moon, and considered that a war-head will be fired from the moon to the earth without any enormous expenditure of energy, since the moon has no atmosphere and little gravity. He declared that the moon 'might provide a retaliation base of considerable advantage over earthbound nations'." (Russell, Bertrand, *Common Sense and Nuclear Warfare* (New York: Simon & Schuster, 1959), page 18.

Mr. Stelle told us that for domestic reasons the United States could not put forward advanced positions on disarmament at this time. The meaning of this was made clearer in an interview I was able to have with Senator Hubert Humphrey. The Senator had been Chairman of the Disarmament Subcommittee of the Foreign Affairs Committee of the Senate, and was looked on as one of the leading proponents of arms control. He had visited Geneva during the sessions, where I had met him. When I saw him on December 4, 1963, he said that the American public would support short moves towards disarmament, peacekeeping and strengthening of the United Nations. But emphasis on the third stage of disarmament (that is, when disarmament would be complete and nuclear weapon vehicles would be eliminated) would lay the administration open to attack by the far right. Owing to the presidential election in the autumn of 1964, the United States would not be pushing disarmament hard.

President Kennedy had been assassinated on November 22, and what attitude President Johnson would take towards disarmament was unknown. It did not seem likely he would be very forthcoming, but the record of the next few years shows that he carried on the line of policy which the late president had initiated.

The disarmament discussions at the eighteenth UN General Assembly ended with resolutions calling on the ENDC to renew attempts to find agreement on general and complete disarmament and various arms control measures, and also to continue, "with a sense of urgency," negotiations with the object of discontinuing all tests of nuclear explosions for all time. As reported in earlier pages, the ENDC, unfortunately, has not been able to make any real progress towards accomplishing either of the tasks set for it in these resolutions.

When the ENDC reopened on January 21, 1964, President Johnson's message proposed that the conference should make special efforts to reach agreement on several of the arms control measures which had been before it for some time, namely, the "Cut-off"; a comprehensive ban on nuclear testing (CTB), which meant to extend the prohibitions of the Moscow Treaty to include underground testing; and non-proliferation. And, as a first step towards solving the problem of reducing nuclear weapon vehicles, he proposed that:

> The United States and the Soviet Union and their respective allies should agree to explore a verified freeze of the number and characteristics of strategic nuclear offensive and defensive vehicles.[10]

---

[10]ENDC/120, January 21, 1964.

At the 162nd meeting on January 31, Mr. William Foster went into the rationale of the freeze proposal. He said:

> It would halt the race for more and better strategic nuclear vehicles and open the path to reductions from present levels in all types of forces. Where the test ban treaty limited warhead size, and the United States proposal for a fissionable material cut-off would limit the amount of explosive materials available for warheads, the present proposal would limit numbers and characteristics of strategic nuclear vehicles.
>
> For many years – even while the conference has been in session – both sides have increased the numbers of their strategic nuclear vehicles to a substantial extent. In so doing, both have simply added to the amounts of their materials of war which must be destroyed if disarmament is to be achieved. To achieve it, we must stop the increase above present levels, increases which seem inevitable in the absence of agreement.[11]

At a later meeting Mr. Adrian Fisher for the US delegation explained how an agreement could be monitored to verify compliance. There would not have to be extensive inspection of Soviet territory. It would only be necessary to keep a check on critical processes in aerospace production centres to control replacements of vehicles expended in launchings for space exploration and for testing the serviceability of the retained ballistic armament.[12]

These proposals seemed reasonable to the Western members of the ENDC, and even got a good reception from most of the non-aligned members. The non-possessors of nuclear weapons would naturally have been pleased to see the arms race halted, no matter which superpower was ahead.

The Hon. Paul Martin, then Secretary of State for External Affairs, who was in Geneva in connection with the UN Conference on Trade and Development, attended the 178th meeting of the ENDC on March 26, and made a statement on how the Canadian Government viewed the negotiations, making the following suggestions, among others:

> My Government believes that the Conference should select from among the following collateral measures those which, taken either singly or in combination, are most likely to lead to early agreement,

---

[11]ENDC/PV.162, pages 16-17.
[12]ENDC/PV.184, pages 13-19.

and should concentrate its attention upon them during the next period of its work;

First, the freeze of strategic nuclear weapon vehicles proposed by the President of the United States;

Second, the destruction of a number of long-range nuclear bombing aircraft proposed in different forms by the Soviet Union and the United States;

Third, the non-dissemination of nuclear weapons;

Fourth, the cessation of production of fissile material for nuclear weapons, and diversion of existing stocks to peaceful uses;

Fifth, the establishment of a system of observation posts to prevent surprise attack;

Sixth, a comprehensive test ban; and

Seventh, the strengthening of the United Nations capacity to keep the peace.

In regard to the freeze, Mr. Martin said:

Let us agree to halt the present upward spiral in the numbers of strategic missiles and bombers: let us agree to stop where we are now. That would help us to find an agreed method to reverse the process, to begin disarmament in this field.

In regard to non-dissemination (the term had not then been changed to non-proliferation) he said:

My country welcomes the importance which this Committee is giving to the vital matter of preventing the wider dissemination of nuclear weapons: that is to say, preventing an increase in the number of States with an independent capacity for waging nuclear war. We are glad that both the Soviet Union and the United States have included this item in their lists of collateral measures.[13]

This statement sets out the Canadian Government policy in regard to disarmament at that time. Of all the measures which Mr. Martin hoped to see worked out, only non-dissemination (non-proliferation) has become a reality. The freeze and the destruction of bombers were almost dead letters when Mr. Martin was speaking, as the following extracts from statements of the Soviet Union delegation will show.

---

[13]ENDC/PV.178, pages 15-23.

Speaking in the 174th meeting on March 12, 1964, Mr. Tsarapkin had the following to say – after a prior rejection of the freeze by Mr. Gromyko in an interview with *Isvestiya* dated the 2nd of March.

> This United States proposal is aimed at maintaining in its entirety the enormous power of destruction now at the disposal of the two military groups confronting each other. Thus, a freeze of the strategic means of delivery of nuclear weapons by itself, without the simultaneous implementation of disarmament measures, cannot lead to any lessening of the threat of nuclear war, since it would not reduce the military arsenals of States by a single missile or a single bomber.

> Secondly, as far as we understand, the United States proposal for a "freeze" would not affect the production of Polaris missiles, nor would it prevent the creation of new armed forces based on these missiles. For instance, the United States proposal for a "freeze" does not cover the United States-West German plan for the creation of so-called NATO multilateral nuclear forces.[14]

After further comments on the unbalanced nature of a freeze that would exclude the tactical nuclear weapon vehicles stationed in Europe, and pointing out that the very large United States programme of constructing ICBM's and SLBM's was now approaching its conclusion, Mr. Tsarapkin expressed this view of the "control" (verification) proposed for a freeze agreement.

> But what does control over the freezing of strategic means of delivery really mean? In the first place, it would be control carried out without any disarmament measures whatsoever and in isolation from such measures, which would mean as a matter of fact opening up to foreign intelligence services the whole production of the most important types of weapons and their testing sites – that is to say, practically disclosing the most important secrets of the defence industry and the defence system of a country in the conditions of a continuing arms race and intensive military preparations.[15]

The unstated reason for the Soviet rejection of the freeze was that it would halt the arms race when the United States was well ahead, as the following table shows.

---

[14]ENDC/PV.174, page 45.
[15]ENDC/PV.174, pages 49-50.

Growth of ICBM/SLBM Strength: 1960-1970 (mid years)[16]

		1960	1961	1962	1963	1964	1965	1966	1967	1968	1969	1970
USA	ICBM	18	63	294	424	834	854	904	1054	1054	1054	1054
	SLBM	32	96	144	224	416	496	592	656	656	656	656
USSR	ICBM	35	50	75	100	200	270	300	460	800	1050	1300
	SLBM	–	some	some	100	120	120	125	130	130	160	280

The American proposition must have appeared to the Soviet Union authorities like a suggestion to end a poker game by a man who had accumulated most of the blue chips. The subject of the freeze was raised at intervals through the remaining meetings of the ENDC in 1964, but with no change in position on the Russian side.

Another way of reducing nuclear weapon vehicles referred to by Mr. Martin in the statement just quoted was nicknamed by disarmers "The Bomber Bonfire." This was a proposal by the United States that they and the Soviet Union should destroy an equal number of medium-range aircraft capable of carrying the nuclear weapon. This idea came into the open about the turn of the year. In a press interview on January 2, 1964, Secretary of State Rusk said that the United States and the Soviet Union were moving into a period where "certain highly sophisticated weapons are in the process of coming out of inventory." The United States thought it would be a pity if these obsolescent armaments, instead of being destroyed, should find their way into the arsenals of less technically advanced states – as had happened with various kinds of conventional armaments, obsolescent by superpower standards.[17]

The Right Hon. R. A. Butler, then Foreign Secretary of the United Kingdom, made this comment on the proposal in an address to the ENDC on February 25, 1964.

> . . . we have warmly welcomed as a preliminary measure the United States proposal for a "bomber bonfire" that is, the destruction of some aircraft on either side. We are encouraged by the interest which the Soviet Government appears to have shown in this proposal, although the extension of it to cover all bombers immediately, if that is the only meaning of the Soviet Government's counter-proposal, seems to us impracticable, certainly without a great deal more progress

[16]From the Strategic Balance, 1970-71 (London: ISS).
[17]USA *Documents on Disarmament*, pages 2, 3.

towards disarmament in other categories and without agreement on methods of verification.[18]

The Soviet Union counter-proposal referred to by Mr. Butler was contained in the memorandum submitted to the ENDC on January 28, which listed some nine "Measures for Slowing Down the Armaments Race and Relaxing International Tension."[19] The eighth item stated that the Soviet Union was prepared to examine the question of the elimination of bomber aircraft, which, "though obsolete, still remain one of the powerful means . . . used to deliver nuclear weapons many thousands of kilometres from their bases in order to inflict massive blows in the territories of other states." It was made clear that this meant *all* bomber aircraft.

A glance at the following table will show why the Soviet Union's proposal was not acceptable to the United States.

Long-range Bombers, Estimated Strengths: Early 1964[20]

	Bombers (over 5000 m. range)	Medium-Range Bombers (over 2000 m. range)	Carrier-based Bombers
Western Allies	630	780	600
Communist Bloc	200	1400	*nil*

The B 52 intercontinental bombers numbered 630 at that time, and were the element in the United States retaliatory force which could deliver the greatest tonnage of thermonuclear weapons. The Americans were certainly not going to destroy them in the existing state of international relations.

The United States proposal was summarized briefly by Mr. Adrian Fisher at the 176th meeting on the 19th of March. He said:

> We propose that the United States and the Soviet Union agree to destroy an equal number of B 47 and TU 16 bombers on a one-for-one basis, at an agreed rate, with simple verification.[21]

An obvious reason why the Soviet Union would not accept the United States proposal was that their 1400 TU 16 medium-range bombers would continue to be a valuable part of their deterrent. From bases inside the

---

[18]ENDC/PV.169, page 12.
[19]ENDC/123.
[20]From the Military Balance, 1963-64 (London ISS).
[21]ENDC/PV.176, page 8.

Soviet Union they could reach all parts of Western Europe including, of course, the bases where United States forces were stationed. The B 47 bombers which the United States proposed to trade off in the bonfire were operating from such bases, and in case of war would be vulnerable to strikes by Soviet bombers, and IRBM's and MRBM's. The US military authorities had concluded that, as their inventory of ICBM's and B 52 intercontinental bombers grew, the B 47's were no longer necessary as part of their strategic retaliatory force. Unfortunately for the United States bargaining position in this matter, Mr. McNamara had told the Congressional Committee that he was proposing to phase out the B 47's. So the Russians naturally concluded that there was no point in agreeing to destroy part of their medium-range bomber forces if the Americans were going to take theirs out of service anyway.

When it was first presented, the Bomber Bonfire had seemed to offer a prospect of real disarmament, or, at the least, a symbolic reciprocal dismantling of some of the carriers of mass destruction. However, the period during which it seemed plausible and possible was brief, compared to the life span of other proposed arms control measures.

Some of the Soviet Union's nine "Measures for Slowing Down the Armaments Race and Reducing International Tension" have been already discussed. Also included in the nine were the reduction of the total manpower in armed forces of States, and reduction of military budgets. Together with the list of arms control proposals in President Johnson's letter, the Soviet nine made a bulky agenda. There was a good deal of wrangling between the co-chairmen about which measures should be dealt with first, which was finally resolved by the unsatisfactory expedient of allowing any delegation to speak about any of the measures it wished, at any of the meetings devoted to arms control, or, as we called them, collateral measures. Of course, this did not make for orderly negotiation, and as might be expected little progress was made on any of the proposals.

The Soviet delegation pressed budgetary reduction strongly, and the idea generally was supported by the non-aligned. However, Mr. Foster said that the United States could not accept it because it would conflict with their constitutional processes for controlling expenditure. It was a presidential election year, and for the then President of the United States to have espoused a ten to fifteen per cent. reduction of military expenditure would not help him get reelected.

One may speculate whether Mr. Khrushchev's pressing for the reduction of military forces and financial allocations made him unpopular with the Soviet Union armed forces. It has been suggested that the loss of the support of the military was a factor in his fall from power in October.

On March 17, at the 175th meeting, I made a statement summing up the position on the limitation and reduction of nuclear weapon vehicles, as the Canadian delegation saw it.

> We have heard a great deal about the horrors of nuclear war, and we all agree. We all want to get rid of the possibility of a nuclear war as soon as feasible – and I emphasize that – ; but, in getting rid of the possibility of nuclear war, we do not want to leave the possibility of conventional war. . . .

> What now deters the nations which possess nuclear armaments from using them to enforce their policies in the international field? The fact . . . that both sides . . . have the means to inflict such devastation that no political object would be worth the risk of incurring it. In other words, we have a balance of nuclear power – or of nuclear terror, if you like.

> Furthermore, this balance of nuclear power also inhibits any large-scale use of conventional military forces, because in the existing circumstances, any war on the continent of Europe at any rate, would immediately become a nuclear war. But this is an unstable balance and can be upset. . . .

> Therefore it is vital to find the means, first, to stop the arms race, the desperate search for ever new weapons systems, and then to start reducing the present roughly-balanced nuclear deterrents to a minimum as quickly as that can be done without upsetting the balance or raising fears that the nuclear terror will be replaced by another kind of terror – the fear of interference in the affairs of other nations by various means involving varying degrees of violence up to the maximum of another conventional war.

After some comments on the Soviet Union arguments against the United States percentage reduction plan, and the freeze, I went on:

> At our meeting of 18 February I asked how Mr. Gromyko's proposal was to be verified, and I pointed out that so far we had been told only that inspectors might be present on the declared intercontinental ballistic missile launching pads at the second stage. I further said that the Soviet proposals for destroying all nuclear weapon vehicles in the first stage, except the limited number postulated in the Gromyko

proposals, were open to the same objections that the Western countries had raised against the original Soviet proposal before the Gromyko amendments.

If the West is to take the Soviet proposals as a serious basis for negotiation, it is necessary for the Soviet Union to put forward a tentative, or at least an illustrative, programme of how the territory of the Soviet Union and its allies, and at the same time, the territory of the United States and its allies would be opened up for inspection to prove that there were no rockets other than those declared at the launching pads.

We have also tried to find out . . . the approximate number of intercontinental ballistic missiles which is envisaged by Mr. Gromyko's umbrella. So far we have had no reply to indicate what is meant in figures by a "strictly limited" number, or a "definite, limited number", or a "minimum quantity", to quote the phrases used by Mr. Tsarapkin.[22]

At the same meeting Mr. Tsarapkin repeated the previously-stated Soviet Union objections to the freeze, and added a new one, that freezing the production of the most powerful types of nuclear weapon vehicles would leave still open and arms race in other types of armaments, including tactical nuclear weapons. He said:

What is the significance of this "new" word for peace, when, given the proposed freeze, the whole world will be even more armed than it is now, although even at the present time the peoples live constantly under the threat and terrible danger of nuclear annihilation? This new United States proposal, by freezing the existing situation in the nuclear arms race, would in fact "freeze" – that is preserve – the terrible nuclear threat hanging over mankind.

. . . we see that the freeze of strategic means of delivery of nuclear weapons proposed by the United States is in fact a device, a convenient screen, for switching resources, production capacities and scientific and technical forces to the development of other types of nuclear weapons and their means of delivery. It is known that tactical means of delivery of nuclear weapons, just like conventional armaments, will increase in quantity and be improved in quality with still greater rapidity. That is the real nature of the United States proposal for a freeze.[23]

---

[22]ENDC/PV.175, pages 17, 20, 21.
[23]ENDC/PV.175, page 30.

There was some substance in this criticism of the freeze. In later statements, the United States delegation suggested that other categories of armaments could be added to the original list of those to be frozen, but there was no encouraging response from the Soviet Union.

There was no advance from the state of affairs illustrated by these quotations during the remainder of the first session of the ENDC in 1964. We recessed from April 28, to June 9, hoping that the representatives of the great powers would be able to get further instructions modifying their positions, which would allow forward movement. The ENDC reconvened on June 9, and it was not long before we saw that these hopes were to be disappointed. There were no changes in positions.

Shortly after the ENDC resumed meetings I received a visit from Mr. Zorin, who had come back to lead the USSR delegation for a while. What he had to say gave me the impression that at this time the Soviet Government really wanted some progress in disarmament. Perhaps he had been sent to Geneva to get some further agreement on instructions from Mr. Khrushchev, whose credit with the party probably needed bolstering by another success for his disarmament policy. (He was to be ousted from power the following October.) In spite of his reputation as a tough negotiator, during this period Mr. Zorin appeared to be somewhat more flexible than Mr. Tsarapkin had been during the previous session.

As an example of his negotiating style during this session, he had the following to say at the meeting on the 18th of June. His remarks are also interesting in showing the Soviet Union's switch from insistence on the primacy of general and complete disarmament. They are also an acknowledgement that arms control measures would be easier to agree upon, and afford a better means of advancing towards the desired goal.

> At the present time, States may be said to have acquired some practical experience in reaching agreement on individual measures aimed at reducing international tension. In the past year alone a number of important measures have been taken by States in this direction, which have had a very positive effect on international relations. From the military point of view the agreements reached in the past year, even though they have not put a stop to the arms race, have nevertheless succeeded in limiting it to some extent. They have shown in a visible and tangible way that the endless growth, accumulation and improvement of the nuclear arsenals of States are not an inevitable destiny for mankind.[24]

---

[24]ENDC/PV.191, page 11.

In our interview on June 12, Mr. Zorin began by remarking that in earlier negotiations Canada had come up with some useful suggestions, which helped towards some bringing together of East-West positions. Of late we had not seemed to do much in this line, and he thought this was a pity. (Later in the year Mr. Tsarapkin, who had taken over as USSR delegation leader again, made much the same pitch to me.) Whether the Russians would genuinely have liked the Canadian delegation to become more of an intermediary is of course doubtful. There were always those on the Western side who said that every separate approach to one of the lesser NATO allies by Soviet representatives was intended to weaken the solidarity of the alliance. But on the occasions mentioned, Mr. Zorin's argument was not that Canada should persuade the United States to adopt the Soviet positions, but rather that we might help negotiations by suggesting compromises. It was flattering to hear this, and in fact we should have liked very much to have been able to help in such a way. However, the combined intelligence of the delegation and the people behind us in Ottawa was not able to find formulae which could be acceptable to the men of power in Washington and Moscow equally.

No more fortunate were the diligent and judicious attempts of the eight non-aligned members of the ENDC to find ways out of the deadlock created by the superpowers' contradictory positions. One had to think of the analogous attempts to mate the giant pandas, the British Chi-Chi and the Russian An-An. They could be brought into proximity, but nothing productive followed.

Looking back on the debates from 1960 to 1964 over the ways to rid the world of the menace of sudden nuclear destruction, we who sat in the disarmament conferences, whether we represented great powers or lesser nations, may well feel now that what we were doing was only tenuously related to the reality of international relations, the world power struggle. But what was realism? The notion that, to be secure, a great power had to maintain an arsenal of weapons capable of destroying hundreds of millions of human beings? Or the notion that great and small powers alike would be more secure if the nuclear powers would dismantle or destroy these weapons, and that a world authority should ensure that no more of them would be made?

In the early sixties, it did not seem unreasonable to believe that the great powers would lay aside the implements of mass destruction, which since Hiroshima had been unusable. But those of us who believed, and still believe, that disarmament is necessary to make the world safer did not realize the tenacity with which national leaders – men of *realpolitik* –

would cling to the grisly symbols of power, would fear to move from the precarious national security given by the possession of great armaments.

Some theorists have comforted themselves by imagining that the nuclear weapon is unusable, and will continue to be unusable. But history shows that up to now no weapon which man has invented, however horrible it seemed when it first came to light, has not been used, sooner or later. Though international efforts were made to ban the use of some such means of war, they failed. Our present hope should be that the enormous development in the modes of international relations in the twentieth century, consequent upon instantaneous communication and air transport, will provide the possibility for controlling the cataclysmic weapons which the century has given birth to. The means to mass murder through nuclear power which scientists and engineers have constructed with such genius and industry can be resolved into their component parts, converted into innocuous or even beneficial uses or scrap. The ideas for disarmament under effective international control exist. What is lacking is the will to put them into effect, and to make the necessary compromises to allow this to happen. What is most wanting is the realization, from the man in the street up to the men in the Kremlin and in the Capitol, that in the long run nuclear weapons can confer no security.

The nineteenth session of the United Nations General Assembly in the autumn of 1964 was thrown into confusion by the confrontation between the Soviet Union and the United States, each with its group of supporters, over payment of the debt incurred by the Congo peacekeeping operation. The Soviet Union, France and some others refused to pay their allotted share, on the grounds that the actions of the force, directed by the Secretary-General, were illegal, although the World Court gave an opinion that all member nations were liable to pay part of the costs. An attempt was made to get a majority of members to vote for the application of the penalty prescribed for states in arrears with their payments to the organization – loss of vote in the General Assembly. The Soviet Union threatened to walk out of the UN if this sanction were applied – and it was not. The ENDC had ended its sessions with deadlock on all important questions, and had hoped that the discussions and resolutions in the nineteenth General Assembly would enable it to make a fresh start, but it was impossible to proceed with the ordinary business of the Assembly – including disarmament matters – and so there was a hiatus in disarmament negotiations.

I recall a conversation I had with Mr. Tsarapkin about the end of the frustrating General Assembly. He was pretty gloomy about the prospects for resumption of negotiation in the ENDC. I suggested that one way to get round the lack of directions and encouragement by the UN general membership would be to convene the UN Disarmament Commission – whose membership was the same as the General Assembly, but in which the complication over the right to vote would not arise. He did not think that it would be possible to arrange a meeting of this body, but within the next month or so the Soviet Union did propose it, and it was accepted. Most of the proceedings of the UNDC, during its meetings from April to July, were concerned with the non-proliferation question, which will form the subject of the next chapter.

CHAPTER 17

Non-proliferation Treaty/Sea-bed Treaty/
Convention against biological warfare

From mid-1965 until mid-1968, the ENDC spent most of its time working out the treaty on non-proliferation. The positions of the two sides concerning the reducing of long-range nuclear weapon vehicles, and the associated proposals of the Gromyko Umbrella, the Freeze and the Bomber Bonfire, remained in deadlock over this period. Discussion was desultory. The underground test ban, required to make the Moscow Treaty comprehensive, was debated frequently, but with no change from the impasse over verification.

At the 195th meeting on July 2, 1964, Mr. Zorin had said:

If the Western Powers are really anxious for a positive solution of the problem of the non-dissemination of nuclear weapons, we are prepared to negotiate on this problem without putting forward any preliminary conditions. However, from the very beginning there must be mutual understanding on the main thing: that our common aim is to conclude such an agreement on the non-dissemination of nuclear weapons as would preclude any possibility of their dissemination and would close every loop-hole of access to those weapons to those who do not now possess them.[1]

[1]ENDC/PV.195, page 15.

In this excerpt from Mr. Zorin's speech two expressions occur which became key words in the negotiation over the next four years. What did the Soviet Union mean by a "loop-hole," and by "access"? It did not take long to discover that their main concern was that the Federal Republic of Germany should not find any loophole in the prospective treaty through which they could have access to nuclear weapons and their vehicles. "Access," as the Russians used the word, had its ordinary meaning of being able to see, reach, touch and examine. If the Germans had such access, they could learn how to make the weapon, the Russians implied.

At the 201st meeting, on July 23, 1964, I stated the Canadian position on non-dissemination.

Canada is firmly opposed to any further increase in the number of States having nuclear weapons in their arsenals and having the independent power to use those weapons on their own decision. In order to prevent any further increase in the number of countries in that category, we consider that it is urgent to conclude an appropriate international agreement on non-dissemination which would be binding on nuclear and non-nuclear States alike. My Government believes that the basis for this agreement already exists in the language of United Nations resolution A/RES/1665 (XVI) – generally referred to as the Irish resolution – which received the support of all members of the United Nations when it was adopted in 1961.

Despite [this] ... no international agreement has been concluded. The main reason for this, so far as our Committee is concerned, is that the Soviet Union and its allies are strongly opposed to certain multinational arrangements which have been made, or are presently contemplated, providing for the participation of several members of the NATO defensive alliance in the creation of a joint nuclear deterrent. The Soviet Union and its allies have been arguing that such arrangements would be contrary to the principle of non-dissemination. As far as the Canadian Government is concerned, arrangements which are at present in effect for the control of nuclear weapons within the Western alliance and arrangements which are presently under discussion are consistent with the terms of the Irish resolution, on which we believe a non-dissemination agreement should be based. ...

We favour negotiation in the Eighteen-Nation Disarmament Committee of an international agreement which would contain specific provisions that no nuclear Power would hand over control of nuclear weapons to any nation not possessing them. To make this principle clear, we must define what we mean by "control" and "possession."

"Control" over nuclear weapons we define as the independent power and authority of a nation to order a nuclear weapon to be launched. By "possession" of nuclear weapons, we mean independent possession, having control over them as just defined. "Possession" would imply that the nation either had manufactured the weapons itself or had been given possession of them by some other nation. A non-dissemination agreement should provide against either of these things happening.

I then quoted the following from the March 1964 White Paper on Defence.

There has never been any serious question of Canada becoming a member of the nuclear club – that is, one of those nations which by its own national decision can launch nuclear weapons. This ability could only be obtained by the national manufacture of nuclear weapons. It is not contemplated.[2]

The expression "handing over control" requires some explanation. UN Resolution 1665 (XVI), just mentioned, contained in its first operative paragraph a call for an agreement under which "nuclear States would undertake to refrain from *relinquishing control* of nuclear weapons and from transmitting the information necessary for their manufacture to States not possessing such weapons."

Resolutions on the subject passed in the two previous General Assemblies had similar wording. When the question of non-dissemination was first brought up, draft resolutions had some such wording as that nuclear powers should not *transfer* nuclear weapons to States not possessing them. But an agreement in these terms would have disallowed the arrangements under which the United States provided some of its NATO allies (including Canada) with nuclear bombs and warheads to be delivered by vehicles owned by the ally. This would have meant abandoning the so-called "Two-key" system under which the NATO allies, other than Britain, were able to have tactical nuclear weapons in their military forces. The "Two-key" system meant that the warhead or bomb could not be used without the consent of the United States (one key) and of course the weapon could not be delivered unless the ally owning the vehicle wanted to do it (the second key). The United States maintained control of the nuclear weapons provided under this system, through physical custody and electronic locks.

---

[2]ENDC/PV.201, pages 27, 28, 29.

By the time the statement just quoted was made, the Canadian forces had been provided with bombs for the CF 104 aircraft, and the Honest John rockets in NATO, and for the Bomarcs and F 101 interceptors in Canada. This being part of our military policy, we could not agree to a treaty that would have prohibited the arrangement. What is more, the United States could not have accepted it (and had made this clear from the beginning) since it would have disrupted NATO defensive arrangements, which depended on tactical nuclear weapons being available if an attack could not be stopped by our conventional forces.

So much for the Canadian position with regard to existing arrangements for use of nuclear weapons by the NATO nations which did not possess them. Our attitude towards the projected MLF was somewhat different. The government had been approached by the American MLF-promotion team to persuade us to join in the project, but had wisely decided to stand aside. However, the Canadian disarmament officials were given to understand that when Prime Minister Pearson visited President Kennedy, shortly after the 1963 election, the matter had been discussed. Mr. Pearson had explained Canada's decision not to participate in the MLF, but agreed to the President's request not to take a position opposing it, in NATO councils or publicly. The Canadian attitude was, briefly, "Include us out, but we won't knock the scheme." This decision to remain silent was slightly embarrassing to the Canadian delegation when the MLF was being discussed in the ENDC. I had written a brief several years before the MLF proposal actively surfaced, giving reasons why such a proposal should not be considered, not only for its negative effect on disarmament negotiations, but also because of its defects as a measure of defence, or nuclear deterrence. (See Appendix I.)

At the 203rd meeting on July 30, 1964, Mr. Tsarapkin commented on the points I had made at the 201st meeting, bringing out the Soviet Union's main objection to the Western position on non-proliferation.

> In these definitions carefully formulated by Mr. Burns there is one very important flaw: they cover only national control and national possession of nuclear weapons, and do not at all affect that way of spreading these weapons which is opened up within the framework of the NATO multilateral nuclear force – that is, through the multilateral control and multilateral possession of nuclear weapons. That is the whole point; and no matter what you say, Mr. Burns, you cannot conceal the fact that the Western Powers are striving to limit the scope of an agreement on the non-dissemination of nuclear weapons by placing the NATO multilateral nuclear force outside the scope of its application.

It is impossible to agree with such an approach. An agreement on the non-dissemination of nuclear weapons must be comprehensive without any exceptions. . . . The NATO multilateral nuclear force is contrary to and incompatible with such an agreement.[3]

I made the following reply at the same meeting.

The question is why this idea of a multilateral force should have developed in the NATO alliance. The answer is that it is felt that there is need for participation of the European members of NATO in a deterrent to the possible use of nuclear weapons against their countries. It is well known and has been stressed here many times that there are no less than 800 to 1,000 intermediate and medium-range missiles deployed in Russia and directed towards Western Europe. That is a fact. The other reasons for which it is considered that it is desirable for the nations of Europe other than those which at present possess nuclear weapons to have some share in and more responsibility for providing a deterrent against those threats can well be ascertained from many publications and many speeches in many places.

The Canadian delegation does not maintain that this is necessarily a desirable development; but it is designed as an alternative to the possible proliferation of national possession, which I think all those concerned would admit to be worse. . . . I think this proposal should be judged in that light.

. . . while certain great nations maintain the nuclear power to destroy others, they cannot expect that others will not think of means to protect themselves. We cannot freeze the present state of affairs, in which certain Powers possess this nuclear weapon which could destroy others, and keep all other nations in a state of nuclear powerlessness. In other words, we cannot have nuclear sheep – the present nuclear Powers – and nuclear goats – those which do not have the nuclear weapon and are never going to get it.

. . . these things ought to be given some consideration in looking at this whole problem. It is not a problem that can be solved in any absolute way by freezing the present state of affairs. It can only be solved if there is a real move on the part of the nuclear powers to begin to divest themselves of some of the power they now have. Then they will be in a better position to insist that any nation which might possibly think of acquiring nuclear power for itself must be inspired

---

[3]ENDC/PV.203, page 23.

by a spirit of revenge and a determination to destroy others, in contrast with the virtuous views and intentions of the present possessors of nuclear weapons.[4]

In the last chapter we saw that it was not possible in the nineteenth United Nations General Assembly (Autumn 1964) to hold the usual debate on disarmament in the First Committee, and that, after a pause, it was agreed to hold discussions in the UN Disarmament Commission, which it was hoped would give some needed impetus and direction to the stalled negotiations in the ENDC.

The Commission met from April to June, 1965, and devoted the greater part of its time to discussing non-proliferation. On June 15 it adopted a resolution calling on the ENDC to reconvene as soon as possible and to:

> . . . accord special priority to the consideration of the question of a treaty or convention to prevent the proliferation of nuclear weapons, giving close attention to the various suggestions that agreement could be facilitated by adopting a programme of certain related measures.[5]

The related measures referred to in the resolution were the comprehensive test ban, the freeze, the cut-off and guarantees against nuclear attack for States not possessing nuclear weapons.

Soviet Union statements quoted already made it clear that its primary goal in the negotiations was to prevent West Germany from becoming a nuclear power. Of course it included warnings against the danger of general nuclear proliferation, but its attention never strayed far from the German factor. We must admit that the Russians had, through history, reason to fear German prowess in war; but in the existing situation, a comparison of armaments and especially of territorial extent makes such fear seem excessive. It has often been suggested that the Russians may have found it useful to go on growling about the German bogey in order to ensure the subservience of the foreign and other policies of its East European allies (as, for example, in justifying the application of the so-called Brezhnev doctrine in Czechoslovakia in 1968).

Whether the Soviet Government was really fearful that Germany might start a nuclear war, or merely pretended to fear it, the argument over what restrictions should be imposed by a non-proliferation treaty on NATO members which did not possess nuclear weapons was a protracted one. The break only came when President Johnson decided in 1965 that

---

[4]*Ibid.*, page 4.
[5]UN Doc. DC/225.

if he wanted to make progress towards disarmament, and get a non-proliferation agreement as a first move in that direction, the MLF project would have to be dropped. When we heard that in Geneva, the prospects for a treaty began to look better.

For some months before the ENDC reassembled in July 1965, the disarmament specialists in the United Kingdom and in Canada had separately been preparing drafts for a treaty. This was done in the hope that, if a definite text could be laid on the table for discussion, progress would be more rapid.

The Canadian draft contained several provisions which did not appear in the 1965 texts produced by the superpowers,[6] but were incorporated in one form or another, either in the final version of the treaty, in the related Security Council resolution, or in declarations by nuclear powers. The purpose of most of these provisions was to make non-proliferation more acceptable to the States not possessing nuclear arms.

One proposed provision was that all parties to the treaty, nuclear powers and other states alike, should place all their *non-military* atomic energy activities under the safeguard procedures of the International Atomic Energy Agency (IAEA). Although in the final treaty there is no such obligation laid on nuclear powers, as it is on states party to the treaty not possessing nuclear arms, the United States and the United Kingdom have declared that they will submit to inspection voluntarily. The Soviet Union has made no such declaration.

Another proposed provision was to the effect that the nuclear powers would come to the assistance of any state not possessing nuclear weapons which was a party to the treaty, and which was subject to or threatened with nuclear attack, provided that it was not formally allied to a nuclear power. This kind of obligation is not included in the final treaty, but has been undertaken in the form of parallel declarations by the United States, the Soviet Union and the United Kingdom, and in Security Council Resolution No. 255 of June 19, 1968, which they sponsored. A "guarantee" (against nuclear attack) was considered of high importance by most nuclear states, as we shall see in later pages.

A third proposal in the Canadian draft was that entry into force of the treaty should depend on ratification by a number of states which were judged capable, in the short term, of making a nuclear weapon. Among the potential nuclear-weapon-makers were cited Canada, the Federal Republic of Germany, India, Israel, Japan and Sweden. After discussion this

---

[6]USA draft treaty, August 17, 1965, ENDC/162; USSR draft treaty submitted to UNGA September 24, 1965; A/5976.

proposal was judged too difficult to implement, and likely to create a block to the eventual treaty's coming into force. Nevertheless, unless the states mentioned do adhere to the treaty, it will not be effective for many years. India and Israel have not signed the Treaty. Canada and Sweden have ratified it. The FGR and Japan have signed but not ratified (as of December 1971).

The fourth proposal was that the treaty should be of limited duration, since non-possessors of nuclear weapons would not wish to bind themselves in perpetuity to nuclear abstention unless the nuclear powers should themselves carry out some measure of disarmament. In the final treaty, Articles 8 and 10 respectively provide that there should be a review of the treaty every five years, and that twenty-five years after entry into force there should be a conference to determine whether the treaty should continue indefinitely, or for some specified additional period.

After some weeks of discussion in Geneva, the four NATO countries agreed on a text which was presented in the name of the United States on August 17, 1965.[7] The key provisions of this draft were contained in Articles I and II, which stated respectively the obligations of the nuclear powers, and those of other states parties to the treaty.

It is unnecessary here to go into the detail of how these key provisions of the treaty were modified in the course of the next three years. The difficulty was to get Soviet Union agreement to a text which would allow the existing "Two-key" system in NATO still to operate, and which would be acceptable to the European allies of the United States. The Soviet Union had to be satisfied that the text would prohibit any arrangement which could give the FGR an independent nuclear role. Perhaps it would be more precise to say that they had to be convinced that the United States Government had no intention of ever doing anything to facilitate this. On the other hand, the European allies made the point that the existing European Economic Community might come to a greater degree of political unity, approximating a federation. This might permit the establishing of a ruling body which could have the authority to control a common deterrent force. Such a development should not be prevented by the emerging non-proliferation treaty.[8]

Mr. William Foster and Mr. Adrian Fisher, representing the USA

---

[7]ENDC/162.

[8]For a detailed account of the negotiation of the various articles of the treaty see the present author's article "The Non-proliferation Treaty: Its Negotiation and Prospects," in *International Organization*, Volume XXIII, No. 4, 1969. Also see International Negotiations on the Treaty on the Non-proliferation of Nuclear Weapons; ACDA, Washington, 1969.

alternately in Geneva, held meeting after meeting first with Mr. Tsarapkin and then with his successor Mr. Alexei Roshchin. The American negotiators had to work very hard to find a formula which would be acceptable to the Soviet Union and yet which would not compromise the existing NATO arrangements for the use of nuclear weapons in defence. Besides the work with the Russians, they had to discuss the terms of the treaty with the leading countries in NATO which were not represented in the ENDC, and assure them that their vital interests would not be compromised. Sometimes there were meetings with the NAC, and sometimes with the authorities of separate members of the alliance.

The allied country which was most vitally interested in the terms of the treaty was the Federal Republic of Germany. Their security against Soviet aggression and threats depended on the effectiveness of the defensive arrangements of NATO, and in particular on the possibility of using tactical nuclear weapons if war should break out, backed up by the enormous nuclear power of the United States. So West Germany was naturally concerned by any agreement which might disturb the delicate balance of the nuclear deterrent. Furthermore, there were certain German politicians who liked the idea of the Multilateral Force, and who hoped that, through this or in some other way, their country could gain more influence in the determining of the nuclear strategy of the alliance. Perhaps they even hoped that the FGR some day would acquire nuclear weapons and so become equal to the second-rank nuclear powers, Britain and France. The number and influence of such politicians was, of course, constantly exaggerated by the Soviet Union propaganda, with its reiterated denunciations of West German militarists and revanchists.

On September 15, 1965, the eight non-aligned members of the ENDC had submitted a memorandum, in which they stated that they believed that a treaty on non-proliferation was not an end in itself, but only a means to an end; namely, the achievement of general and complete disarmament, and, more particularly, nuclear disarmament. They were:

> convinced that measures to prohibit the spread of nuclear weapons should, therefore, be coupled with or followed by tangible steps to halt the nuclear arms race and to limit, reduce and eliminate the stocks of nuclear weapons and the means of their delivery.[9]

It can be said that the Canadian viewpoint was substantially that expressed in the memorandum, although it was not possible for us to join in presenting it. (Nor were we invited to do so!)

[9]ENDC/158.

Earlier in 1965, during the discussions on non-proliferation at the meetings of the Disarmament Conference, the representative of India, Mr. Chakravarty, had said that the solution of the problem of preventing nuclear proliferation should comprise the following elements:

1 / An undertaking by the nuclear powers not to transfer nuclear weapons or nuclear weapons technology to others;
2 / An undertaking not to use nuclear weapons against countries which do not possess them;
3 / An undertaking through the United Nations to safeguard the security of countries which may be threatened by powers having a nuclear weapons capability, or about to have a nuclear weapons capability;
4 / Tangible progress towards disarmament, including a comprehensive test ban treaty, a complete freeze on production of nuclear weapons and means of delivery, as well as a substantial reduction in the existing stocks; and,
5 / An undertaking by non-nuclear powers not to acquire or manufacture nuclear weapons.[10]

Mrs. Myrdal, representing Sweden, called for a package linking a non-proliferation agreement with a comprehensive test ban and the "Cut-off."[11] The representative of Nigeria, Chief Adebo, felt like the Indian representative that a non-proliferation treaty should provide for the security of non-nuclear states.[12] The UAR representative thought that the security problem was very complex and "should be carefully and cautiously examined because of its far-reaching implications."[13] In this comment he was undoubtedly right. Not long afterwards, the Soviet Union representative warned that an attempt to write a security clause into the treaty would so complicate the problem that it would delay indefinitely the production of an agreement.

The security problem was of particular concern to the Indian Government. They were apprehensive that the People's Republic of China, having exploded a nuclear weapon, and thereby being recognized as a nuclear power might, as its nuclear armament was built up, be tempted to use it against India, or might threaten to do so. The memories of the defeat inflicted by the Chinese in the border war of 1962 were still bitter, and it is not surprising that the Indians should have been apprehensive. The

[10]UNDC, Official Records, 75th meeting, pages 2-6.
[11]*Ibid.*, 77th meeting, pages 8-13.
[12]*Ibid.*, 78th meeting, page 3.
[13]*Ibid.*, 75th meeting, pages 10-13, para. 131.

Government had explored the possibility of obtaining guarantees of protection against Chinese nuclear aggression from both Moscow and Washington. This protection would have amounted to that afforded by the great nuclear powers to their allies. But as India wanted the guarantee without any corresponding undertakings or obligations on its part, it is not surprising that no satisfactory answers were received.

During the next three years in the negotiations, the Indian line was to become more critical of the one-sidedness of non-proliferation, as it was dealt with in the draft treaties put forward by the superpowers. Mr. Vishnu Trivedi, who had invented the terms "horizontal" and "vertical" proliferation, argued that it was essential to stop both kinds of proliferation, and that a treaty which dealt only with the "horizontal" kind would be discriminatory and ineffective. At one point he remarked that the draft treaties resembled a law which would forbid alcoholic beverages to teetotallers, while leaving the known drunkards to pursue their anti-social behaviour unchecked.

Of course it is true that the non-proliferation treaty is discriminatory. However, the question was could "vertical" and "horizontal" proliferation be dealt with in the same treaty or convention? Or to put it in less fanciful and obscurantist terms, could an agreement be reached on a treaty which would (1) prevent dissemination of nuclear weapons and (2) halt the great power nuclear arms race? The obstacles which stood in the way of any agreement between the superpowers to halt their competition in armaments have been set out in the preceding chapters. In 1965 and the three years which followed, there was no indication that these obstacles would disappear in the near future. What remained to be done was to move in the direction of disarmament through arms control measures. Non-proliferation in the sense of non-dissemination was clearly the most significant measure on which the interests of the superpowers coincided sufficiently to make agreement possible.

As previous pages show, the Canadian viewpoint was that a treaty on non-dissemination, if it was to endure, had to be followed by a halt to the arms race. But we also saw that this order of negotiation offered the possibility of progress, while the reverse did not. While halting the nuclear arms race remained the great objective, leading to effective general disarmament, what could be done in the immediate future was to have a non-proliferation agreement. It was our feeling also that, if the states not possessing nuclear arms renounced their acquisition, they would be in a stronger moral position to press the nuclear powers to halt their piling up of the implements of mass destruction. A contrary view was sometimes expressed, that the nuclear powers might better be influenced to halt, limit and even reduce their armament, under threat of a number of other countries "going nuclear." But this view did not have much to support it.

An important document produced in the course of the negotiations was UN Resolution 2028 (xx) of November 19, 1965. This was worked out after prolonged discussion in the First Committee and harked back to the memorandum by the non-aligned members of the ENDC. The resolution called on the ENDC to reconvene as early as possible with a view to negotiating an international treaty to prevent the proliferation of nuclear weapons, based on the following main principles:

a / The treaty should be void of any loop-holes which might permit nuclear or non-nuclear Powers to proliferate, directly or indirectly, nuclear weapons in any form;
b / The treaty should embody an acceptable balance of mutual responsibilities and obligations of the nuclear and non-nuclear Powers;
c / The treaty should be a step towards the achievement of general and complete disarmament, and, more particularly, nuclear disarmament.

There were two more "principles" but the above are the significant ones. As usual in the United Nations, the compromise resolution could be taken to mean different things by different parties.

The first principle will be seen to conform, more or less, to language previously employed by the Soviet Union. But with the Trivedi formulation that proliferation was both "horizontal" and "vertical," Indian representatives later could argue that the draft treaties presented by the superpowers said nothing about preventing "vertical" proliferation (that is, halting the nuclear arms race), and therefore did not conform to Resolution 2028. The superpowers and their allies took the stand that what principle (a) really meant was that the treaty should prevent dissemination of nuclear weapons, or, in other words, the birth of more independent nuclear powers.

Obviously, there was room for much argument about what would be an "acceptable balance" of obligations, as between nuclear powers and other states. The main thrust of the arguments of the non-aligned members was for the nuclear powers to obligate themselves in the treaty to agree on such measures as the comprehensive test ban, the freeze, the cut-off, and eventual reduction of nuclear armaments. And there was strong pressure for a clause which would bind the nuclear powers not to use nuclear weapons against any country not possessing them.

The Soviet Union was prepared to offer what came to be known as a "negative guarantee." Premier Kosygin declared that his government would be willing "to include in the draft treaty a clause on the prohibition of the use of nuclear weapons against non-nuclear States parties to the treaty which have no nuclear weapon on their territory."[14] This was unacceptable to the NATO members of the ENDC, on the grounds that it would force a choice on the nuclear-weaponless members of the alliance to clear all tactical nuclear weapons off their territory, if they wanted the immunity offered. The disruption to NATO defensive arrangements if the proposal were accepted, and its divisive intent, seemed all too clear. If agreed to by the West, it would have almost the same result as the Soviet Union's favourite plan to eliminate all foreign bases. Furthermore, to ensure that no nuclear weapons were on the territories of Warsaw Pact and European allies would have required verification by inspection – which would have been most complicated to arrange, if indeed the Soviet Union would have accepted it at all. And finally, there was the usual objection by the West to all merely declaratory measures, unaccompanied by any real disarmament or verifiable restrictions—"Ban-the-Bomb" and its various successors. This "negative guarantee" was a partial banning of the use of nuclear weapons.

The "positive guarantee" was first exemplified by President Johnson's statement in a TV address on October 18, 1965. This address followed the important events of Chairman Khrushchev's fall from power (October 15) and the explosion of the first Chinese nuclear device (October 16). Part of the President's address was concerned with the prospects for arms control measures in the light of these events. In the course of it he said:

> The nations that do not seek national nuclear weapons can be sure that, if they need our strong support against some threat of nuclear blackmail, then they will have it.[15]

This statement could hardly be expected to inspire great confidence among the nuclear-weaponless states, of which the most concerned was India. Neither were the Indians reassured by the statement in Premier Chou En-Lai's message to heads of government, the day following the nuclear explosion, that

> The Chinese Government solemnly declares that at no time and in no circumstances will China be the first to use nuclear weapons.[16]

Nevertheless, President Johnson's approach was eventually developed into the declarations of the nuclear powers and Security Council Resolution 255 of June 19, 1968, intended as an assurance of protection of

---

[14]ENDC/167, February 3, 1966, page 3.
[15]US *Documents on Disarmament*, 1964, page 468.
[16]*Ibid.*, page 455.

nuclear-weaponless nations signatory to the treaty against the use or threat of nuclear weapons against them. But before discussing this measure, and the objections which have been raised to it, we shall briefly refer to other provisions of the Treaty on Non-proliferation which were intended to meet the criticisms of the non-aligned and nuclear-weaponless states.

Article VI of the NPT reads as follows:

> Each of the Parties to the Treaty undertakes to pursue negotiations in good faith on effective measures relating to cessation of the arms race at an early date and to nuclear disarmament, and on a treaty on general and complete disarmament under strict and effective international control.[17]

This was the limit of the commitment which the nuclear powers would make in the way of "responsibilities and obligations" to balance the renunciation of the acquisition of nuclear weapons by the other parties to the treaty. It is generally accepted that the Strategic Arms Limitation Talks between the superpowers which have been in progress since November 1969 are evidence of their intention to "negotiate in good faith" on a cessation of the arms race and nuclear disarmament. We shall be discussing SALT, the problems which they face and the possible outcome in the next chapter.

During the years of negotiation, the nuclear-weaponless states, in the ENDC and elsewhere, had expressed fears that the terms of the projected non-proliferation treaty would hamper their development of nuclear energy for peaceful purposes. Article IV of the treaty is intended as a reassurance that their interests in this respect will be protected. It reads as follows:

1 / Nothing in this Treaty shall be interpreted as affecting the inalienable right of all the Parties to the Treaty to develop research, production and use of nuclear energy for peaceful purposes without discrimination and in conformity with Articles I and II of this Treaty.

2 / All the Parties to the Treaty undertake to facilitate, and have the right to participate in, the fullest possible exchange of equipment, materials and scientific and technological information for the peaceful uses of nuclear energy. Parties to the Treaty in a position to do so shall also co-operate in contributing alone or together with other States or international organizations to the further development of the applications of nuclear energy for peaceful purposes. . . .

---

[17]For a text of the Non-proliferation Treaty, see Appendix IX, *The United Nations and Disarmament*, 1945-1970.

This would appear to be adequately comforting to those states which feared, or professed to fear, that the NPT was to be an instrument perpetuating a monopoly of nuclear energy technology among the existing nuclear powers. However, another point concerning the peaceful uses of nuclear energy caused considerable difficulty, and failure to solve the problem to their satisfaction has been cited by some non-signatory states as their reason for not adhering. This was the question of "peaceful nuclear explosions." To understand the problem, it is desirable to examine the terms of Article II, which sets out the obligations of the parties other than the nuclear powers.

> Each non-nuclear-weapon State Party to the Treaty undertakes not to receive the transfer from any transfer or whatsoever of nuclear weapons or *other nuclear explosive devices* or of control over such weapons or explosive devices directly, or indirectly; not to manufacture or otherwise acquire nuclear weapons or *other nuclear explosive devices*; and not to seek or receive any assistance in the manufacture of nuclear weapons or *other nuclear explosive devices*.

What was meant by the expressions italicized above? The insertion of this term beside "nuclear weapons" grew out of the argument that the NPT should not prohibit signatories which were not nuclear powers from carrying out "peaceful nuclear explosions" on the lines of those which had been widely publicized by the "Plowshare" programme of the USA AEC. That programme was intended to determine, by experiment, whether it would be possible to use the enormous explosive power of nuclear fissile material to execute various engineering projects, such as excavating for canals, making new harbours, and similar vast undertakings. The idea was that they could be carried out more cheaply than would be possible with ordinary chemical explosives. It also was proposed to use underground nuclear explosions to liberate oil and gas which could not be economically tapped by standard methods. A great deal of enthusiastic propaganda as to the possibilities of this technology emanated from the AEC, and the nuclear scientists of countries which believed they had, or soon would have, the ability to make a nuclear explosion were captivated. As it turns out, the difficulties in using nuclear explosions for peaceful purposes are much greater than anticipated, and relatively little has been heard of the Plowshare experiments for some time. The programme has recently been suspended by the US Government as an economy measure. The Russians have announced from time to time that they were pursuing investigation into this kind of technology, but details have been usually vague.

However, the fact is that any kind of device which can produce a nuclear explosion is a potential nuclear weapon. Therefore it would be of no use prohibiting making nuclear weapons, while allowing the production of "peaceful nuclear explosions." This fact was repeated many times to those members of the ENDC, principally India and Brazil, who argued that there should be no prohibition on their freedom to conduct "peaceful nuclear explosions"; and that any such prohibition would be an unwarranted interference with their liberty to develop their economies through the use of nuclear energy. The United States, the Soviet Union, Sweden and Canada repeatedly made it clear that the production of a nuclear explosion equalled the production of a nuclear weapon. This contention was confirmed unanimously by the Secretary-General's Committee of Experts on the effects of nuclear weapons, during one of its sessions at Geneva. Nevertheless, the argument continued.

There was justification for the demand that the benefits of the use of nuclear explosives for peaceful purposes (if these turned out to be significant) should not be withheld from parties to the treaty other than the nuclear powers. So Article v was introduced, to provide for this.

> Each Party to the Treaty undertakes to take appropriate measures to ensure that, in accordance with this Treaty, under appropriate international procedures, potential benefits from any peaceful application of nuclear explosions will be made available to non-nuclear-weapon States Party to the Treaty on a non-discriminatory basis. . . .

An international body to control any such arrangements was to be set up, by negotiation to begin as soon as possible after the treaty came into force. The matter, however, seems to have dropped from sight, as the two countries which were most strenuous in their demands for freedom to carry out "peaceful nuclear explosions" (India and Brazil) have not signed the treaty. There is frequent speculation that if India should decide to move towards producing nuclear weapons, the first step will be to carry out a "peaceful" nuclear explosion underground. But there is no indication that the Indian Government has decided to authorize such a step.

The operative paragraphs of Security Council Resolution 255 of June 19, 1968 are as follows:

> 1 / Recognizes that aggression with nuclear weapons or the threat of such aggression against a non-nuclear-weapon State would create a situation in which the Security Council, and above all its nuclear-weapon State permanent members, would have to act immediately in accordance with their obligations under the United Nations Charter;

2 / Welcomes the intention expressed by certain States that they will provide or support immediate assistance, in accordance with the Charter,
to any non-nuclear-weapon State Party to the Treaty on the Non-
Proliferation of Nuclear Weapons that is a victim of an act or an object of a threat of aggression in which nuclear weapons are used;

3 / Reaffirms in particular the inherent right, recognized under Article 51
of the Charter, of individual and collective self-defence if an armed
attack occurs against a Member of the United Nations until the Security Council has taken measures necessary to maintain international peace and security.

The key portions of the texts of the declarations of "intention" expressed by the United States, the United Kingdom and the Soviet Union
are not significantly different from the resolution.

This mode of security assurances was less than satisfactory to the
states not possessing nuclear weapons. It was argued that the agreement
of the nuclear powers to act in the way specified added nothing to their
existing obligations under the charter. All experience had shown that
action by the Security Council to maintain peace, or suppress threats to
the peace was uncertain, subject to veto, and at best slow. A state could
be destroyed by nuclear attack before the machinery of the Council could
move.

In private discussion with some of the representatives who depreci-
ated the value of the resolution and declarations, I pointed out that it was
remarkably significant that the superpowers, at odds on nearly every question of power in international relations, should have joined together, along
with Britain, to make these declarations. Furthermore, the reference to
Article 51, on the right to individual and collective self-defence, was an
indication that one or both superpowers might act to protect a threatened
friendly state, before the Security Council took a decision. This fact, and
the agreement of the superpowers on this question, were of great psycho-
logical importance. But the effect of the resolution and declaration cannot
usefully be argued without considering actual circumstances in the world
today. The India-China situation is the most important case. But before
examining this, another objection to the resolution should be looked at.
This was the contention that in restricting the protection offered to states
which were party to the treaty, the sponsors of the resolution were dero-
gating from the protection of all states which the charter was supposed to
guarantee.[18]

---

[18]For an extended discussion of the Security guarantee question, and particularly
the effect of the Security Council Resolution 255 and the accompanying declarations, see de Gara, *Nuclear Proliferation and Security* (New York: Carnegie
Endowment, May 1970), pages 35-52.

The viewpoint of the Canadian delegation was that a state not possessing nuclear weapons which determined not to adhere to the treaty was thereby announcing its intention to make a nuclear weapon itself, and rely on its own nuclear armament for protection. Therefore it was not entitled (unless through a positive alliance) to great power protection in the event of its being threatened with nuclear attack. India is reserving her "option" to make nuclear weapons, in spite of having supported UN resolution 1653 (XVI), which declared that any state using nuclear and thermonuclear weapons is to be considered as violating the charter of the United Nations, as acting contrary to the laws of humanity, and as committing a crime against mankind and civilization.

The Non-proliferation Treaty entered into force on March 5, 1970. As has been frequently mentioned already, its durability as a means of preventing more states acquiring independent power to use nuclear arms depends, in the long run, on the nuclear powers halting the arms race and beginning to reduce their nuclear armament. In the short run, that is the next five years (after which a conference of the parties is to review the operation of the instrument) what will be important are the actions of a few states which have the scientific, technological and economic assets required to enable them to produce a nuclear weapon. Key states in this category are India, Japan, the Federal Republic of Germany and Israel. All of these states have large problems of national security, and have had interior debates on the advisability of acquiring nuclear weapons. Of these states, the FGR and Japan have signed but not ratified the treaty. The others have not signed it.

The FGR appears to be holding up ratification until there is a settlement of some outstanding questions related to the negotiations in connection with the present government's policy of seeking détente with the Soviet Union and its allies, and settling such questions as access to Berlin. The negotiations under which states which are members of Euratom are working out the manner in which the IAEA safeguards will be applied to them, as required by Article III of the NPT, are protracted, and offer a convenient excuse for delay. But it is highly unlikely, in the present politico-military conjunction in Europe, that West Germany would take the dangerous and destabilising step of producing nuclear weapons.

Israel is credited with the ability to produce an atomic bomb, but has limited quantities of fissile material, and so could not make enough weapons for a really effective nuclear deterrent system. It is beyond the scope of this book to examine the effect of the undertakings in Security Council Resolution 255 if Israel should acquire a nuclear weapon, but it may be said that it would be a very perilous way to attempt to win greater security. The official Israel Government position is that Israel will not be the first country to introduce nuclear weapons in the Middle East.

There have been repeated statements by Prime Ministers of India and other high authorities that, despite their keeping open the "nuclear option" by not adhering to the Non-proliferation Treaty, India has no present intention to develop nuclear weapons, and that "this position is based on a national evaluation of all aspects of the problem, including that of security."[19]

However, Shelton Williams, at the end of his valuable book *The U.S., India, and the Bomb*, reaches the following conclusion:

> Considering India's political conceptions delineated in this study, nuclear weapon development by India would seem to be the logical course. If the NPT does not promote general disarmament, if the superpowers will not grant adequate security guarantees, if China is a direct and growing threat to India's security, and if India desires to avoid the obligations and responsibilities of alliance membership, it seems only a matter of time before India will initiate the development of nuclear weapons.[20]

Of the factors cited in this excerpt, we have discussed all but the political conceptions which would seem to lead India, sooner or later, towards the decision to manufacture the bomb.

Many influential Indian politicians and intellectuals see India's future as one of the great powers of Asia. This inevitably involves rivalry with the People's Republic of China. China now occupies a permanent seat on the Security Council, from which it was long excluded. China has produced a nuclear weapon. Some Indians argue that the possession of the nuclear weapon is the criterion of a great power – apparently oblivious to the fact that it is not a nuclear weapon that makes a great power, but a great power that makes a nuclear weapon.

Even if guarantees by the superpowers against nuclear aggression could be relied upon, to be dependent for protection on a foreign power would limit India's freedom in international relations, and upset her long-standing policy of non-alignment, let alone the hopes for future great power status. Furthermore, a guaranteeing power or powers would insist

[19]India Information Service: "India's Position on the Proposed Draft Treaty on Non-Proliferation of Nuclear Weapons, 1968, page 2.
[20]Williams, Shelton, *The US, India and the Bomb* (Baltimore: Johns Hopkins, 1969), page 64.

on exercising control over India's foreign and military policies, if these might lead to a clash with China.

Finally, Indian politicians and the public have been assured that India has the capacity to make the bomb. The history of the development of nuclear weapons and other technology in western countries and the Soviet Union shows that for scientists, and their military bosses the ability to make a weapons system produces a tremendous urge to make the possibility a reality, and the pressure spreads to the politicians.

Against all these arguments for making the bomb, the counter-arguments are, firstly, that if India were to contribute to the breakdown of the NPT by producing a nuclear weapon, she would lose much sympathy and support from the USA and the Soviet Union, and probably from many other countries.[21] Then it is doubtful whether, even if China is really a military threat to India, acquiring nuclear weapons is the surest way to counter it. Other ways to expend the money and effort available for Indian defence might be more appropriate. The analysis given by Major-General D. Som Dutt, in *India and the Bomb*,[22] sets out this point of view, and his conclusion is that the time is not ripe for India to take this very costly way of attaining security. The results of acquiring nuclear weapons could be quite unpredictable.

There is also the matter of cost. Those in India who favour making the nuclear weapon greatly underrate the enormous cost of producing a system of delivery which could be effective as a deterrence against China's nuclear threat. The information on costs is, of course, readily available in general form in the UN Secretary-General's Report on the Effects of the Possible Use of Nuclear Weapons and the Security and Economic Implications for States of the Acquisition and Further Development of These Weapons.[23]

Finally, there is the question: Since 1962, has the People's Republic of China shown that it threatens India's essential security? This can only be assessed for the next five to seven years – the span over which reasonably objective planning of defence systems, based on facts, can be extended. China's support of Pakistan during the India-Pakistan war of 1965 and since, and her aid to communist and nationalist factions within India and near her borders, are certainly unfriendly meddling. Neverthe-

---

[21]So far India's refusal to sign the NPT has not noticeably altered the attitudes of either superpower towards her. Canada and the United States continue to give technological aid for the construction of Indian nuclear reactors, which will produce plutonium, usable for a nuclear weapon if India so decides.
[22]Adelphi Paper No. 30, November 1966.
[23]UN Publication E.68.IX.1.

less, it must be realized by many knowledgeable Indians, besides those in the armed services, that the 1962 war was an unnecessary one. The hostilities came about because of ineptitude and arrogance in India's political and diplomatic handling of the border dispute, followed by gross incompetence in the military actions intended to enforce India's claim to disputed border territory. The guilt for this rests on the politicians then in charge of India's defence, and the officers they had selected to hold the highest positions in the military establishment. It resulted in an impossible task being set to formations of the Indian Army which had proud records in World War II – and their consequent defeat, and undeserved humiliation.

Does this quarrel of the 1960's mean that China is India's implacable enemy, ready to threaten use of its nuclear weapons to extend its power and influence at India's expense? No one sitting in North America can state what the answer of responsible Indian opinion to this question ought to be. The treaty of friendship concluded between India and the USSR, and the notable abstention from "nuclear blackmail" or any form of military action by the People's Republic of China for the purpose of supporting Pakistan in the December war, may cause those Indians who advocate the acquisition of nuclear weapons to reassess their ideas. The power struggle in Southern Asia has entered an active phase. Whether events will reinforce the arguments of the pro-nuclear Indian faction or not, time will tell.

Japan has signed but not ratified the NPT. Her foreign minister, at the time of signing, indicated that ratification would depend on the arrangements for IAEA inspection, and particularly that in any IAEA agreement Japan should obtain terms no more onerous than those the Euratom countries might negotiate for themselves.

Only a few years ago it was generally assumed that there was such revulsion against the nuclear weapon in Japan that no government would propose the acquisition of nuclear armament. But it is twenty-six years since Hiroshima, and the new generation did not experience the cataclysmic shock. Japan has developed immense economic and technological power. Restrictions on national freedom of action, and seeming relegation to second-class status, based on defeat in World War II, are becoming less and less acceptable. Sentiment for increased independence in defence grows. Japan probably has more to fear from Chinese nuclear armament than India. The nuclear umbrella held over her by the United States will not be there forever. It is a fair prediction that unless the great powers make some serious moves to halt the arms race and reduce their own huge armaments, it will not be many years before Japan will move towards nuclear power status.[24]

Since the completion of the Non-proliferation Treaty, the main achievement of the disarmament negotiations has been agreement on a Treaty on the Prohibition of the Emplacement of Nuclear Weapons and Other Weapons of Mass Destruction on the Sea-bed and the Ocean Floor and the Subsoil Thereof.[25] In 1969 the Eighteen-Nation Committee on Disarmament was enlarged by ten members, and changed its name to the Conference of the Committee on Disarmament. It was in the enlarged conference that the final agreement on the form of the treaty was reached.

The treaty may be considered as another in the series which limit the environments in which nuclear weapons may be located. Of these the first was the Antarctic Treaty (1959), followed by the Outer-Space Treaty (1967), and the Tlatelolco Treaty for the Prohibition of Nuclear Weapons in Latin America (1967). It is another step in the process of closing an environmental stable door *before* the technological armament horse has bolted.

The subject came into the sphere of disarmament negotiations following the discussion, in the 1967 UN General Assembly, of the "question of the reservation for peaceful purposes of the sea-bed and the ocean floor, and the subsoil thereof . . . and the use of their resources in the interests of mankind." The General Assembly concluded that there should be an international régime for the exploitation of these resources, to ensure that all countries, and not only the most advanced technologically, would share in the wealth. There was also concern that the environment should be used for peaceful purposes only.

In a memorandum submitted to the ENDC on July 16, 1968, the Soviet Union proposed that negotiations should start on prohibiting the establishment of fixed military installations on the sea-bed and ocean floor. In a message to the ENDC on the same date, President Johnson called on the ENDC to begin negotiating on an agreement which would prohibit the emplacement of weapons of mass destruction in the new environment. So the difference between the positions of the two superpowers at this stage was that the Soviet Union wanted to prohibit all military activity, while the United States proposed to prohibit only the emplacement of arms of mass

[24]For a discussion of Japanese attitudes in this matter see Quester, George H., "Japan and the Nuclear Non-Proliferation Treaty," *Asian Survey* (Berkeley: University of California, September 1970).

[25]See Chapter 8 ("The Problem of the Prevention of an Arms Race on the Sea-Bed") *UN and Disarmament, 1945-1970*.

destruction (nuclear weapons). No progress in resolving this contradiction was made at the General Assembly in 1968, but in the course of the negotiations in the ENDC/CCD in 1969, the USSR came to accept the United States position. By October 7, the superpowers had produced a joint draft treaty[26] which would ban from the sea-bed, beyond the twelve-mile limit, nuclear weapons or any other weapons of mass destruction, as well as launching installations, or facilities for storing, testing or using such weapons.

Canada had proposed that a 200-mile security zone should be established beyond the twelve-mile contiguous zone, in which only the coastal states could carry on defensive military activities permitted under the treaty. This measure for protecting coastal states' rights on the continental shelf attracted interest and support from other members of the committee with similar interests, but was not incorporated in the final text of the treaty.

The question of verification, as usual, created difficulties; although in this case it was between the smaller nations and the superpowers, and not between the superpowers. A number of the members of the CCD suggested amendments. In particular, Canada, Italy, Brazil, India, Sweden and Yugoslavia were not content with the provisions allowing for the verification that no prohibited activities were being carried on in the twelve-mile contiguous zone.

To verify what was being done within these zones, and also on the sea-bed and ocean floor, would require the use of submarines capable of operating at the relevant depths, and having special equipment. Possibly special underwater craft would have to be built for the purpose. Only the great powers would have the resources to produce and operate such inspection vessels. The problem for the lesser coastal states was to devise safeguards, so that if they were not satisfied with the innocence of any particular activity in the waters over which international law gave them control, the question could be brought into the international arena. It would not do to rely on bland assertions by the great powers that no contravention had been committed.

The problem was a difficult one: How could an obligation be created for the possessors of the necessary means of investigation to cooperate in the investigation of what might be their own contravention of the treaty? How would it be ensured that verification procedures would not be entirely under control of the great powers, which, in certain hypothetical circumstances, might adopt attitudes which would not be in the

---

[26]CCD/269, October 7, 1969.

interests of the smaller states, especially those with an extensive continental shelf – such as Canada had. It was towards finding the best possible terms for this Article III on verification that Mr. George Ignatieff, who led the Canadian delegation, devoted the most attention. A working paper on procedures which should govern the "right to verify" was drawn up, and presented to the CCD on October 8, 1969.[27] While the Canadian proposals were not finally accepted *in toto,* the difference between Article III, as it was in the draft treaty of October 7, 1969 and as it is in the draft treaty in its third revision, of September 1, 1970[28] shows the result of the pressure exercised by the Canadian delegation and delegations of other members of the CCD who agreed with our views on this question.[29]

In the CCD meeting of September 1, 1970, Mr. Ignatieff, commenting on the revised draft which had just been presented by the USA and the USSR, welcomed the latest revisions in Article III, providing for international assistance in the verification, through appropriate procedures within the framework of the United Nations. He said that the Canadian delegation realized that the co-chairmen had made a real effort to meet the views of the other members of the Committee in this matter, and were prepared to recommend the approval of the draft treaty in its present form to the Canadian Government.[30]

Brazil had been particularly concerned that the treaty should not contain anything which would interfere with the rights of coastal states to exploit the resources of their continental shelf. This concern was expressed in a working paper of August 21, 1969.[31] It was stated:

> It is indeed necessary to prevent situations where, under the allegation that a normal verification of compliance is being sought, operations would actually be deployed that could threaten the security and the sovereignty of the Coastal State or to violate its exclusive rights of exploitation of the continental shelf.

Argentina played a large part in ensuring that the treaty should in no way jeopardize existing or future Latin American claims to territorial waters. The revised wording of Articles I, II and IV contained in the Argentine document a/C.1/997, tabled in the UN General Assembly on December 11, 1969, was incorporated almost verbatim in the final draft of the Sea-bed Treaty.

---

[27]CCD/270, October 8, 1969.
[28]CCD/269/REV 3, September 1, 1970.
[29]For example, in the memorandum of nine members, CCD/297, July 30, 1970.
[30]CCD/PV.492, page 18.
[31]ENDC/264.

Sweden pressed for inclusion of an obligation on the parties to continue negotiations for measures to prevent an arms race on the sea-bed and ocean floor, which appeared in the final treaty as Article V.

The latest revision of the draft treaty was presented to the 25th UN General Assembly. It received the support of the vast majority of those who spoke on it. A resolution commending the treaty, and hoping for the widest possible adherence to it was introduced by the USA and the USSR and thirty-four co-sponsors, including Canada. The resolution was adopted on December 7, 1970 by a vote of 104 in favour, 2 against, and 2 abstentions. Peru voted against because in its opinion acceptance of the treaty might prejudice its position in respect of rights in the adjacent sea. Peru was supported by El Salvador.

During its 1971 sessions, the CCD succeeded in drafting a convention on the prohibition of the development, production and stockpiling of bacteriological (biological) and toxin weapons. Negotiations on this issue began with an initiative of the United Kingdom delegation in 1968. Action was delayed through three sessions mainly because the USSR, the socialist states and some neutral nations would have liked chemical and biological means of warfare to be dealt with in the same document. But this could not be agreed upon.

The main reason for this negotiation was that it was felt that there should be a strengthening of the 1925 Geneva Protocol, which prohibited the use of chemical and bacteriological means of warfare, but did not prohibit their development, production and stockpiling.

Negotiations were made difficult in the early years by the American use of defoliants and riot-control gases in the Vietnam war, but when this was discontinued, progress was easier. The draft convention was submitted to the UN General Assembly at its twenty-sixth annual session, and was approved without a negative vote in December.

The preamble refers to the Geneva Protocol and previous debates on chemical and bacteriological warfare in the United Nations. The following are the convention's principal articles.

ARTICLE I

Each State party to this Convention undertakes never in any circumstances to develop, produce, stockpile or otherwise acquire or retain:
1/Microbial or other biological agents, or toxins whatever their origin or method of production, of types and quantities that have no justification for prophylactic, protective or other peaceful purposes;

2/Weapons, equipment or means of delivery designed to use such agents or toxins for hostile purposes or in armed conflict.

ARTICLE II

Each State party to this Convention undertakes to destroy, or convert to peaceful purposes, as soon as possible but not later than nine months after the entry into force of the Convention, all agents, toxins, weapons, equipment and means of delivery specified in Article I . . . .

Other articles provided that no transfers of the prohibited agents should be made, that domestic laws necessary to give effect to the convention should be passed, and that complaints could be made to the Security Council if any party suspected any other party of violations.

The reasons why a similar prohibition of chemical warfare agents could not be agreed upon are the following. There was no strong opposition by the military generally to the prohibitions embodied in the draft convention and set out above. This was because biological methods of warfare had never been tried, and no research had produced a convincing picture of technology and tactics which would make them effective in war. But chemical weapons had been used, in World War I, with inconclusive results. However, the invention of the nerve gases greatly increased lethal potentialities. No military adviser could agree that a mere verbal (or treaty) promise to destroy all stocks and make no more could be relied upon. And the scientists who interested themselves in the problem have until now been unable to propose a means of inspection which would be internationally acceptable, and would be sufficient guarantee to ensure that no production or stockpiling could take place. So the powers prefer to maintain stocks of chemical weapons to prevent use of chemical warfare means against themselves by the threat of retaliation. It is widely accepted that the threat of retaliation was what prevented the use of chemical agents in World War II.

CHAPTER 18

Strategic Arms Limitation Talks

The Strategic Arms Limitation Talks between the United States and the Soviet Union began at Helsinki in November 1969, and have continued in meetings there and at Vienna alternately. After it was announced that there would be a meeting in Helsinki in July 1971, President Nixon made a statement which slightly lifted the veil of secrecy which had shrouded the talks until then. He said that as a result of negotiations at the highest level, the United States and the Soviet Union:

> Have agreed to concentrate this year on working out an agreement for the limitation of the deployment of anti-ballistic-missile systems (ABM's).

> Have also agreed that, together with concluding an agreement to limit ABM's, they will agree on certain measures with respect to the limitation of offensive strategic weapons.

> The two sides are taking this course in the conviction that it will create more favourable conditions for further negotiations to limit all strategic arms.[1]

A simultaneous announcement to the same effect was made by the Soviet Government.

---

[1]A. P. despatch from Washington, in the Toronto *Globe and Mail*, May 21, 1971.

When the session of SALT in Vienna ended in July 1970, there were newspaper reports that the United States had proposed a freeze on ABM systems, which would allow the USSR to keep its ABM defences around Moscow, and allow the United States to build a limited Safeguard system, for the defence of Minuteman complexes in Montana and elsewhere; or, as an alternative, build an ABM defence around Washington. It was understood that the United States had also proposed that to accompany the halt in the ABM build-up there should be a freeze on some of the long-range nuclear weapon vehicles.

It is generally assumed that what the superpowers intend to achieve through SALT is a halt to the arms race. It would not seem that merely to *slow down* the race, or to set up rules under which the competition should continue would be a reasonable purpose for either of the participants. A halt to the arms race would mean that at some point in time, through agreement, the superpowers would freeze the contest in the development, production and deployment of nuclear weapon delivery systems, offensive and defensive, and consequently their overall nuclear weapon power. Such a freeze would leave the superpowers in one of the three following relationships, in general terms:

a / The USA would retain superiority; the USSR would acquiesce in this.
b / The USA and the USSR would be equal in nuclear-weapon power: parity.
c / The USA would acquiesce in the USSR achieving superiority.

No public statement by the governments of either superpower suggests that outcomes (a) or (c) could be accepted. So an agreement which can be seen by each superpower as maintaining a position of equality and security *vis-à-vis* the other is left as the only possible solution, if there is to be a positive outcome.

"Parity," of course, does not require that each superpower have the same number of ICBM's, each with the same explosive power, the same number of missile-launching submarines and of intercontinental-range bombers. In 1969 President Nixon said that the purpose of the United States in determining the level of its strategic armament was not "superiority" but "sufficiency." So we ask: How much is sufficiency? Recent theory on the use of nuclear weapons would seem to define sufficiency as the ability to visit "unacceptable destruction" on the opponent after absorbing a first strike of the maximum power which he could mount. So it could be argued that, for "parity," each side need only have a "sufficiency" of strategic armaments. If any agreement for limiting them is to be durable, a large element of stability must be built in. According to what appears to be official thinking in the West, for one thing, that means that the absolute quantity of strategic armaments should be great enough that the balance could not be upset by temporary unserviceability of deterrent weapons systems, nor by marginal miscalculations of the opponent's strength. It also has to be remembered that any strategic balance would not be static, but dynamic, and would depend to a degree on estimates and perceptions of the opponent's intention and determination, which in turn would be affected by the view taken of his international policies and the aims which they appear to embody.

In *The Military Balance 1971-1972*, published by the Institute of Strategic Studies of London, the estimate of comparative strategic strengths, Appendix 1 gives the following figures for USA and USSR nuclear strike forces.

	ICBM	IRBM, MRBM	SLBM	Intercontinental-range bombers
USA	1054	0	656	460
USSR	1510	700	330 (a)	140
			90 (b)	

(a) in nuclear submarines
(b) in diesel-engine submarines.

On the face of it, the USSR's superiority in numbers of ICBM's, and the steady increase in the number of their SLBM's might give cause for alarm to those responsible for the defence of the United States. But the above figures leave out of account the programme of modifying US Minuteman missiles to receive MIRV; and to replace most of the Polaris submarine-launched missiles by Poseidons, which are MIRVed. The modified Minuteman will have three targetable reentry vehicles; the Poseidons ten. These RVs will, of course, be of less explosive power than the original single warheads, but the overall effect is calculated to be more devastating.

What we may take to be the official USA view of the balance, taking all factors into account, was expressed by Secretary of Defense Laird, in his statement to the House Armed Services Committee on March 9, 1971.

> We continue to believe that an effective defense of our population against a major Soviet attack is not now feasible. Thus we must continue to rely on our strategic offensive forces to deter a Soviet nuclear attack on our cities.

> Since we rely on these forces for deterrence, we must ensure that they are adequate to convince all potential aggressors that acts which could lead to nuclear attack or nuclear blackmail pose unacceptable risks to them.

Recent analyses of strategic force effectiveness indicate that planned strategic forces should continue to provide an adequate deterrent for the near term. We do have reliable and survivable strategic retaliatory forces, and their capabilities for retaliation today cannot be denied by nuclear attack.[2]

This may be taken as indicating that the Department of Defense believes that the United States has, and will continue to have a "sufficiency" of strategic armaments, and it may be deduced that there would not be thought to be a USA "sufficiency" if there were a USSR "superiority."

Since the announcement that SALT would be held in 1969 there has been a lot of thinking and writing about possible outcomes to the negotiations by many persons with expertise in arms control, strategic studies and relevant spheres. The extensive exploration of the subject has, of course, gone on without the benefit of published information on the positions of the two sides. As has been mentioned, the secrecy of the talks has been maintained to a degree extraordinary in diplomatic intercourse; and in great contrast to the proceedings in any previous conferences on disarmament and arms control since World War II. It is doubtless because open discussions have had so little result in checking the arms race that the superpowers decided to try more-than-quiet diplomacy. The United States, from time to time, has informed its NATO partners of the progress of the talks (or lack of it). But no significant hard information has transpired from the North Atlantic Council, and nothing from any other source, until President Nixon's announcement of July 20, 1971.

If parity in nuclear weapon power is to be the aim, the negotiators are faced with an extremely complex problem. They will have to devise an equation making the sum of the power of the nuclear weapon systems on the one side equal to the sum of the power of those on the other. The latest data published by the Institute of Strategic Studies shows each side with an array of ICBM's, SLBM's and long-range bombers of varying load-carrying capability. Numbers and load would be the main parameters in this equation. I suppose it would not be impossible for a non-involved mathematician to work out the sums to make one side equal to the other. If we start with the idea that an establishment of NWV's for each side which would result in overall parity should be worked out, the difficulty is that what is in question is not the absolute power of a nuclear weapon system,

---

[2]*Statement of Secretary of Defense Melvin R. Laird on the Fiscal Year 1972-76 Defense Program* (Washington, D.C.: Superintendent of Documents, U.S. Government Printing Office).

measured as the product of its range, load, invulnerability (or in the bar-
barous neologism "survivability") and penetration capability. Instead it is
the view which the military of the opposing side have of the overall significance of the system, and the threat to their own national security which
it appears to them to create; for example, USA/USSR views of the Soviet
Union's very large ICBM, the SS 9.

Rather than to attempt any hypothetical balancing of nuclear delivery systems which might produce a theoretical parity, in this chapter we
will try to foresee what might follow if the superpowers could agree, as the
announcements from Washington and Moscow suggested they could, on
the halting of the build-up of ABM systems at a point where, for example,
the USSR would have its Moscow complex, and the USA its complexes protecting Minuteman. But before considering what might be the favourable
consequences of such a result we might briefly review the claims and
counter-claims which were registered during the 1969-70 controversy in
the United States over the government proposals to construct ABM systems.

As we have seen, ever since the United States and the Soviet Union
began their programmes of developing and producing long-range nuclear-
headed ballistic missiles, they have also been striving to find a defence
against what was labelled on its first appearance as the "absolute
weapon." They have succeeded in intercepting a single incoming ICBM
with an anti-rocket missile.[3] This has encouraged research and development in an attempt to solve the enormously more difficult and complex
problem of intercepting a very high proportion of a large number of
missiles coming from several directions.

The R and D teams and their military sponsors claim that systems
have been developed which will do this. After long resistance, Secretary
McNamara, put forward proposals in 1967 for a relatively modest instalment of ABM defence, intended, so he said, to be a protection against
China's predicted capability to hit US cities with ICBM's in the middle
1970's, which was likely to degrade the confidence which the United
States allies and clients in the West Pacific area would have in the protection provided them by the US nuclear umbrella.

From 1967 on, there was a very active controversy over whether the
United States should take the decision to construct or deploy anti-missile
defence, and what the purpose and extent of these defences should be. It
became a political-military question of the highest importance. The de-

---

[3]For example, by the interceptions by Nike-Zeus missiles on Kwajalein of
missiles fired from the Vandenberg Base in California, in 1964-5.

bates and votes on the subject in Congress, and the public debate carried on by military experts, scientists and strategic analysts showed much more concern than there had been in anything related to national security and arms control for many years.

The most persuasive argument put forward by those who favoured an ABM build-up was that it would be more reasonable and more moral to spend the defence dollars in a system that would protect human lives – American lives – than in continuing to support the "assured destruction" concept of deterrence, which had been the basis of the defence policy expounded by Secretary McNamara in his last years in office. Donald Brennan,[4] a leading spokesman for the "defensive emphasis philosophy," put it as follows in an address given during the Carleton University conference on the prospects for SALT in March 1970.

> The somewhat political phrase that I sometimes use to describe this change in emphasis is that one should be more concerned with buying live Americans than with buying dead Russians. Many of the choices about strategic hardware present choices of the kind where you can in essence on the one hand with defenses buy more live Americans or, if you preferred, put the money into strategic offensive forces and buy more potentially dead Russians.[5]

One must admit the attractiveness of the idea that spending billions of dollars on ABM defences (BMD) could save millions of American lives, and that continuing to maintain a defence establishment the primary purpose of which is to be able to visit "assured destruction" on the Soviet Union, killing seventy million or so Russians, is indeed repulsive – as has been argued or implied throughout the present book. But the question of whether to build an American BMD cannot be decided on this moral plane alone. There has to be answered the question of whether such a development would set off another spiral to the arms race between the superpowers, as many opponents of BMD argued, and whether it would make agreement difficult on measures of arms control and disarmament, and prevent the lessening of tension between the superpowers which could bring a more lasting degree of security against the threat of nuclear war. And the other question: Could the designed systems really work, and really reduce American casualties to the degree claimed in the event of an

---

[4]Former President of the Hudson Institute, one of the most noted American military "think-tanks."

[5]Brennan, Donald G., *The Strategic Arms Limitation Talks: Possible Objectives*, Occasional Paper No. 11 (Ottawa: School of International Affairs, Carleton University, 1970).

all-out Soviet Union nuclear attack? In simpler terms, could the proposed ABM defences really stop as many incoming missiles as was claimed by creators and sponsors?

The argument for ballistic missile defence, put forward by the military, was set down clearly and forcefully by General Leon W. Johnson, USAF (retired).[6] He first cited the objections to the "assured-destruction" strategy as follows:

1 / It is not a war-waging strategy and provides no war-termination capability. Should deterrence fail and general nuclear war develop, it can be expected to result in the destruction of the United States as a viable nation.

2 / It makes it essential that the United States consider Soviet interests most carefully, and avoid transgressing them, recognizing all the while that it is impossible to know exactly what the Soviets consider those interests to be.

3 / As the United States strategic offensive forces have little coercive value and little other value except for the deterrence of general nuclear war, other major forces must be provided, or else lack of such forces must be accepted as an important limitation on national policy.[7]

This criticism exemplifies the frustration which military men in the United States are bound to feel when they analyse the balance of nuclear power between their country and the Soviet Union, and the effect of this on the traditional function of the military forces. They see themselves unable to fight and win a war, and consequently unable to promote the policies of the United States by those "other means" in the Clausewitz dictum. Worse still, they see themselves unable to defend their people and their territory from devastating blows, if war should come. The trauma for the defenders of a country that has not known foreign invasion since 1812, and which has "never lost a war" is necessarily very great.

General Johnson goes on to argue the advantages of adding an effective ballistic-missile defence to the offensive strategic forces, as follows:

1 / It would deter Soviet nuclear attack upon the United States unless the Soviets were convinced that the United States was about to launch an all-out attack upon them.

---

[6]General Johnson is a specialist in strategic studies with the Stanford Research Institute, after a career in which he held many important posts in which his duties related to defence policy.

[7]*Anti-Ballistic Missile: Yes or No?*, Report of Conference held by the Center for the Study of Democratic Institutions (New York: Hill and Wang, 1968), pages 40-41.

2 / It should produce a war-waging posture that should permit war ter-
mination under conditions favourable to the United States.

3 / It would permit the United States to pursue its foreign policy with
forthrightness and with consideration, but not compelling fear, of the
Soviets.

4 / It should permit the United States to use general-purpose forces in
limited situations with more freedom of action than does the present
policy. The Soviets would have to act with more care in supporting
wars of national liberation and in pushing world revolution, or in
employing direct conventional military pressures.

5 / Should over-all deterrence fail, it would give the President the option
of a flexible response rather than a Spasm Response as the nation
would not lie naked to the Soviet attack....

6 / It might lead the Soviets to a more reasonable attitude toward meaningful arms control measures [and] might convince the Soviet leaders
of the folly of challenging us further in the arms race, and make them
turn their attention to less threatening forms of competition.[8]

Summarized briefly, these arguments add up to the suggestion that
adding an *effective* ballistic missile defence to the existing United States
strategic armament would put them again in a position of military superiority, with the advantages this could create in world politics. I have italicized the word "effective." The crux of the question, to my mind, is, could
the system be effective in preventing "unacceptable destruction" (to use
another term used in descriptions of the United States strategic policy).
General Johnson, up to a point, recognizes this, in the arguments he quotes
against producing and deploying an American BMD.

1 / It may be that it is not technologically attainable at the present
moment. However, it is certain that the present ABM potential could
reduce the damage that the United States might suffer. It should be
able to . . . let us survive as a nation for a period before it attains the
capability of reducing casualties to a large extent here.

2 / It might engage the United States in an all-out arms race with the
Soviets, which could be expensive both in dollars and in talent. However, it is a race that we should be able to win. . . .[9]

The essentials of General Johnson's arguments in favour of the American BMD can be found in the statements of many other proponents. It does

---

[8]*Ibid.*, pages 41-2.
[9]*Ibid.*, page 42.

not seem necessary to quote these, as General Johnson sets out the pro arguments clearly, concisely and unemotionally.

Before referring to the arguments advanced by the opponents of the ABM, we might consider what is implied in the second and fifth advantages General Johnson lists for a ballistic missile defence. These seem to hark back to the hopes of the US military to somehow develop nuclear armament and its associated installations to the degree that it will be possible to get back to the state of affairs described by Secretary McNamara, in his speech announcing the strategy of controlled response (which, incidentally, was soon thereafter modified into the strategy of flexible response).

> The United States has come to the conclusion that, to the extent feasible, basic military strategy in a possible general nuclear war should be approached in much the same way that more conventional military operations have been regarded in the past. That is to say, principal military objectives, in the event of a nuclear war stemming from a major attack on the Alliance, should be the destruction of the enemy's military forces, not of his civilian population.[10]

It is difficult to understand how military men, who have studied military history and have thereby attained an understanding of the real nature of war, can follow such delusive dreams. Once nuclear weapons belonging to the superpowers are discharged, events will not depend on the decisions and actions of supermen with the icy control and concentration of chess masters. From the man in the White House and the men in the Kremlin down to the captains and corporals at the computer manuals, all will be subject to rage, passion and hate, and the terrible pressure of the immediate need to act in the hope of averting the total defeat and destruction of their country. "War is a dreadful and impassioned drama," wrote Jomini many years ago. It was not less true in World War II or in Vietnam. It is not an exercise that can be played out on computers, with predicted results.

Now for the views of the opponents of Ballistic Missile Defence. First, is it "technologically attainable"? Will the proposed system work?

In *ABM: An Evaluation of the Decision to Deploy an Antiballistic Missile System*,[11] Steven Weinberg, Leonard Rodberg, J. C. R. Licklider and Hans Bethe all produce strong arguments that neither the presently authorized Safeguard, the object of which is to protect the Minuteman mis-

---

[10]Speech at Ann Arbor, Michigan, June 16, 1962.
[11]Ed. Wiesner and Chayes (New York: Signet Books, 1969).

siles, nor a greatly extended system for the protection of cities, would be able to prevent penetration by a substantial number of ICBM's sufficient to destroy the targets. Other experts have produced counter-arguments, particularly in supporting the Department of Defense's proposals before committees of Congress. The outside inquirer, not an expert in missilery, electronics, radar, computers is caught in a crossfire of conflicting evidence. What makes independent judgement more difficult is that much of the key information bearing on the problem is top secret. I refer to the results of the tests of offensive ballistic missiles for reliability and accuracy, and the kind of tests that have been applied to the components of the Safeguard system and their results.

Jerome Wiesner summed up the dilemma when he wrote:

> . . . when [scientists] attempt to evaluate something that has not been built, they have to make assumptions about what can be done. . . . Different people make different assumptions about all these elements. That is what is involved in the argument about anti-ballistic-missile systems. One man's assumptions give one set of conclusions; another man's assumptions give a different set. Some of the assumptions are essentially undefinable—we are talking about things we do not and cannot know anything about, no matter how we try. And so you can take whichever set of assumptions you choose. . . .

> We assume it [Sentinel] is going to work as specified, or we quite arbitrarily use some reliability estimate like .95. But we can't know whether that is even close to correct, because we have never built or operated anything like the Sentinel before . . . it is probably the most complicated electronic system anyone has ever tried to put together. Here it is, the most elaborate, sophisticated, dynamic combination of rocketry, radars, computers, electronics and other technology ever proposed, and we are expecting that it will work and work well, and not just well but perfectly the first time it is tried in a large-scale test. All kinds of mock tests can be invented for it, but the first genuine one will be when it is used in earnest.[12]

Whether BMD will work or not, it certainly will cost. Safeguard Phase I already carries a high price tag. Much of the opposition in Congress to authorizing expenditure for the programme proposed by Secretary Laird in 1970 was because the legislators felt they would only be making a down payment, and that the instalment payments would go on and on and

---

[12]*Anti-Ballistic Missile: Yes or No?*, page 5.

up and up. Recent experience has been that any new armament component or system when actually produced comes to cost enormously more than was estimated when the programme for it originally received congressional authority. Safeguard Phase I is supposed to be only for the protection of the missiles in the Grand Forks (North Dakota) and the Malmstrom (Montana) complexes, but plans exist for ten other installations, which if completed will blanket the whole continental United States, much as the sidetracked Sentinel system was planned to do.[13] With this experience and evidence, it would be astonishing if Senators and Congressmen, opposed to blank cheques for the Pentagon, did not suspect that they are once again being led up the garden path of open-ended expenditures for strategic weaponry.

The resistance shown by Congress to the whole BMD project and the restrictions placed on the expenditures actually authorized are heartening to those who believe that security for the United States (and its immediate neighbour) lies in agreement with the Soviet Union to limit armaments, and not in an unending competition in armaments.

Among the considerations which affect the attitudes of the Congress to the BMD question are the vested interests of the so-called military-industrial complex. Adam Yarmolinsky states the case as follows:

> The interest of the defense industry in maintaining a constant (or expanding) level of procurement coincides with the interest of military officers in developing new weapons systems for which they have been assigned program responsibility. It coincides also with the interest of the labor union leaders in keeping their members on the job; with the interest of individual Congressmen in maintaining full employment and prosperity in their Congressional districts; and with the interests of lawyers, bankers, public relations men, trade associations, executives and journalists and a host of others whose professional and personal fortunes depend on this major sector of the US economy.
>
> The coincidence of these interests does not suggest any nefarious combination or conspiracy among the various elements of the military establishment. The overwhelming majority is motivated by a genuine concern for national security. But when one view of the requirements for national security happens to coincide with personal and financial interests, and another view does not, it is difficult for an individual or

---

[13]*ABM: An Evaluation.* See the map on page 45, reprinted from *Scientific American.*

a group to maintain an unbiased judgment of where the national security interest lies.[14]

Has the controversy about Ballistic Missile Defence in the United States been settled by the announcement of the President that it has been agreed with the Soviet Union to seek an agreement to limit the deployment of these systems? Can we make the assumption that in agreeing to deal with this element of strategic armament first, the top political authorities in both Washington and Moscow have come to the conclusion that the arguments of the anti-ABM antagonists are valid; and that what the further development of existing systems offers is a prospect of enormous expense, with a minimum degree of effectiveness in reducing damage from an enemy nuclear attack. For purposes of further argument here, let us assume that this is so, or at least that the governments of both superpowers are sincere in their announced intention to find agreement on this point.

The development of MIRV's in its origin was a response to the deployment of ABM defences. The planners of offensive action had to consider the possibility than an extensive system of ABM defence could intercept and destroy a single ICBM aimed at a particular target, or even a salvo of several ICBM's. So means had to be found to penetrate such a defence— assuming, of course, the "worst case" from the offensive viewpoint, that is, that the opponent's ABM system would really work effectively. A similar problem had faced the planners of nuclear attacks where long-range bombers were the carriers of the weapon. Apart from developing various aids to penetration which could confuse and deceive the enemy, or rather his radars and computers, an obvious answer was to increase the number of incoming targets the limited number of defensive missiles would have to deal with. To increase by a factor of three or more the number of ICBM's would have been extremely costly, but to make one rocket, or "booster" carry several warheads which would separate on approaching the target area was less expensive. So MRV, or multiple reentry vehicle systems, came into being, and now are carried by a proportion of the USA Polaris and Minuteman missiles.

Having gone so far, the next step was to make each reentry vehicle guidable after separation from the "booster," so that in theory, instead of an ICBM distributing warheads on a shot-gun principle, each of its warheads, or reentry vehicles, could be directed at a specific and separate target. If such a system could be perfected, or at least be brought to a fairly high degree of reliability and accuracy, the possible effects on the

---

[14]*Ibid.*, page 48.

vulnerability of the opponent's retaliatory deterrent force of missiles would be alarming. We see such alarm registered in Secretary of Defense Laird's statement about the threat posed by the Soviet Union's large ss 9 ICBM's. The gist of what he said was that the growth of Soviet forces could present a severe threat to the survival of the Minuteman and bomber forces by the mid-1970's. The worst case foreseen was that the Soviet Union would deploy a MIRV on the ss 9, improve the ICBM accuracy, and continue building ICBM's at the then current rate. The United States would then be faced with a threat much too large to be countered by the proposed Safeguard system, which would have to be substantially modified and improved.[15]

If agreement is reached between the superpowers to deploy no more ABM systems, the argument that MIRV's are needed to penetrate ballistic missile defences, and so maintain the validity of the deterrent, disappears.

The other purpose of MIRV, as visualized, would be as a counterforce weapon; to be able to destroy the opponent's retaliatory missile forces, and so break down the mutual deterrence status. In other words, the MIRV would be a delivery system which would make a preemptive strike possible. We have seen in previous chapters that the fear of a preemptive strike, or preventive war, is one which motivated decisions to increase strategic armaments. The vision of the country disarmed, that is, deprived of the means to deliver nuclear weapons, and faced by an opponent still possessing them, who threatens to destroy industry and population unless the disarmed state surrenders, is a horrifying one. To eliminate the possibility that this threat might be made a reality through extensive deployment of MIRV's and improvements in their reliability and accuracy should be the next object of SALT, if an agreement on ABM limitation is reached.

To repeat: if the superpowers agree to halt BMD, then there is no reason to continue the development of MIRV, unless to provide capability for a first strike – euphemized as "damage-limitation." It should therefore be the next stage in the limitation of strategic arms to halt the further development and deployment of MIRV's.

This has been recognized by a number of authorities writing on possible outcomes of SALT. Herbert Scoville, while citing the difficulties in the way of such an agreement, principally that of verifying that it was being complied with, notes that:

. . . to allow the unrestricted deployment of MIRV's would seriously

---

15Statement by Secretary of Defense Laird before a joint Session of the Senate Armed Services and Appropriation Committees, February 20, 1970, Supt. of Documents (Washington), page 48.

reduce the efficacy of an arms control agreement, since in a few years the number of offensive nuclear warheads could be increased to a very high level. . . . Their deployment might thus increase the incentive for preemptive strikes against land-based ICBM's in time of crisis. . . .[16]

The Federation of American Scientists released a statement in November 1970, on the eve of the resumption of SALT at Helsinki, which expressed apprehension that the two powers might execute an agreement that would limit only numbers of weapons, and not their qualitative features, thus permitting wholesale replacement of older weapons with more advanced versions. As well as advocating the ban or severe limitations of ABM's, the Federation had this recommendation to make regarding an agreement on MIRV's:

> The US should make every effort to persuade the Soviets to agree to a MIRV production, test and deployment ban and should demonstrate its seriousness by halting further MIRV production, testing and deployment as long as the Soviets reciprocate.

The statement went on to consider one difficulty in negotiating such an agreement, which is that the United States had a considerable lead in developing and testing MIRV's, and had already deployed a certain number. It might be necessary to agree to allow the USSR a certain period in which to test, and catch up. This would not necessarily make agreement impossible. We might remember the history of efforts to prohibit nuclear testing in the atmosphere, during which both sides stopped testing, started again, and then finally agreed to a definite halt under the 1963 Moscow Treaty.

Then there was the difficulty of being sure that testing of MIRV's might not be carried out by disguising the firings as routine tests of standard ICBM's. (Such tests would probably be allowed under any agreement so long as nuclear deterrents were in existence. A proportion of all kinds of ordnance in government stocks is tested, as a matter of routine, to determine that it is still serviceable.) However, other experts believe that any extensive programme of MIRV testing would inevitably be detected.

The importance of extensive testing of MIRV's is clear. Without it, the claimed advantages of being able to destroy many targets with the nuclear heads from one ICBM could not be accepted by the military as a basis for planning their targeting, even for counter-city roles, much less for counterforce use.

---

[16]Scoville, Jr., Herbert, *Toward a Strategic Arms Limitation Agreement* (New York: Carnegie Endowment, 1970), pages 27, 28.

Another way to prevent, or at least restrain further technological development of MIRV would be for the superpowers to agree to a Comprehensive Test Ban. If new warheads could not be tested, this would create a considerable obstacle to the qualitative arms competition – and would also be in the way of new entrants to the nuclear power circle. What stands in the way of agreement to prohibit underground testing of nuclear weapons now, as has been remarked previously, is the intention of the superpowers to continue testing to develop and refine their weaponry for which, if it is really their intention to halt the arms race, there is no need. The arguments put forward by the United States for on-site inspection to provide "fool-proof" verification that no nuclear weapons are clandestinely exploded underground demand a degree of fulfilment which is hardly afforded by any other obligations entered into between states. As Senator Hubert Humphrey remarked:

> The truth is that we have been demanding more certain guarantees of success of those who have urged the positive course of negotiated disarmament than we have of those who insist that prudence requires us to rely on the negative protection of nuclear deterrence.[17]

Eighty per cent. reliability seems to be accepted for the launching towards target of an ICBM, but US negotiators have been demanding ninety-nine and a half per cent. assurance that all underground nuclear tests will be detected by seismological means before the unnegotiable on-site inspection requirement for a comprehensive nuclear weapon test ban will be abandoned.

As 1971 ended, SALT continued to meet, without any agreement having been announced. The American programme of MIRVing Minuteman and converting Polaris to Poseidon goes on. Some hawkishly-inclined observers say with gloomy satisfaction that it is too late to halt the general deployment of MIRV's by both superpowers. They may be right, and, if they are, hopes for truly limiting the arms race in its qualitative as well as quantitative aspects will not be great.

If we can be so optimistic as to suppose that the negotiators can agree on the limitation of ABM systems, and of MIRV's, what could be the next aspect of nuclear arms control to be agreed upon? Most of the experts who have written about the forms of agreement which SALT might produce, have begun with the problem of the parity equation, already discussed. To devise limitations which would involve any reductions of existing

---

[17]*Anti-Ballistic Missile: Yes or No?*, page xxvii.

nuclear weapon vehicles would be very complex and difficult. But if the governments of the superpowers agreed to limit BMD and cease developing MIRV systems, they would thereby have demonstrated their intention not to seek to equip themselves with means to carry out a disarming strike. In the context of such agreements, a non-first-use convention might carry credence. If such agreements could be reached, the problem of what to do about existing contra-superpower delivery systems might lose much of its difficulty. It does not seem appropriate here to enter into lengthy discussion of the various alternatives which have been proposed. Dr. Herbert Scoville examined the question in detail in an article. I shall quote only part of the conclusions he reached.

> The most immediately practical method of controlling offensive weapons would involve a freeze on existing systems, a ban on the construction of new launchers and a restriction on any changes in deployed systems to those that do not change their external characteristics. Such an agreement would provide some valuable limitations on qualitative improvements and would be adequately verifiable by unilateral means. . . .
>
> An agreement that limited strategic weapons to specific numbers without any restrictions on replacement or substitution would do little if anything to halt the arms race and in fact might provide strong incentives for accelerating it along new directions.[18]

Dr. Scoville's article was written before President Nixon's announcement that priority would be given to an agreement to limit BMD. If bargaining on limitations of existing strategic armaments did not have to begin before limitations on BMD and MIRV had been agreed to, it would present a much less difficult problem. This would be mainly because the bargaining or trading-off of superiority in numbers or payload in one category or other of nuclear weapons vehicles would be taking place in the greatly improved atmosphere which would exist after the superpowers had mutually declared their intention not to build up means which would allow a first strike.

If the USA and the USSR could agree in SALT to limit BMD, MIRV and offensive nuclear weapon vehicles, it would be an immense advance. But these agreements would relate to what might be called the intercontinental balance. The armament of NATO and the Warsaw Pact in Europe, both nuclear and conventional, would not be affected. However, it is now

---

[18]Scoville, Jr., Herbert, "The Limitation of Offensive Weapons," *Scientific American* (January 1971), page 25.

accepted by many observers that the limitation and reduction of armaments in Europe must be negotiated separately. It could be a mutual balanced forces reduction, in a European security conference. Of course, the possibility of a favourable outcome for such negotiations would be greatly affected by the outcome of SALT. But there must be agreement on European armaments if a stable relationship between the superpowers and a definitive halt to the nuclear arms race is finally to be established. Another point: It would seem that questions of the future size and role of the British and French nuclear deterrents would enter into the European armaments balance, rather than the USA-USSR balance.

Then there is the question of China. It is certain that the United States and the Soviet Union would not reduce their nuclear armament to a degree which might lay them open to threats by a China which had developed comparably powerful nuclear forces. So China must be brought into the negotiation, either when the first USA-USSR limitation agreements have been concluded, or soon thereafter. The People's Republic of China has made various statements as to the position it might take regarding nuclear disarmament negotiations. Premier Chou En-lai, in the course of a dinner given to the Canadian trade delegation on July 2, 1971, said that he believed that the nuclear powers would eventually agree on the prohibition of nuclear weapons, but that China would refuse to participate in a five-nation conference on the subject, as proposed by the Soviet Union. Participating in talks limited to the nuclear powers would run counter to China's policy of shunning big-power politics, and, accordingly, China would continue to insist that the talks be open to all nations.[19]

On June 22, 1971, at a dinner for three American reporters, including Seymour Topping from whose despatch to *The New York Times* the following is extracted, Premier Chou En-lai said:

> . . . that he had received the Soviet proposal for a disarmament conference among the five nuclear states—the United States, the Soviet Union, Britain, France and China. He said that his Government will discuss it but he indicated personal reservations about the plan. . . . He said "First of all, we are not a big power although the extent of our territory is vast and we have a vast population. From the point of view of power we are rather weak and backward. Secondly, we are in an experimental stage of our testing of nuclear weapons. We cannot call ourselves a big nuclear power. Thirdly, every time we conduct a nuclear test, that is necessary in a limited way, we issue a statement as follows: 'We will not at any time and under any circumstances be

---

[19]*The Globe and Mail*, Toronto, July 3, 1971.

the first to use nuclear weapons. Never!' Fourthly, we advocate that all countries of the world, regardless of their size, should sit down together and agree on the complete prohibition and complete destruction of nuclear weapons."[20]

It will be noted that the position set out by Premier Chou En-lai is very similar to that which the Soviet Union held in the days when it was much inferior to the United States in nuclear weaponry.

When the Soviet Union's proposal for a world disarmament conference was being debated in the plenary of the UNGA (in November 1971), the newly-seated representative of the People's Republic of China attacked the disarmament policies of the superpowers, and denounced the nuclear test ban and the Non-proliferation Treaty. In rejecting the Soviet-proposed world disarmament conference, the Chinese representatives reiterated their suggestion, mentioned in the quotation from Chou En-lai, that there should be a world summit conference to "discuss the questions of the complete prohibition and thorough destruction of all nuclear weapons."

The Chinese view appeared to be that all agreements on arms control so far reached are "essentially a camouflage for their own nuclear arms expansion in the name of nuclear disarmament. . . . It was a means to consolidate the nuclear monopoly of the two superpowers."[21]

While it cannot be denied that the Chinese criticism has some validity, such an attitude shows that prospects are dim for the PRC to play a constructive part in disarmament negotiations in the near future.

Writing about disarmament and arms control and the negotiations on them is a kind of journalism; whatever the author sets down as the state of affairs when he completes his book or article may be vastly changed by the time it is published.

One final word.

Most of the information on which governments must take defence decisions comes from military sources. Experienced politicians of both superpowers often have considerable reservations as to the accuracy of military men's judgements. Nevertheless, when they are told that the potential enemy is building up his stocks of this or that dreadful engine of destruction, it is difficult for them entirely to disregard their advisers' recommendations to take countermeasures. It seems that the habit of the top brass in Moscow and Washington is to peer at each other through

---

[20]*Ibid.*, New York Times Service, June 23, 1971.
[21]Reuters despatch from the UN in the Toronto *Globe and Mail*, November 25, 1971.

powerful telescopes incorporating filters which transmit only images of implacable hostility and offensive postures. So it can be inferred that if the warlords would change this habit, progress in making the world safe from nuclear war could be more substantial. But this is not likely to happen soon. Meanwhile the top politicians must be prepared to take brave decisions, balancing the possible risk to national security through arms limitation against the greater risk of nuclear war if the arms race goes on unchecked.

Appendix

*Memorandum by the author to the Secretary of State for
External Affairs, December 1960* (extracts)
The USA may put forward certain proposals for providing NATO, either as
a group, or the NATO nations separately, with nuclear weapons. There is
also the question of whether the Royal Canadian Air Force in Europe
should be equipped with F 104 G's—an aircraft which has no other purpose than to serve as a vehicle for a nuclear warhead; and whether the
Canadian Army in Europe should be equipped with the Honest John
rockets—a short-range nuclear vehicle.

I have argued in another paper that any spreading of nuclear arms in
NATO would be to go in a direction contrary to disarmament, and would
therefore be undesirable if our long-range policy is that only through disarmament can Canada really find peace and security in the nuclear age.
In the present paper I propose to set forth arguments of a military-political
nature against the adoption of either of the courses of action mentioned
in the first paragraph above.

It has been argued, I believe, that the Canadian forces in Europe, for
their own effectiveness and security, should be equipped with the means
of delivering nuclear warheads referred to above. General Norstad has
recently made it clear to the visiting Parliamentarians that the warheads,
without which the vehicles are useless, are held and will continue to be

held in the custody of the USA. General Norstad also stated that the decision to use the nuclear arms would be made at a "high level"; presumably meaning at a level higher than that of the Canadian commander of the troops or air force units concerned. That would mean that the decision would have to be made by a USA officer, since the warheads are held in US custody. It is therefore possible that the Canadian army formation might find themselves engaged in fighting in which their commander might consider it essential that the nuclear weapons should be used, but permission would be refused.

Why might permission be refused? Because it is most probable that the initial use of nuclear weapons, on the "tactical" level, will result, through the "escalator" principle, in the more powerful kinds of nuclear weapons being brought into use, and very rapidly. No military man, or professional so-called expert has, so far as I know, given any convincing reason why this "escalator" effect should not take place; no one has demonstrated that there can be any such thing as restricted nuclear warfare. Hence, once the nuclear weapon is used at all, its use will in all probability be unlimited.

Conditions are different now to what they were when the decision to equip NATO with nuclear arms was taken in 1957. That was before the USSR had shown its ability to make ICBM's which could hit targets in the United States. Now, hardly anyone doubts that the USSR has so many of them that it could cause terrific destruction and loss of life in the continental United States, and there is nothing the USA can do to stop this – except the deterrent provided by the ability of her own nuclear carriers to mete out similar or greater destruction in Russia. What nearly every European thinker on the subject now doubts, is whether the USA would take the decision to initiate nuclear warfare to stop an aggression in Europe by the USSR with conventional forces. A decision to retaliate with nuclear weapons, previously seen in the context of a decision to unleash the United States Strategic Air Command, which requires the authority of the President of the United States, would seem now to be required before the "tactical" nuclear weapons with which certain forces in NATO have been equipped could be used; that is, before the warheads for these vehicles could be released from United States custody. Does it make sense to equip a Canadian brigade with a weapon – a so-called tactical weapon – which requires the authority of the President of the United States for its use?

The same considerations apply generally in the case of the RCAF Division. Unless it were authorized to receive the nuclear warheads – bombs – the F 104 G aircraft is designed to deliver, it would have no combat usefulness at all; except perhaps in a reconnaissance role for which cheaper aircraft would be equally useful. General Norstad expects the role of light bombers or fighter-bombers to be taken over by MRBM's beginning 1963. Is it desirable for Canada to equip her air component with an aircraft which will be obsolete in a few years or which perhaps, if an emergency arises, may never receive the nuclear bombs it is designed to deliver?

There is a further consideration against equipping the Canadian forces with these vehicles for the delivery of nuclear weapons. That is, if a situation threatening war should develop, and the Russians knew that the Canadian brigade and the RCAF division were equipped with nuclear weapons, would our forces not become a selected target for medium-range nuclear-headed Russian rockets? Thus, equipping the Canadian forces with these weapons would reduce their security, not add to it. We should be giving them a short-range delivery for Russian nuclear weapons, and rendering them priority targets for Russian nuclear rockets of much longer range. This is not equalizing their equipment with that of the prospective enemy.

For these several reasons, I believe that the Canadian Government should reconsider its previous decision (if such a decision has indeed been taken) to obtain the nuclear delivery vehicles mentioned above. On the other hand, the opinion is growing in many of the NATO nations that there is a real need to strengthen NATO's conventionally-armed forces. Canada might compensate for her refusal to accept nuclear arms by offering to increase moderately her contribution in land and air forces, equipped with modern conventional weapons.

The matter of a separate NATO deterrent force would seem to be less urgent, and also of less direct interest to Canada. However, it may be discussed at the Ministerial meeting, and could be of importance in the context of disarmament. There are several questions which suggest themselves in this connection.

If the USA handed over to NATO a quantity of nuclear weapons, and their vehicles, it would let the decision to initiate nuclear warfare in Europe pass out of US hands. This might reassure Europeans who now fear that the USA would not use their nuclear deterrent in response to a USSR threat to Europe's vital interests or territory, for fear of the destruction which the USSR ICBM's could cause in the USA. However, the Americans must think, before handing over a "nuclear capability" on any large scale to the control of NATO, whether if a nuclear war were initiated in Europe, would the Russians confine their riposte to European targets? Might the Russians not reason that even if they could practically destroy Europe, the damage they would themselves suffer would be such that afterwards, the USA, with its nuclear striking capacity intact, could destroy the rest of Russia while suffering relatively little damage itself? In such a case, would the USSR not be likely to begin any nuclear war by concentrating on destroying USA nuclear striking power, or as much of it as they could, devoting a relatively minor part of their effort to European targets? With this possibility, would it not be very dangerous for the Americans to let the decision to employ the nuclear arms pass out of their control?

Apart from this difficulty, there is also a great difficulty in devising a method of organizing a command for a NATO nuclear striking or deterrent force. When decisions to use such a force have to be taken in a matter of minutes, committee decisions by majority are out of the question. Would the NATO nations be able to agree on a commander for such a deterrent force whom all could trust to do the right thing in the decisive moment, and not think more of the interest of the country of which he happened to belong than of the interests of other member countries? The problem seems almost insoluble. Yet the present situation of relying on the US-controlled deterrent is unsatisfactory, and seems likely to become more so.

This dilemma may open the door to a proposal to examine once more the possibilities of making a nuclear-free zone in Europe, of wider extent than has previously been considered. Such an idea, in connection with protection against surprise attack, was discussed in general terms between the five Western members of the Ten-Nation Disarmament Committee in elaborating the disarmament plan which they drew up and presented in Geneva on March 16, 1960.

The NATO military authorities might be called upon to study and make a plan for freeing Europe of nuclear arms, in the context of a general disarmament plan; with, of course, all the indispensable measures of control and verification. At the same time, they might study the problem of the composition and control of a NATO deterrent. Meanwhile, further dissemination of the control of nuclear arms could be halted, pending the outcome of the next round of serious disarmament negotiations between West and East.

Glossary of terms

ABM	Anti-Ballistic-Missile
ACDA	Arms Control and Disarmament Agency
ARROW	A high-performance aircraft developed by AVRO of Canada
ATLAS	An American ICBM
BLACK BOXES	Automatic seismological stations used to monitor the extent and intensity of nuclear tests
BOEING 707	An American civil airliner
BOMARC	An American anti-aircraft missile designed to use either conventional or nuclear warheads
BOMBER COMMAND	The subdivision of Britain's Royal Air Force concerned with the direction of Britain's strategic nuclear bombers
BUNDESWEHR	The West German Defence Forces
B 47	An American medium-range nuclear bomber

B 52	An American long-range nuclear bomber
B 58	An American medium-range super-sonic nuclear bomber
B 70	An American intercontinental super-sonic strategic bomber under development
CCD	Conference of the Committee on Disarmament
CEP	Circular Error Probable: a measure of delivery accuracy represented by the radius of a circle about the target point within which, on the average, fifty per cent. of a specific type of nuclear weapon can be expected to fall
CF 104	A modified version of the F 104 Starfighter built under licence in Canada for use by the Royal Canadian Air Force
CTB	Comprehensive Test Ban
CUT-OFF	A term used in reference to non-production and reduction of stocks of fissionable material
DC 3	A World War II vintage American transport aircraft (called the Dakota by British)
DOD	Department of Defense
DOVES	Political figures who stress disarmament and a peaceful world
ENDC	The Eighteen-Nation Disarmament Committee
F 104	The Lockheed Starfighter: a dual-purpose fighter-bomber of American design
GCD	General and Complete Disarmament
GROUND-TO-AIR MISSILES	The general classification of anti-aircraft and anti-missile missiles launched from the ground (also called SAM; surface-air missile)

HAWKS	Those individuals who stress security through armed force, and a hard policy line vs. USSR and communism.
H.E.	High explosive
HONEST JOHN	An American-built tactical nuclear missile
HOUND DOG	An air-to-ground missile designed to be launched from the American B 52 bomber
ICBM	Intercontinental Ballistic Missile
IDO	International Disarmament Organization
IRBM	Intermediate-Range Ballistic Missile
ISS	Institute for Strategic Studies
JCS	Joint Chiefs of Staff
JUPITER	An American IRBM
KILOTON	A measure of the explosive power of a nuclear weapon; equal to 1,000 tons of TNT
MEGATON	A measure of the explosive power of a nuclear weapon; equal to 1,000,-000 tons of TNT
MIDAS	An American intelligence-gathering satellite (Missile Alarm Defence System)
MINUTEMAN	An American ICBM
MIRV	Multiple Individually-targetable Re-entry Vehicle
MLF	Multilateral Force
MRBM	Medium-Range Ballistic Missile
MRV	Multiple Reentry Vehicle
NIKE-ZEUS	An anti-aircraft missile system developed by the US Army
NPT	Non-proliferation Treaty
NSC	National Security Council
NWV	Nuclear Weapon Vehicle
PLUTONIUM	A fissionable material used in nuclear warheads
POLARIS	An American submarine-launched ballistic missile

258

‎‎‎‎ ‎‎‎

POSEIDON	An improved American submarine-launched ballistic missile
REGULUS	An air-breathing missile for discharge from naval vessels
SAC	Strategic Air Command
SALT	Strategic Arms Limitation Talks
SAMOS	An American intelligence-gathering satellite (Satellite and Missile Observation System)
SKYBOLT	A proposed long-range, air-to-ground missile development (cancelled)
SLBM	Submarine-launched Ballistic Missile
SPUTNIK	First Soviet space satellite
STRATEGIC RETALIATORY FORCES (SRF)	An American designation for the B 47's, B 52's, B 58's, Minuteman, Atlas and Titan missiles and Polaris submarines in the strategic arsenal of the US
THOR	An American IRBM
TITAN	An American ICBM
TNCD	Ten-Nation Committee on Disarmament
TU 16	A medium-range Soviet nuclear bomber
UNDC	United Nations Disarmament Commission
UNGA	United Nations General Assembly
U 2	High-performance reconnaissance and photographic aircraft used by the US
U 235	Fissionable material used in nuclear warheads
V-BOMBER	The British strategic nuclear bomber force consisting of Vulcan and Victor bombers
WING	An air force unit, consisting of two or more squadrons of aircraft
WIZARD	An anti-missile system once under development by the US Air Force

Bibliography

Military Policy and Strategy

Adelphi Paper, No. 65: *Soviet-American Relations and World Order: Arms Limitations and Policy* (ISS, London, Feb. 1970).

Adelphi Paper, No. 66: *Soviet-American Relations and World Order: The Two and The Many* (ISS, London, March 1970).

Brodie, Bernard: *Strategy in the Missile Age* (Princeton University Press, Princeton, 1959).

Buchan, Alistair: *NATO in the 1960's*, Studies in International Security (ISS, London, 1960).

Burns, Lt.-Gen. E. L. M.: *Megamurder* (Clarke, Irwin & Company Ltd., Toronto, 1966).

Dinerstein, H. S.: *War and the Soviet Union*, revised ed. (Praeger, New York, 1962).

Documents on Disarmament; 1945-49; . . . 1967 (U.S. Department of State; U.S. Arms Control and Disarmament Agency: Washington, D.C.).

Gallois, General Pierre: *Stratégie de l'Age Nucléaire* (Calmann-Lévy, Paris, 1960).

Garthoff, Raymond: *Soviet Strategy in the Nuclear Age*, revised ed. (Praeger, New York, 1962).

Gavin, Lt.-Gen. James M.: *War and Peace in the Space Age* (Harper and Brothers, New York, 1958).

Halperin, Morton H.: *Contemporary Military Strategy* (Little, Brown, Boston, 1967).

Halperin, Morton H.: *Defense Strategies for the Seventies* (Boston, 1971).

Holloway, David: *Technology, Management and the Soviet Military Establishment*, Adelphi Paper, No. 76 (ISS, London, April 1971).

Huntington, Samuel P.: *The Common Defense* (Columbia University Press, New York, 1961).

Juvilier, Peter H.: Morton, Henry W.: *Soviet Policy-Making: Studies of Communism in Transition* (Praeger, New York, 1967).

Kennedy, Robert F.: *Thirteen Days* (W. W. Norton, Co., New York, 1969).

Lyon, Peyton: *Canada In World Affairs, 1961-63* (Oxford (CIIA), Toronto, 1968).

McLin, Jon B.: *Canada's Changing Defense Policy 1957-1963: The Problems of a Middle Power in Alliance* (Johns Hopkins Press, Baltimore, 1967).

McNamara, Robert S.: *The Essence of Security* (Harper and Row, New York, 1968).

Military Balance (annual) 1962 . . . 1970 (ISS, London, 1962).

Newman, Peter C.: *Renegade in Power: the Diefenbaker Years* (McClelland and Stewart, Toronto, 1964).

Nixon, President Richard: *U.S. Foreign Policy for the 1970's: A New Strategy for Peace*, A Report to the Congress (U.S. Government Printing Office, Washington, Feb. 18, 1970).

Power, General Thomas S.: *Design for Survival* (Coward-McCann, New York, 1964).

Schelling, Thomas C.: *Arms and Influence* (Yale University Press, New Haven, 1967).

Schelling, Thomas C.: *The Strategy of Conflict* (Oxford University Press, London, 1960).

Schwarz, Urs: *American Strategy: A New Perspective* (Doubleday Anchor, Garden City, 1967).

Smart, Ian: *Advanced Strategic Missiles: A Short Guide*, Adelphi Paper, No. 63 (ISS, London, Dec. 1969).

Sokolovski, Marshal V. D., ed.: *Soviet Military Strategy* (Prentice-Hall, Englewood Cliffs, 1963).

Sipri (Swedish International Peace Research Institute) Yearbook of World Armament and Disarmament, 1969/70 (Humanities Press, New York, 1970).

Taylor, General Maxwell D.: *The Uncertain Trumpet* (Harper and Brothers, New York, 1959, 1960).

Von Riekhoff, Harald: *NATO: Issues and Prospects* (Canadian Institute of International Affairs, Toronto, 1967).

Wolfe, Thomas W.: *Soviet Power and Europe 1945-1970* (Johns Hopkins Press, Baltimore, 1970).

Disarmament

Bloomfield, Lincoln P.; Clemens, Walker C., Jr.; Griffiths, Franklyn: *Khrushchev and the Arms Race* (M.I.T. Press, Cambridge, 1966).

Cook, Fred J.: *The Warfare State* (Macmillan, New York, 1962).

Dean, Arthur H.: *Test Ban and Disarmament; The Path of Negotiation* (Harper and Row, New York, 1966).

Frisch, David H., ed.: *Arms Reduction: Programs and Issues* (Twentieth Century Fund, New York, 1961).

Howard, Michael: *Projects of Disengagement* (Penguin, London, 1958).

Inglis, David R.: *Testing and Taming of Nuclear Weapons* (Public Affairs Pamphlet No. 303, Public Affairs Committee Inc., Sept., 1960).

Jacobson, Harold Karan, & Stein: *Diplomats, Scientists and Politicians* (University of Michigan Press, Ann Arbor, 1966).

Kolkowicz, Roman, *et al.*: *The Soviet Union and Arms Control: A Super Power Dilemma* (Johns Hopkins Press, Baltimore, 1970).

Lall, Arthur S.: *Negotiating Disarmament* (Centre for International Studies, Cornell University, Ithaca, 1964).

Larson, Thomas B.: *Disarmament and Soviet Policy, 1964-1968* (Prentice-Hall, Englewood Cliffs, 1969).

Noel-Baker, Philip: *The Arms Race* (Stevens & Sons Ltd., London, 1958).

Nutting, Anthony: *Disarmament: An Outline of Negotiations* (Oxford University Press, London, 1959).

Rathjens, George W.: *The Future of the Strategic Arms Race* (Carnegie Endowment for International Peace, New York, 1969).

Report of the Secretary General of the United Nations Consultive Group, 1968: *Effects of the Possible Use of Nuclear Weapons and the Security and Economic Implications for States of the Acquisition and Further Development of These Weapons.*

Robles, Alfonso Garcia: *The Denuclearization of Latin America* (Carnegie Endowment for International Peace, New York, 1967).

Russell, Bertrand: *Common Sense and Nuclear Warfare* (Simon and Schuster, New York, 1959).

Schelling, Thomas C.: Halperin, Morton H.: *Strategy and Arms Control* (The Twentieth Century Fund, New York, 1961).

Wright, Sir Michael: *Disarm and Verify* (Chatto and Windus, London, 1964).

Non-proliferation Treaty

Beaton, Leonard: *Secondary and "Almost-Nuclear" Powers* (Occasional Paper, The Centre of Policy Study, the University of Chicago, University of Chicago Press, Chicago, 1970).

Burns, Lt.-Gen. E. L. M.: "The Non-proliferation Treaty: Its Negotiation and Prospects," *International Organization*, Vol. XXIII, No. 4, 1969.

de Gara, John P.: *Nuclear Proliferation and Security* (Carnegie Endowment, New York, May 1970).

International Negotiations on the Treaty on the Non-proliferation of Nuclear Weapons (United States Arms Control and Disarmament Agency, Publication 48, Washington, Jan. 1969).

Quester, George H.: "Japan and the Non-proliferation Treaty," *Asian Survey*, Vol. X, No. 9 (University of California, Berkeley, Sept. 1970).

Williams, Shelton: *The US, India and the Bomb* (Johns Hopkins, Baltimore, 1969).

World of Nuclear Powers?: Report of the International Assembly on Nuclear Weapons, June 23-26, 1966 (Canadian Institute of International Affairs, Toronto, 1966).

ABM

Brennan, Donald G.; Johnson, Leon W.; Wiesner, Jerome P.; McGovern, George S.: *Anti-Ballistic Missile: Yes or No?* (Hill and Wang, New York, 1968).

Chayes, Abram; Wiesner, Jerome B., eds.: *ABM* (The New American Library, New York, 1969).

Holst, Johan J.; Schneider, William, Jr., eds.: *Why ABM?* (Pergamon Press, New York, 1969).

Libby, Willard F.; Thaler, William J.; Twining, General Nathan F.: *The ABM and the Changed Strategic Military Balance* (Acropolis Books, Washington, 1969).

Rabinowitch, Eugene; Adams, Ruth: *Debate the Anti-Ballistic Missile* (The Bulletin of the Atomic Scientists, Chicago, 1967).

Stone, Jeremy J.: *The Case Against Missile Defense*, Adelphi Paper, No. 47 (ISS, London, April 1968).

Strategic Arms Limitation Talks

Brennan, Donald G.: *The Strategic Arms Limitation Talks: Possible Objectives*, Occasional Paper No. 11, School of International Affairs, Carleton University (Ottawa, May 1970).

Bull, Hedley: *Strategic Arms Limitation: The Precedent of the Washington and London Naval Treaties*, Occasional Paper, The Center for Policy Study, the University of Chicago (The University of Chicago Press, Chicago, 1971).

Burns, Lt.-Gen. E. L. M., ed.: *The Prospects for Strategic Arms Limitation Talks*, Occasional Paper No. 10, School of International Affairs, Carleton University (Ottawa, May 1970).

Caldwell, Lawrence T.: *Soviet Attitudes to SALT*, Adelphi Paper, No. 75 (ISS, London, Feb. 1971).

Gray, Colin S.: "Security Through SALT," *Behind the Headlines*, Vol. XXX, Nos. 3-4, April 1971 (CIIA, Toronto).

Holst, Johan J.: *Comparative US and Soviet Deployments, Doctrines and Arms Limitation*, Occasional Paper, The Center for Policy Study, the University of Chicago (University of Chicago Press, Chicago, 1971).

Scoville, Herbert, Jr.: *Toward a Strategic Arms Limitation Agreement* (Carnegie Endowment for International Peace, New York, 1970).

Slocombe, Walter: *The Political Implications of Strategic Parity*, Adelphi Paper, No. 77 (ISS, London, May 1971).

Index